INTRODUCTION TO THE SOCIOLOGY OF MUSIC

INTRODUCTION TO THE SOCIOLOGY OF MUSIC

Theodor W. Adorno

Translated from the German by E. B. Ashton

A Continuum Book
THE SEABURY PRESS · NEW YORK

The Seabury Press, Inc.
815 Second Avenue
New York, N.Y. 10017

Published by arrangement with Suhrkamp Verlag. Originally published under the
title *Einleitung in die Musiksoziologie.* Copyright © Suhrkamp Verlag, Frankfurt-am-
Main, 1962. All rights reserved.

Printed in the United States of America

LIBRARY OF CONGRESS CATALOGING IN PUBLICATION DATA

Adorno, Theodor W 1903–1969.
    Introduction to the sociology of music.

    (A Continuum book)
    Translation of Einleitung in die Musiksoziologie.
    1. Music and society. I. Title.
ML3797.1.A3413   780′.07   75-33883
ISBN 0-8164-9266-2

CONTENTS

FOREWORD TO THE 1968 EDITION

The didactic character which the new edition of *Introduction to the Sociology of Music* is meant to retain has prevented major revisions. That the lectures are not as meticulously formulated as other works of the author's may be commercially useful. Since the book is to serve as an introduction, not only to musical sociology but to the sociological conception of the Frankfurt School, it reckons with readers who would flinch from more demanding texts. Beyond the emendation of misprints and errors, the author has therefore confined himself to a very few, though centrally placed, additions. Entirely new is only the postscript "Sociology of Music," a fragment intended to correct some fragmentary aspects of the book.

In general, the author tends not so much to say what he is doing and how, but to do it. This is the consequence of a theory which does not adopt the accepted separation of matter and method and is suspicious of abstract methodology. Over the past few years, however, the dispute about methods in musical sociology has continued to seethe. Perhaps the author is permitted, for that reason, to point to an essay which in some measure outlines his position in that dispute. It is entitled *"Thesen zur Kunstsoziologie"* and has been published in the little book *Ohne Leitbild.*

While many sociologists have chided the procedure of this *Introduction* as metaphysical, philosophical, or at least nonsociological, one music critic's exceedingly kind review has assured the author that his book really contains nothing not already known, more or less vaguely, to every musician. Nothing could please the author more than having his allegedly wild speculations confirmed as solely helpful in lending a voice to prior knowledge. To resolve the tension between this motive and one of a thought free from leading-strings is the purpose of this book.

January, 1968

PREFACE

These lectures, each followed by a discussion, were delivered in the winter term of 1961–62 at Frankfurt University; major portions were broadcast over the North German Radio.

The history of the publication may not be irrelevant to its form. In 1958 the author was invited to contribute an article, *"Ideen zur Musiksoziologie,"* to *Schweizer Monatshefte.* In that piece, later incorporated in his volume *Klangfiguren,* he developed principles of music-sociological activity without separating them from questions of substance; and precisely this remains the specific feature of his method. Whatever procedures he may be following in musical sociology are still controlled by that article.

It no sooner appeared than the musical sociologist Alphons Silbermann kindly suggested expanding it into book form. At the time this was prevented by other commitments as well as by the maxim that what has been tersely expounded ought not to be subsequently expatiated on. The idea took root, however, and ripened into the design of a more detailed presentation of music-sociological thoughts and findings, quite independently of that previous text. Another impulse from outside was helpful: an invitation in 1961 to read two short papers of a music-sociological nature on the "University of the Air" program of RIAS (Radio in the American Sector) in Berlin. They became the core of the first two of these lectures.

Utilized in them are American papers from the time when the author directed the Princeton Radio Research Project. The typology of listening to music, roughly sketched as early as 1939, had continued to occupy him; many of the ideas found in the second lecture had been laid down in an essay "On Popular Music" (pp. 17ff. of *Studies in Philosophy and Social Science*, Vol. IX, No. 1—an issue devoted entirely to the sociology of the mass media). Unintentionally unfolded in the problematics of the two lectures was the conception of the whole, although its complex origin made repetitions impossible to avoid altogether, whether within the lectures or between them and others of the author's publications.

Under no circumstances would he tamper with the lecture character. The book contains only minor retouchings and supplementations of what was actually spoken. Digressions, even leaps, were left standing to the extent that seems permissible in extemporaneous speech. Whoever had experienced the incompatibility of an autonomous text with the act of addressing an audience will not try to hide the differences and ex post facto to force the communicative word into ruthlessly adequate phrasings. The more apparent the difference, the less false pretensions. In this sense the book is akin to *Soziologische Exkurse* from the series published by the Institut für Sozialforschung. The word "Introduction" in the title may also be taken to mean that readers are not supposed to be introduced to the material field alone but to the type of sociological thought served by *Exkurse*.

The author has resisted the temptation to use materials, documents, and references as fillers for what essentially has been spontaneous reflection—a kind of reflection into which none of that entered unless it was present in the author's immediate experience. No effort was made to be systematic. Instead, the reflections were focused on neural points. Not many topical questions of musical sociology are likely to have been neglected, and yet the possible result should not be mistaken for a scientifically complete one—because, if for no other reason, the author treated his topics in line with a principle of Freud's: "It is not so often that psychoanalysis will deny somebody else's contention; as a rule it does no more than add something new, and occasionally, of course, this previously ignored, now newly added thing happens to be the very essence." There is no intention to compete with existing expositions of musical sociology, not even where their intentions conflict with the author's own.

What should be self-understood in the whole approach is that all aspects of the present situation which the book deals with are incomprehensible without a historic dimension. It is precisely in the intellectual realm that the concept of the bourgeois dates back much farther than the full political emancipation of the bourgeoisie. Categories whose emergence is attributed to bourgeois society in the narrow sense can be suspected already—or their origins can be sought—where a bourgeois spirit and bourgeois forms existed without being obeyed as yet by society as a whole. Inherent in the very concept of the bourgeois seems to be that phenomena taken for unmistakable parts of one's own era have been around for a long time. *Plus ça change, plus c'est la même chose.*

In his lecture course the author had at least tried to show the students that his presentation was not all there is to musical sociology. He tried by inviting three guest lecturers: Hans Engel, author of *Musik und Gesellschaft*, a work with the accent on history; Alphons Silbermann, the exponent of empirical research in the sociology of music; and Kurt Blaukopf, who opened highly productive perspectives of the connection between musical sociology and acoustics. All of them are due this public expression of thanks for their cooperation—and particularly Alphons Silbermann, the author of *Introduction à une sociologie de la musique,* for his generous consent to the author's use of the same title in German. A different one would hardly have conveyed the meaning, since this book is neither an outright sociology of music nor a monograph.

The lectures themselves occasionally touch on the relation to empirical sociology. The author is conceited enough to believe that he is supplying the musical branch of that discipline with enough fruitful questions to keep it meaningfully occupied for some time and to advance the link between theory and fact-finding—a link that is constantly called for and constantly put off again, not without changes in the overly abstract polarity of both occurring in the process. But he is not conceited enough to posit, as already valid, whatever theses of his might be plausible in theory, insofar as they imply empirical assertions. By empirical rules, many of those would be hypothetical. At times—in the typology, for instance—it is fairly clear how research techniques might serve to test the ideas; in other chapters, as in the ones on function or on public opinion, it is less obvious. Working out the process in detail would have exceeded the limits which the author placed on his task.

What ought to be done is hard to say; it would need to be most carefully thought out and then carried out step by step, with the research instruments subject to critical correction. The constitutive strata that have been defined theoretically, like the ones of function, of social differentiation, of public opinion, also the unconscious dimension of the social psychology of conductor and orchestra—all these are impervious to direct questioning. Their penetration is barred by the verbalization problem as well as by the affective side of those complexes. Besides, we can say of theses derived from research instruments that the more differentiated they become, the greater, generally, is the threat of their elimination for lack of distinctiveness, and that without a decision being made about truth or untruth of the so-called hypothesis itself. But that such differentiation is indispensable if the instruments are not to miss from the start what the respective research would be concerned with—this will be clear to anyone who gets down to the serious work of translation.

Occurring further in the network of reflections are numerous statements whose evidential value is of a different sort than might be nailed down with research methods. A general discussion of these questions will be found in the essay *"Soziologie und empirische Forschung,"* now contained in the volume *Sociologica II*. Empirical inquiries aimed at confirming or refuting theorems of this book would have to stick to its principle, at least: to grasp and analyze subjective modes of behavior toward music in relation to the thing itself and its definable content, rather than to disregard the quality of the object, to treat it as a mere stimulus of projections, and to confine oneself to determining, measuring, and classifying subjective reactions to the object, if not sedimented modes of conduct.

A sociology of music in which music means more than cigarettes or soap in market researches takes more than an awareness of society and its structures, and more than a purely informational knowledge of musical phenomena. It requires a full understanding of music itself, in all its implications. A methodology that lacks this understanding and therefore depreciates it as too subjectivistic will only lapse the more deeply into subjectivism, the median value of researched opinions.

Frankfurt, July 1962

INTRODUCTION
TO THE SOCIOLOGY
OF MUSIC

1

TYPES OF MUSICAL CONDUCT

Asked to say offhand what a sociology of music is, one would probably start by defining it as knowledge of the relation between music and the socially organized individuals who listen to it.

Such knowledge would call for the most extensive empirical research. But it could not be productively undertaken, would not rise above the compilation of inarticulate facts, if the problems were not already structured in theory—if we did not know what is relevant and what we want to inform ourselves about.

To this end, raising specific questions may be more helpful than any general reflections on music and society. At first, therefore, I shall deal theoretically with typical modes of conduct in listening to music under the conditions that prevail in present-day society. Yet earlier situations cannot be simply ignored lest we lose a grasp of today's characteristic features. On the other hand, as in many sectors of material sociology, we lack comparable and reliable research data on the past. In scientific debate one likes to use the absence of such data to blunt all criticism of the status quo, arguing that presumably the old days were no better. The more our research aims to establish discoverable data—regardless of the dynamics they are involved in—the more apologetic will be its nature, the more inclined to accept its own thematic condition as the ultimate, to "recognize" it in a twofold sense.

We are told, for instance, that uncounted multitudes have received their first taste of music from mechanical means of mass reproduction, and that, according to concepts of statistical universality, these means have thus raised the listening level. Here I would rather avoid this question, which seems less than promising; dauntless convictions of cultural progress and the culture-conservative jeremiad about "leveling" are worthy of each other. Materials for a responsible answer to the problem can be found in E. Suchman's study "Invitation to Music," published in New York in the volume *Radio Research 1941*.

Nor am I going to expound gravid theses on the distribution of listening types. I conceive them solely as qualitatively characteristic profiles that will illuminate something about hearing music as a sociological index, also perhaps about its differentiations and determinants. Whenever I make statements that sound quantitative—even in theoretical sociology this can hardly be avoided altogether—they are made in order to be tested; they are not meant as outright assertions. And it is all but needless to stress that the listening types do not occur in chemical purity. They are unquestionably subject to the universal skepticism which empirical science, notably psychology, harbors about typologies. What such a typology inevitably classifies as a "mixed type" is in truth no mixture at all; rather, it is evidence of the fact that the chosen principle of stylization has been imposed upon the material. It is the expression of a methodological difficulty, not of a quality of the thing itself.

And yet the types are not arbitrary conceptions. They are points of crystallization, determined by reflecting on principles of the sociology of music. Once we posit the premise that among the ways in which social problems and complexities express themselves are contradictions in the relation between musical production and reception, that indeed those ways are expressed in the very structure of listening—once we adopt this point of departure we shall not be able to expect an unbroken continuum to lead from fully adequate listening to an unrelated or surrogated one. Instead, we shall expect those contradictions and contrasts to influence even the way and the habits of listening to music. Contradictoriness means discontinuity. What contradicts each other appears as set off against each other. It is reflection on the underlying social problematics of music as much as extensive observation and its frequent self-correction that has led to the typology.

Once translated into empirical criteria and sufficiently tested, the typology would of course have to be modified and differentiated once more, especially regarding the type that listens to music as entertainment. The cruder the mental products investigated by sociology, the more refined must be the procedures necessary to do justice to the effect of such phenomena. It is far more difficult to see why one popular song is a hit and another a flop than why Bach finds more of an echo than Telemann, and a Haydn symphony more than a piece by Stamitz. What the typology intends, being well aware of social antagonisms, is to come from the thing itself, from music itself, to a plausible grouping of the discontinuous reactions to music.

The typology is thus to be understood as merely one of ideal types—a trait it shares with all typologies. The transitions have been eliminated. If the underlying thoughts are valid, the types, or some of them at least, should be more plastically distinct from each other than seems likely to a scientific frame of mind whose groups are formed purely instrumentally, or from a conceptless arrangement of empirical materials, not according to the sense of the phenomena. It should be possible to state solid earmarks for the several types, marks solid enough to tell whether the types are rightly or wrongly assigned, to establish their distribution in a given case, and also to make out some social and socio-psychological correlations. To bear fruit, however, empirical inquiries of this sort would have to take their bearings from society's relation to the musical objects. Society is the totality of those who listen to music and those who do not, yet it is by objective structural features of the music that audience reactions are apt to be determined. Accordingly, the canon guiding the construction of the types does not—as in the case of purely subjectively directed empirical findings—refer exclusively to tastes, preferences, aversions, and habits of the audience. Rather, it rests upon the adequacy or inadequacy of the act of listening to that which is heard. A premise is that works are objectively structured things and meaningful in themselves, things that invite analysis and can be perceived and experienced with different degrees of accuracy. What the types want, without claiming to be complete and without tying themselves too strictly to their goal, is to stake out realms of their own, realms that range from fully adequate listening, as it corresponds to the developed consciousness of the most advanced professional musicians, to a total lack of understanding and complete indifference to the material—an indifference, by the way, which should by no means be confused with musical insensitivity. But the arrangement is not one-dimensional; from different points of view, the type closest to the subject matter may be now this, now that. Characteristic modes of conduct matter more than logically correct classification. Any pronouncements on the significance of the emerging types are suppositions.

To make scientifically sure of the subjective content of a musical experience, beyond superficial indices, is an all but prohibitively difficult task. Experiments may tell us about degrees of the intensity of the reaction; they will hardly reach its quality. The literal, perhaps physiological and thus measurable, effects which a specific music exerts—even accelerated pulse rates have been noted—are far from identical with the esthetic experience of a work of art as such. Musical introspection is a most uncertain thing. Besides, most people who have not mastered the technical terminology will encounter insurmountable obstacles in verbalizing their own musical experiences, quite apart from the fact that the verbal expression itself is already prefiltered and its value for a knowledge of primary reactions is thus doubly questionable.

This is why differentiation of the musical experience with respect to the specific quality of the object—the quality that makes the conduct discernible—seems to be the most fruitful method of transcending trivialities in that sector of the sociology of music which deals with people, not with music itself. As for the expert, whom we tend to view as competent in that sector, the question of his cognitive criteria is itself subject to both social and intramusical problematics. The *communis opinio* of a committee of experts would not suffice as a basis. The interpretation of musical content is decided by the inner composition of the works and is as one therewith by virtue of the theory linked with the works' experience.

The *expert* himself, as the first type, would have to be defined by entirely adequate hearing. He would be the fully conscious listener who tends to miss nothing and at the same time, at each moment, accounts to himself for what he has heard. For a start, if a man has his first encounter with the second movement of Webern's Trio for Strings and can name the formal components of that dissolved, architectonically unsupported piece, such a man would qualify as an expert. Spontaneously following the course of music, even complicated music, he hears the sequence, hears past, present, and future moments together so that they crystallize into a meaningful context. Simultaneous complexities—in other words, a complicated

4

harmony and polyphony—are separately and distinctly grasped by the expert.

The fully adequate mode of conduct might be called "structural hearing." [1] Its horizon is a concrete musical logic: the listener understands what he perceives as necessary, although the necessity is never literally causal. The location of this logic is technique; to one whose ear thinks along with what he hears, its several elements are promptly present as technical, and it is in technical categories that the context of meaning is essentially revealed.

Today this type may be more or less limited to the circle of professional musicians. Not all of them meet its criteria; indeed, many reproductive artists are apt to resist them. Quantitatively the type is probably scarcely worth noting; it marks the limit value of a typological series that extends away from it. One hasty assumption to guard against is that the professionals' privilege to constitute this type might be explicable by the social process of alienation between individuals and objective spirit in the late bourgeois phase. That explanation would discredit the type itself. The tendency of most musicians, from their first recorded utterances on, has been to grant full comprehension of their works to their own kind only, and the increasing complexity of compositions can hardly have failed to further reduce the circle of the fully qualified. At all events, it will have done so relatively to the growing numbers that listen to music at all.

Under the prevailing social conditions, making experts of all listeners would of course be an inhumanly utopian enterprise. The compulsion which the work's integral form exerts upon the listener is not only incompatible with his nature, with his situation, and with the state of nonprofessional musical education, but with individual liberty as well. This is what bestows legitimacy on the type of the *good listener* as opposed to the expert. The good listener too hears beyond musical details, makes connections spontaneously, and judges for good reasons, not just by categories of prestige and by an arbitrary taste; but he is not, or not fully, aware of the technical and structural implications. Having unconsciously mastered its immanent logic, he understands music about the way we understand our own language even though virtually or wholly ignorant of its grammar and syntax.

This is the type we mean when we speak of "a musical

5

person"—assuming that this phrase is still a reminder of the capacity for direct, meaningful hearing, that it is not enough for us to find that someone "likes" music. Historically, such musicality required a certain homogeneity of musical culture; furthermore, it needed some solidity of the total condition, at least in the groups reacting to works of art. The chances are that something of this sort survived at courts and in aristocratic circles as late as the nineteenth century. There is a letter written by Chopin in which, though deploring the distracted way of life in high society, he credits it with real comprehension while chiding the bourgeoisie for appreciating only the stunning performance—"the show," one would say nowadays. Characters of this type are drawn by Proust in the Guermantes sphere—Baron Charlus, for example.

With society irresistibly turning bourgeois and the exchange and performance principles victorious, the good listener—again in proportion to the increasing numbers that will listen to music at all—may be presumed to keep growing rarer and threatening to disappear. There are signs of a polarization toward the extremes of the typology: today one tends to understand either everything or nothing. Partly at fault, of course, is the decay, under pressure from mass media and mechanical reproduction, of any nonprofessional musical initiative. The amateur's best chance of survival may be where remnants of an aristocratic society have managed to hold out, as in Vienna. In the petty bourgeoisie the type is hardly apt to occur any more, with the exception of polemical lone wolves who are already tending to expertise. In the past, by the way, there was a far better understanding between good listeners and experts than exists today between the so-called educated class and the products of the avant-garde.

The sociological heir to this type has come to be a third type, the properly bourgeois one in control of opera and concert audiences. We may call this type the *culture consumer*. He is a copious, sometimes a voracious listener, well-informed, a collector of records. He respects music as a cultural asset, often as something a man must know for the sake of his own social standing; this attitude runs the gamut from an earnest sense of obligation to vulgar snobbery. For the spontaneous and direct relation to music, the faculty of simultaneously experiencing and comprehending its structure, it substitutes hoarding as much musical information as possible, notably about biographical data and about the merits of interpreters, a subject for hours of inane discussion. It is not rare for this type to have an extensive knowledge of the literature, but of the sort that themes of famous, oft-repeated works of music will be hummed and instantly identified. The unfoldment of a composition does not matter. The structure of hearing is atomistic: the type lies in wait for specific elements, for supposedly beautiful melodies, for grandiose moments. On the whole, his relation to music has a fetishistic touch.[2] The standard he consumes by is the prominence of the consumed. The joy of consumption, of that which—in his language—music "gives" to him, outweighs his enjoyment of the music itself as a work of art that makes demands on him.

Two or three generations ago this type used to pose as a Wagnerian; today he is more likely to call Wagner names. At a violinist's concert his interest will focus on what he calls "tone production," if not indeed on the violin itself. In a singer's case it is the voice that interests this type; in a pianist's, it may be the tuning of the grand. Such people are appraisers. The one thing they primarily respond to is an exorbitant and, so to speak, measurable performance—breakneck virtuosity, for instance, wholly in the sense of the "show" ideal. Technique, the means, impresses them as an end in itself; in this respect they are quite close to the presently widespread mass audience. Of course, they posture as elitists hostile to the mass. Their milieu is the upper and uplifted bourgeoisie, with links to the petty one; their ideology may be mostly reactionary, culture-conservative. Almost always they are enemies of the vulnerable new music, proving their value-conserving and at the same time discriminating level to themselves by railing jointly at the "crazy stuff."

Conformism and conventionality largely mark their social character. Quantitatively, though having notably more representatives than the second type, this third one is still rather unsubstantial even in countries with so strong a musical tradition as Germany and Austria. It is a key group, however, and to a great extent determines the official life of music. It furnishes not only the subscribers to the leading concert societies and opera houses, not only the pilgrims to festivals like Salzburg and Bayreuth, but more importantly, the membership of the programming and scheduling bodies—above all, the philharmonic concert committee ladies in

America. They are the ones to guide that reified taste which wrongly deems itself superior to that of the culture industry. More and more of the musical cultural commodities administered by this type are transformed into commodities of manipulated consumption.

Next in line would be another type, one defined not by the relation to the specific quality of what is heard, but by its own mentality, grown independent of the object. This is the *emotional listener*. His relation to music is less rigid and indirect than the culture consumer's, but in another respect it is even farther removed from perception: to him, the relation becomes crucial for triggering instinctual stirrings otherwise tamed or repressed by norms of civilization. Often music becomes a source of irrationality, whereby a man inexorably harnessed to the bustle of rationalistic self-preservation will be enabled to keep having feelings at all. Often he has virtually nothing to do any more with the form of what he has heard: its preponderant function is that of such a trigger. The listening process follows the theorem of specific sense energies: a sensation of light results from a punch in the eye. Yet this type may indeed respond with particular strength to music of an obvious emotional hue, like Tchaikovsky's. He is easily moved to tears, and his links with the culture consumer are continuous; the latter's arsenal too is rarely without an appeal to the emotional values of genuine music.

In Germany—perhaps under the spell of the cultural respect for music—the emotional listener seems less characteristic than in Anglo-Saxon countries, where the stricter pressures of civilization necessitate evasions into uncontrollably introverted realms of feeling; in technologically backward countries, notably in the Slavonic ones, it is also likely to retain a role. The contemporary output tolerated and mass-produced in the Soviet Union is tailor-made for this type; in any event its musical ego ideal is patterned after the cliché of the violently oscillating, now ebullient, now melancholy Slav. As in music, the type is probably naive, or ostensibly naive, at least in his overall habitus. The immediacy of his reactions tallies with an occasional stubborn blindness to the thing he is reacting to. He does not want to know anything and is therefore easily influenced from the outset. The musical culture industry can plan for him—in Germany and Austria with the synthetic folk song species, for example, from about the early nineteen-thirties on.

Socially the type is hard to identify. He may be credited with some warmth; perhaps he is really less callous and self-satisfied than the culture consumer who outranks him, according to established concepts of taste. And yet this may be the very listening type to cover the drudges and notorious "tired businessmen" who seek, in a realm that will not affect their lives, to compensate for what they must deny themselves otherwise.

The type extends from those whom music, of whichever kind, will stimulate to visual notions and associations to men whose musical experiences approach the torpor of vague reveries. Akin to it, at least, is the "sensuous" listener in the narrow sense of the word, the culinary taster for isolated sonic stimuli. At times such people may use music as a vessel into which they pour their own anguished and, according to psychoanalytical theory, "free-flowing" emotions; at other times they will identify with the music, drawing from it the emotions they miss in themselves. Problems of this sort are difficult and as much in need of investigation as the question whether auditory emotions are fictitious or real. Probably the two are not sharply severed at all. Whether the differentiations in the mode of musical reaction correspond in turn to differentiations of the total person, and ultimately to sociological ones, must remain open for the time being.

To be suspected is the anti-intellectualist effect that may be exerted on the emotional listener by a prefabricated ideology of official musical culture. Conscious listening may come to be confused with a cold and outwardly reflecting attitude toward the music. The emotional type fiercely resists all attempts to make him listen structurally—more fiercely, perhaps, than the culture consumer who for culture's sake might put up even with that. As a matter of fact, without an affective factor adequate listening is not conceivable either. Only, here the factor is the thing itself, and the psychological energy is absorbed by the concentration on it, while the emotional listener considers music a means to ends pertaining to the economy of his own drives. He does not give himself up to the thing, which thus cannot reward him with feelings either; instead, he refunctions it into a medium of pure projection.

What has developed in Germany, at least, is a stark anti-type to the emotional listener, a type which instead of using music to evade the mimetic taboo, the civilized ban on feelings, appropriates the taboo, virtually choosing it as the norm of musical conduct. The ideal of this type is a static-musical listening.[3] He scorns the official life of music as washed-out and phantasmic, but he does not strive beyond it; rather, he flees back of that life, back to times which he fancies are proof against reification, against the dominant commodity character. In his rigidity he pays tribute to the very reification he opposes. This essentially reactive type might well be christened the *"resentment listener."*

The type includes those devotees of Bach against whom I once defended him, and even more the sticklers for pre-Bachian music. In Germany, up to the very recent past, almost all the adepts of the youth movement were ensorcelled by that mode of conduct. Seemingly nonconformist in his protest against current musical activities, the resentment listener will mostly sympathize with orders and collectives for their own sake, along with all socio-psychological and political consequences. Witness the concentration of obtusely sectarian, potentially wrathful faces at so-called "Bach evenings" and other nocturnal musicales. They are well-trained in their special sphere, also in active music-making, which proceeds like clockwork; but everything is coupled with *Weltanschauung* and twisted. The inadequacy consists in the jettisoning of entire musical spheres whose perception would be crucial.

The consciousness of people of this type is pre-formed by the goals of their organizations, most of which follow crassly reactionary ideologies, and by their historicism. Loyalty to the work, which they set against the bourgeois ideal of musical showmanship, becomes an end in itself, not so much a matter of adequately presenting and experiencing the meaning of works as of guarding zealously against any minute deviation from what—impeachably enough—they take for the performing practice of past ages. If the emotional type tends to corn, the resentment listener tends to a spurious rigor, to mechanical suppression of his own stirrings in the name of shelteredness in the community. They once called themselves *Musikanten;** it took an administration of practiced

---

* Originally simply the German for musicians, this word came in the nineteenth

anti-romanticists to make them drop the name. Psychoanalytically this type remains most characteristic, an appropriation of precisely what they are against. It attests ambivalence. What this type wants is not only the counterpart of the romantic musicmaker; the wish is inspired by the most vehement affect against his *imago*.

The resentment listeners' inmost impulse is probably that of raising an age-old taboo—the civilized ban on the mimetic impulse[4]—in the very art which lives by that impulse. They want to liquidate what has not been domesticated by the solid order, the untamed vagary whose last, sorry traces are the *rubati* and exhibitions of soloists; in music, which the operetta used to grant them as a private sphere, the gypsies are to croak now as they did before, in concentration camps. Subjectivity, expression—to the resentment listener all this is profoundly linked with promiscuity, and that he cannot bear to think of. And yet, according to Bergson's insight in *Deux sources*, the longing for an open society is too strong for even that hatred to proceed to its abolition, and it is that longing which is sedimented in art. The compromise is the absurdity of an art from which mimesis has been expurgated, a germ-free art, so to speak. That art as its ideal is the secret of the resentment audience.

Strikingly undeveloped in this type is the sense for qualitative differences within the preferred literature. The ideology of unity shriveled the sense for nuances. As a general rule, whatever is differentiated comes under puritanical suspicion. The size of the resentment audience is difficult to make out; well-organized and propagandistically active, with vast influence on musical education, it functions as another key group, as the body of those who are *musisch*.* But whether it has very many representatives beyond the organizations themselves is uncertain. The masochism of a mode of conduct where one must incessantly forbid himself something or other indicates a necessary premise: collective coercion. Internalized, such coercion may well remain a determinant of the type even

---

century to acquire the slightly belittling connotation of street entertainers, hurdy-gurdyists, etc.—Transl.

* Defined in German dictionaries as "dedicated to the Muses; gifted and trained in the arts." Not only the word and its antonym, *amusisch,* but the very concept is peculiarly German.—Transl.

where the listener's real situation is an isolated one, as often in the case of broadcast music. Contexts of this sort are far too complex to be unraveled simply by correlations such as the one made between people's membership in organizations and their taste in music.

While socially the type remains to be deciphered, the direction of its deciphering can be shown. It is recruited largely from the upper petty bourgeoisie, which faced social decline. For decades, members of this stratum had become more and more dependent, less and less able to turn into outwardly self-determining and thus inwardly unfolding individuals. This also hampered their experience of the great music that is mediated—and by no means since Beethoven only—by the individual and his liberty. But at the same time that stratum's old fear of proletarization in the midst of the bourgeois world made its members cling to the ideology of social eminence, of elitism, of "inner values." [5] Their consciousness as well as their attitude toward music results from the conflict between social position and ideology. They settle it by pretending to themselves and others that the collectivity they are condemned to, the collectivity in which they are afraid of losing themselves, is superior to individuation—that it is tied to Being, meaningful, humane, and whatever else. What supports this pretense is their substitution of the preindividual state, suggested by the synthetic *Musikanten*-music and by most of the so-called Baroque, for the real, post-individual state of their own collectivization. They think they are thus investing this with an aura of health and integrity. According to the ideology of "inner values," the forced regression is falsified into something better than what the resentment listeners are denied—a process formally comparable to the fascist manipulation that invested the compulsory collective of the atomized with the insignia of a precapitalist, nature-grown "people's community."

Recently we find discussions of jazz featured in the periodical literature of this type. While jazz had long been suspect there—as subversive—one can note increasing signs of sympathies possibly linked with its domestication, long accomplished in America and no more than a question of time in Germany. The type of *jazz expert* and *jazz fan*—the two differ less than the jazz experts flatter themselves—is akin to the resentment listener in the habitus of "received heresy," of a protest against the official culture that has been socially captured and rendered harmless. The same kinship shows in the need for musical spontaneity in opposition to the prescribed ever-sameness, and it shows in the sectarian character. In Germany in particular any critical word about jazz, about whichever form of jazz happens at the moment to be worshipped as progressive, will be avenged by the inner circle as a crime of the uninitiated.

The jazz listener also shares the resentment type's aversion to the classic-romantic ideal of music; but he is free of the ascetic-sacral gesture. He boasts of precisely his mimetic side even though he has reduced it to a pattern of "standard devices." At times—not always—he too has an adequate understanding of his subject while sharing in the narrowness of reactivity. Out of a justified aversion to cultural humbug he would like best to exchange esthetics as a norm of conduct for technology and sports. He mistakes himself for a bold avant-gardist although for more than half a century his utmost excesses have been outdone and rendered consistent by serious music.

On the other hand, in crucial points such as expanded-impressionistic harmonics and the simple standardization of form, jazz remains imprisoned within narrow bounds. The undisputed predominance of the beat, from which all syncopic arts must take orders; the inability to conceive music dynamically in the proper sense of the word, as something freely evolving—these endow even this listening type with the character of bondage to authority. Except that here the character has more an Oedipal touch in the Freudian sense: it is a kind of backtalk to the father in which readiness to knuckle under is already implied. With respect to social consciousness the type is often progressive; it is found mostly among the young, of course, and probably bred and exploited by the teenage business. Its protest scarcely lasts long; what endures in many is the readiness to participate. The jazz audience itself is split, with each group plying its own special brand. The fullfledged technical experts vilify the screeching retinue of Elvis Presley. It would take a musical analysis to find out whether the offerings to which those two extremes respond are really worlds apart.

There are those who try desperately to distinguish what they consider "pure jazz" from the commercially disfigured kind, and even they cannot help admitting commercial band leaders to their place of worship. The jazz realm is tied to commercial music by its predominant basic material, the hit songs, if by nothing else. Part of its physiognomics is the amateurish incapacity to account for things musical in exact musical terms—an incapacity which it is futile to rationalize with the difficulty of nailing down the secret of the irregularities of jazz, long after the notators of serious music have learned to fix fluctuations of incomparably greater difficulty. In this type the estrangement from sanctioned musical culture recoils into a preartistic barbarism vainly advertised as a burst of primal feelings. Numerically, even if we count all those whom the leaders take for fellow travelers, this type too is modest for the time being. But in Germany it is apt to grow and probably merge with the resentment audience in the not-too-distant future.

The quantitatively most significant of all the types is certainly the listener to whom *music is entertainment* and no more. If we were thinking purely in terms of statistical criteria, not of the weight of particular types in society and in musical life, and not of typical positions on the subject matter, the entertainment type would be the only relevant one. Even without such a qualification it seems doubtful whether in view of the preponderance of this type it will be worth sociology's while to develop a much more far-reaching typology. The picture changes only when we start to look at music not just as something For Others, a social function, but as an In-Itself—when the present social problematics of music are ultimately fused with the very appearance of its socialization.

The entertainment listener is the type the culture industry is made for, whether it adjusts to him, in line with its own ideology, or whether it elicits or indeed creates the type. Perhaps the isolated question of priority is wrongly put, and industry and audience both make up a function of the state of society, a function in which production and consumption are entwined. Socially the entertainment listener type would have to be correlated with a widely noted phenomenon that can refer to none but a subjective consciousness, however: with a leveled unitarian ideology. We would have to examine whether the social differences that have since been observed in this ideology show up among entertainment listeners as well. One hypothesis would be that the lower stratum will surrender to unrationalized entertainment while the upper will dress it up idealistically, as spirit and culture, and will select it accordingly.

The widespread elevated entertainment music would square very well with this compromise between ideology and actual listening. The ground for the type has been prepared in another type: in the culture consumer, who does not relate to specific music either; to both types it is not a meaningful context but a source of stimuli. Elements of emotional listening play a part there, so do elements of listening as a sport. But all of this is flattened as by a steamroller, leveled by the need for music as a comfortable distraction.

It is quite possible that extremes of this type may not even be gratified any longer by the atomistic stimuli, that music will hardly be enjoyed any longer, in any conceivable sense. The structure of this sort of listening is like that of smoking. We define it more by our displeasure in turning the radio off than by the pleasure we feel, however modestly, while it is playing. No one knows the size of the group that will, as it has often been put, let itself be sprinkled with broadcast music without really listening; but that unknown size illuminates the whole domain. The comparison with addiction is inescapable. Addicted conduct generally has a social component: it is one possible reaction to the atomization which, as sociologists have noticed, parallels the compression of the social network. The addict manages to cope with the situation of social pressure, as well as with that of his loneliness, by dressing it up, so to speak, as a reality of his own being; he turns the formula "Leave me alone!" into something like an illusionary private realm, where he thinks he can be himself.

However, as might be expected of the extreme entertainment listener's misrelation to the subject matter, his inner realm itself stays altogether empty, abstract, and indefinite. Where this attitude is radicalized, where artificial paradises take shape as they do for the hashish smoker, powerful taboos are violated. Yet the addictive tendency is innate in the social contexts. It cannot be simply suppressed. Results of the conflict are all the patterns of conduct which satisfy the addict's need in weakened form without too greatly impairing the dominant work ethic and sociability. Society's position on the use of alcohol—a lenient one, to say the least—is one such pattern; the social approbation of tobacco is another. Addiction to music on the part of a number of entertainment listeners would be a similar phenomenon. It attaches itself to technology, which is affectively engaged in any case. There can be no more drastic demonstration of the compromise character than the conduct of a man who has the radio playing while he works. The unconcentrated attitude in this simultaneity has long been historically prepared by the entertainment listener and is often aided by the material he will hear at such times.

The enormous number of entertainment listeners justifies the assumption that their type is of the sort which in American social research has won notoriety as "Miscellaneous." Probably it is reducing quite heterogeneous things to a common denominator. We might conceive a series leading from the man who cannot work without the blare of a radio to one who kills time and paralyzes loneliness by filling his ears with the illusion of "being with" no matter what; from him to the lovers of medleys and musical comedy tunes; on to those who value music as a means of relaxation; finally to a group one must not underestimate: to the genuinely musical who have been barred from education in general and from musical education in particular, and who therefore, and because of their place in the production process, do not share in genuine music and allow themselves to be fobbed off with staple merchandise. We encounter many such people among the "folk musicians," in provincial areas.

Mostly, however, the representatives of the entertainment type are resolutely passive and fiercely opposed to the effort which a work of art demands. For decades, for instance, members of this group have been writing letters to the Vienna Radio, protesting against broadcasts of what music to which they lend the horrible appellation "opus music" and insisting that preference be given to the "chromatic" one—to wit, to the accordion. If the culture consumer will turn up his nose at popular music, the entertainment listener's only fear is to be ranked too high. He is a self-conscious lowbrow who makes a virtue of his own mediocrity. He repays the culture of music for the social debt it incurred by banishing him from its experience. His specific mode of listening is that of distraction and deconcentration, albeit interrupted by sudden bursts of attention and recognition; conceivably even laboratory tests might have access to this listening structure. The fitting instrument for its primitivity is the program analyzer.

Assigning the entertainment listener to a distinct social group is difficult. In Germany, at least, the truly educated owe it to their own ideology to keep their distance from that type—which does not prove, by the way, that a majority of their stratum actually listens in very different fashion. Americans have no such inhibitions, and they are sure to fade in Europe too. Some social differentiations within the entertainment audience can be expected to show in its favorite materials; the young outside the jazz cult may delight in pop hits, for example, and rural segments of the population in the folk music that swamps them. The American *Radio Research* has come upon a ghostly state of facts: the synthetic cowboy and hillbilly music manufactured by the culture industry is especially popular in areas where cowboys and hillbillies are really still living.

An adequate description of the entertainment listener will be possible only in the context of the mass media, of radio, film, and television. His psychological peculiarity is a weak ego: as a guest at live broadcasting sessions he will applaud enthusiastically whenever light signals urge him to do so. To criticize the offering is as far from him as to make an effort for its sake. He is skeptical only of what takes self-reflection; ready to agree with his own customer's rating; obstinately bonded to the facade of society that grins at him from magazine covers. The type has no political profile. But, as in music, he will probably conform in reality to any rule that does not patently impair his consumer standard.

A word remains to be added on the type of the musically *indifferent,* the *unmusical,* and the *anti-musical*—if we may combine those in a type. Its roots are not, as bourgeois convention would have it, a matter of deficient natural talent, but of processes occurring in early childhood. Let me venture the hypothesis that it was always brutal authority which in those days caused the defects in this type. Children of particularly strict fathers often seem unable even to learn to read notes—now, by the way, the premise of a musical education worthy of humankind. This type evidently coincides with an excessively, one might even say pathologically realistic mentality; I have observed it in people with extreme talents for special technical fields. But neither should it surprise us if the type were found, reactively, in groups exempted from the bourgeois culture by educational privilege and economic situation

—if it constituted their reply to dehumanization, as it were, and confirmed it at the same time. The social significance of being *amusisch** in both the narrow and the broad sense of the word has not been studied yet; it would be a highly educational project.

Rejections of what has been said here may be due to misinterpretations of my draft. My point is neither to disparage representatives of the described listening types negatively nor to distort the picture of reality by deriving judgments on the world situation from the present dubious state of listening to music. To posture mentally as if mankind existed for the sake of good listening would be a grotesque echo of estheticism, just as the converse thesis, that music exists for mankind, merely puts a humane face on the furtherance of thought in exchange categories—a way of thinking to which everything that exists is only a means for something else, a way that degrades the truth of the matter and thus strikes the very men it aims to please. The prevailing condition envisioned by critical typology is not the fault of those who listen one way rather than another. It is not even the fault of the system, of the culture industry that buttresses the state of mind of people so as to be better able to exploit it. Instead, the condition arises from the nethermost sociological layers: from the separation of mental and manual labor, or of high and low forms of art; later from the socialized semiculture; ultimately from the fact that the right consciousness in the wrong world is impossible, and that even the modes of social reaction to music are in thrall to the false consciousness.

Too much weight should not be given to the social differentiations within this draft. The types, or many of them, will cut across society, as we say in the jargon of social research. For the shortcomings of each type mirror the divided whole; each is more representative of an inwardly antagonistic totality than of a particular social variation. Attempts to subsume the types, and the predominance of the entertainment listener, under the massification concept that is so popular among the masses would be particularly wrong-headed. In the entertainment listener, no matter what the old and what the new falsehood inherent in him, the

---

* See Translator's Note, p. 11 above.

masses are not uniting to rise against a culture which they are denied in the very offer. Their movement is a reflex movement; it is the discontent which Freud diagnosed in civilization, turned against civilization. It harbors the potential of something better, just as a yearning for and a chance of human dignity in dealing with music, with art pure and simple, endures in almost every other of the types, albeit in degraded form.

It would, of course, be an erroneous conclusion simply to equate such treatment of art with an unmutilated treatment of reality. The fact which expresses the antagonistic state of the whole is that even musically correct modes of conduct may, by their positions in the whole, cause moments of disaster. Whatever we do will be wrong. The expert listener needs a degree of specialization as probably never before, and the proportional decrease of the "good listener" type—if it should prove true—might well be a function of that specialization. And the price paid for it is often a seriously disturbed relation to reality, including neurotic and even psychotic character deformations. These are certainly not necessary premises of egregious musicality in love with the old-fashioned slogan of genius and dementia, yet an unregimented empiricism cannot but be struck by the fact that such defects occur precisely in the most highly qualified musicians. It cannot be an accident, but must lie in the course of specialization itself, that many of them, faced with questions beyond the realm of their own expertise, will seem naive and obtuse to the point of total disorientation and deviant pseudo-orientation.

An adequate musical consciousness does not even involve a directly adequate artistic consciousness as such. Specialization extends all the way into the relation to the various media; a number of young avant-gardists in the fine arts have been carrying on as jazz fans, all unaware of the difference in level. In cases of such disintegration, of course, we come to doubt the validity of the seemingly advanced intentions. In view of such complications there is nobody in the intimidated, overtaxed, captive audience of millions to shake a finger at and tell that he must know something about music, or at least must take an interest in it. Even the freedom of release from such obligations has an aspect of human dignity—that of a state of affairs in which culture is no longer forced upon one. A man gazing peacefully at the sky may at times be closer to truth than another who accurately follows the "Eroica." But in thus failing culture he compels conclusions about the way culture has failed mankind, and about what the world has made of mankind. The contradiction between the freedom of art and the gloomy diagnoses regarding the use of such freedom—this contradiction is one of reality, not just of the consciousness that analyzes reality so as to make some small contribution to change.

2

POPULAR MUSIC

The concept of popular music[1] is both murky and self-evident. We all know what happens to us when we absentmindedly turn on the radio, and this knowledge seems to relieve us of reflecting upon *single piece of data* what it is. The phenomenon becomes a <u>datum</u> that must be accepted as unalterable, so to speak, a datum whose sheer obstinate existence proves its right. The administrations of culture have long sanctioned the splitting of music into two spheres, with one section flatly reserved for popular music,[2] and now and then this will indeed be deplored as allegedly leveling the general taste or isolating serious music from the mass of listeners. But it is also the lack of reflection on popular music itself which precludes insights into the relation of two realms that have since congealed into rigid disciplines. They have been separated and entwined for just as long as high and low art have been. The people kept out of the cultural establishment by economic and psychological pressures, the ones whose discontent with civilization is always an expanded reproduction of the raw state of nature—these, beginning in Antiquity and definitely since the Roman Mimus, were fobbed off with specially prepared stimuli. Their lower art was mixed with remnants of that orgiastic intoxication which the higher, in the sign of progressive logicity and mastery of nature, would eliminate from itself.

Conversely, as long as the objective spirit was not yet wholly planned and steered by administrative centers, the higher art would recall the extent to which its own principle involved injustices to the many. Time and again it felt the need of something else, of something that would resist the formative esthetic will and that might serve as the touchstone of that will—and so, whether unintentionally or intentionally, it would absorb elements of the lower music. Some of this shows in the old custom of parody, of setting spiritual texts to profane melodies. Bach did not shrink from borrowing from below even in his instrumental works, as in the

Quodlibet of the "Goldberg Variations," and neither Haydn nor the Mozart of *The Magic Flute* or Beethoven would be conceivable without an interaction of what by then were separated spheres. The last instance of their reconciliation, utterly stylized and teetering as on a narrow mountain bypass, was *The Magic Flute*—an instant still mourned and longed for in such structures as Strauss and Hofmannsthal's *Ariadne auf Naxos*. There were times far into the nineteenth century when it was possible to write decent popular music. Its esthetic decay is as one with the irrevocable and irrelative dissociation of the two realms.

If the concept of decay, which cultural philistines love to cite against modern art, is justified anywhere it is in popular music. There it is tangible and precisely determinable. In Offenbach a highly original inventiveness operating on two levels, a colorful imagination, and a felicitous facility coincided with lyrics whose meaningful nonsense made Karl Kraus fall in love with them. Johann Strauss's gift for composing proper may have surpassed Offenbach's (how ingeniously the "Emperor Waltz" theme is devised in counterpoint to the cadence of the waltz pattern!), and yet he is a harbinger of decline in tasteless libretti as much as in an instinctually uncertain tendency to garish operaticism—a tendency, by the way, which the Offenbach of the Rhine nymphs had not withstood either. Popular music in general, all the way to Puccini who half-belongs to its sphere, is the worse the greater its pretensions, and lukewarm self-criticism is the very thing that keeps inducing such pretensions. The peak of bloated cretinism may well have been reached in *Friederike*, the Lehár operetta with the retouched May song. Those who came after Offenbach and Strauss were quick to waste their heritage. Their immediate successors, men like Lecocq who still preserved something from better days, were followed by the abominable monstrosities of the operetta stages of Vienna, Budapest, and Berlin. It is a matter of taste whether Hungarian *schmaltz* is more revolting than Prussian *Puppchen** brutality. Only on rare occasions would the filthy tide spew up loose and charming things such as some Leo Fall tunes or certain authentic ideas by Oscar Straus.

---

* Literally "Little Doll," "Dolly"—an endearment popular among the pre-World War I Prussian middle and lower classes.—Transl.

If the World Spirit had indeed lost its way and strayed into popular music, that music would have got some of its just deserts. Operetta and revue have become extinct, albeit on the threshold of a merry resurrection in the musicals. Their end, probably the most drastic historical phenomenon from the later phase of popular music, will be charged to the advances and the technological and economic superiority of radio and motion pictures—not unlike the way painted kitsch was choked off by the photographic one. But the revue vanished even from films, which in America had absorbed it in the early thirties. So our confidence in the World Spirit is shaken again: it may have been precisely the unrealistic and imaginative side of the revue that discomfited the mass taste. In any case its playful flights of fancy, untamed by any false logic, ranked far above the tragic second finale of Hungarian operettas. In the age of commercials one feels suddenly homesick for the old "Broadway Melodies."

The true reasons for the demise of revue and European-style operetta are difficult to find out, but a trend, at least, may be shown by general sociological reflections. Those types of music were closely connected with the economic sphere of distribution—more specifically, with the garment business. A revue was not only an undress show; it was also a dress show. One of the biggest hit operettas of the Viennese-Hungarian type, the *Autumn Maneuvers* that made Kálmán famous, came directly from the associative field of clothing manufacture, and even in the age of musicals this link remained perceptible in shows like *Pins and Needles* and *Pajama Game*. Just as the operetta's staff, mode of production, and jargon, suggested the apparel business, it could regard people in that line as its ideal audience. In Berlin, the man whom the sight of a sumptuously bedecked and simultaneously bared star moved to exclaim "Simply fabulous!" was the archetypical coat-and-suiter.

And since in Europe, at least, for reasons ranging from economic concentration to totalitarian terrorism, the relevance of this and other distributive trades declined decisively in the past thirty years, those genera of the allegedly buoyant Muse have lost some of their real basis. The loss should not be understood merely in the narrow sense, as extinction of the specific stratum which once upon a time had carried certain types of music. It applies even more in the more delicate sense that the decay of the sphere of distribution caused a

23

fading of concepts and stimuli which had been radiating far into society as long as that sphere provided models for the success of individual initiative.

The ontology of the operetta would be that of the ready-to-wear business. But just as this word has come to sound old-fashioned,* the type of entertainment borrowed from its sphere is threadbare, like a continued gamble on reactions which in a far more strictly organized world are no longer forthcoming anywhere. A detailed comparison of the operetta between 1900 and 1930, on the one hand, with today's musical comedy on the other would probably show the objects differing in the form of economic organization. Artistically, in content and means, not much has changed; but the musical as opposed to operetta and revue is "streamlined." The slick, polished, cellophane-wrapped shows of today make the operettas and their kin look sloppy as well as too much in touch with their audience, if one may put it that way—while the musical comedy serves, in a sense, to retransfer the technological reification of motion pictures to the musical stage. This may explain the global triumphs of *My Fair Lady*, for instance, a show that musically fails to meet the most primitive standards of originality and inventiveness. The galvanization of musical language and exactly, almost scientifically calculated effects goes so far that no gap remains, that precisely the consummate sales-technical organization of the "showpiece" will create the illusion of its being self-evident and natural. Insulated against whatever differs from its universe of well-planned effects, it results in an illusion of freshness, while the older form, in which everything does not yet click, seems both naive and moth-eaten to listeners who want to be up to date.

Contrasting with the crude and drastic history of the decaying types and forms of popular music is a peculiar constancy of their musical language. It makes do, throughout, with the depraved stock of late Romanticism; even Gershwin is a talented transposition of Tchaikovsky and Rachmaninoff into the amusement sphere. To this day, pop music has scarcely participated in the evolution of

---

* The German word, *Konfektion,* had a disdainful ring in the early part of the century, when every gentleman's clothes were made to measure and every lady had Parisian models discreetly copied by her own *salon de couture.*—Transl.

material that has been going on in serious music for more than fifty years. Pop music does not balk at novelties, of course, but it deprives them of function and free unfoldment by using them—down to the seemingly haphazard dissonances of some jazz trends—as mere splotches of color, ornaments added to a strictly traditional tongue. They have no power over that tongue; they are not even properly integrated in it. This is why talk of kinship between some popular music and modern music is so foolish. Even where the same is tolerated it will not stay the same; toleration will transform it into the opposite. We no longer need to worry about the traces of orgiastic memories in Offenbach's can-can or in the fraternization scene of *Die Fledermaus*; an administered, arranged intoxication ceases to be one. What is incessantly boosted as exceptional grows dull, and the festivities to which light music permanently summons its adherents, under the name of feasts for the ears, are dismal everyday fare.

In the advanced industrial countries pop music is defined by standardization: its prototype is the song hit. A popular American textbook on writing and selling such hits[3] confessed that with disarming missionary zeal some thirty years ago. The main difference between a pop song and a serious or—in the beautifully paradoxical language of that manual—a "standard" song is said to be that pop melodies and lyrics must stick to an unmercifully rigid pattern while the composer of serious songs is permitted free, autonomous creation. The textbook writers do not hesitate to call popular music "custom-built," a predicate usually reserved for automobiles.

Standardization extends from the overall plan down to details. The basic rule in the American practice that governs production everywhere is that the refrain consists of 32 bars with a "bridge," a part initiating the repetition, in the middle. Also standardized are the various types of song—not only dances, whose standardization would be plausible and by no means new, but songs celebrating motherhood or the joys of domesticity, nonsense or novelty songs, pseudo-children's-songs or lamentations at the loss of a girlfriend. For the last, which may be the most widespread of all, a curious name has become customary in America: they are called "ballads." Above all, it is the metric and harmonic cornerstones of any pop song, the beginning and the end of its several parts, that must follow the standard schema. It confirms the simplest fundamental structures, whatever deviations may occur in between. Complications remain without consequences: the pop song leads back to a few basic perceptive categories known ad nauseam. Nothing really new is allowed to intrude, nothing but calculated effects that add some spice to the ever-sameness without imperiling it. And these effects in turn take their bearings from schemata.

As mindlessness will rise to heights of acumen whenever an existing evil needs defending, the spokesmen of popular music have toiled to offer an esthetic apology for the standardization that is the primal phenomenon of the reification of music, of its naked commodity character. They have sought to blur the difference between art and directed mass production. Thus the authors of that manual hasten to equate the mechanical schemata of pop music with the strict postulates of canonically exalted forms. "Certainly there are few more stringent forms in poetry than the sonnet, and yet"—I quote verbatim—"the greatest poets of all time have woven undying beauty within its small and limited frame." A composer has "just as much opportunity for exhibiting his talent and genius in popular songs" as the impractical one with allegedly long hair has in other kinds of music.

That the comparison would have stunned Petrarch, Michelangelo, and Shakespeare does not faze the authors; those men were masters, of course, but long dead. Such imperviousness compels a humble attempt to verbalize the difference between the standardized forms of popular music and strict types of the serious one—as if we did not have to abandon all hope as soon as proof is required. The higher music's relation to its historical form is dialectical. It catches fire on those forms, melts them down, makes them vanish and return in vanishing. Popular music, on the other hand, uses the types as empty cans into which the material is pressed without interacting with the forms. Unrelated to the forms, the substance withers and at the same time belies the forms, which no longer serve for compositional organization.

The *effect* of song hits—more precisely put, perhaps: their social role—might be circumscribed as that of patterns of identification. It is comparable to the effect of movie stars, of magazine cover girls, and of the beauties in hosiery and toothpaste ads. The hits not only appeal to a "lonely crowd" of the atomized; they reckon with the immature, with those who cannot express their emotions and experiences, who either never had the power of expression or were crippled by cultural taboos.

To people harnessed between their jobs and the reproduction of their working energies, the hits are purveyors of an ersatz for feelings which their contemporaneously revised ego ideal tells them they should have. Socially the hits either channel emotions—thus recognizing them—or vicariously fulfill the longing for emotions. The element of esthetic appearance, the distinction of art from empirical reality, is restored to that reality in song hits: in the actual psychological household, appearance substitutes for what the listeners are really denied. What makes a hit a hit, aside from the manipulative energy of the moment, is its power either to absorb or to feign widespread stirrings. Couching texts and titles, in particular, in a sort of advertising language plays a part; but according to American research results these carry less weight than the music.

To visualize this, let me recall related processes from other mass media in which words or representational images are used. The growing tendency to integrate all such media entitles us to draw conclusions on pop music. In an imaginary but psychologically emotion-laden domain, the listener who remembers a hit song will turn into the song's ideal subject, into the person for whom the song ideally speaks. At the same time, as one of many who identify with that fictitious subject, that musical I, he will feel his isolation ease as he himself feels integrated into the community of "fans." In whistling such a song he bows to a ritual of socialization, although beyond this unarticulated subjective stirring of the moment his isolation continues unchanged. To phrase such states of fact as verifiable or refutable hypotheses, social psychologists would need research procedures of an extraordinary subtlety that is now hard to imagine. Empiricist resistance to theorems of such plausibility is due not only to the backwardness of the investigative techniques currently available to the sociology of music; what this resistance can teach us is that structural sociological insights cannot always be simply reduced to succinct specific findings.

It is the banality of present-day popular music—a banality relentlessly controlled in order to make it salable—which brands that music with its crucial trait. That trait is vulgarity. We might almost suspect that this is the most avid concern of the audience, that the maxim of their musical mentality is indeed Brecht's line: "But I don't want to be human!" Any musical reminder of themselves, of the doubtfulness and possible uplifting of their own existence, will embarrass them. That they are really cut off from their potential is the very reason why it infuriates them to be reminded by art.

The perfectly phrased antithesis of popular music is Siegmund's query in the death announcement scene of *Die Walküre*: *"Wer ist es, die so ernst und schön mir naht?"* Thunderous, possibly prerehearsed applause, on the other hand, signifies what the bellowers call "humor" and what has meanwhile become the worst; the only thing worse is lack of humor. The vulgarity of the musical posture; the disparagement of all distances; the insistence that nothing a man comes in touch with may be better, or may be regarded as better, than he himself is or thinks he is—all this is social by nature. The vulgarity consists in identification with the abasement from which there is no escape for the captive consciousness it was inflicted on. True, such abasements were more or less involuntarily arranged by the so-called "lower art" of the past, and that art was always at the abased ones' disposal; but today abasement itself is organized and administered, and the identification with it is planned and controlled. That is the disgrace of pop music, not what its branches are chided for in such phrases as "soullessness" or even "unbridled sensuality."

Where serious music satisfies its own concept, every detail gets its concrete meaning from the total course, and this totality in turn receives it from the living interrelation of details that oppose and continue one another, pass into each other, and recur. Where the form is dictated from outside, on the other hand, one will, as Wagner put it, "hear the harness rattle." Of course, in the period from the age of thorough-bass to the tonality crisis there is no lack of invariants, even of embarrassing invariants, in serious music either. But in good pieces even the clichés acquire changing values, depending on the configuration in which they are placed, and they do not confront the specific musical content in alienation. Moreover, at least since Beethoven, the invariants have been sensed as problematical, while in popular music they are today imposed with unproblematical imperiousness. Some of Beethoven's grandest movements, the first of the "Appassionata," for instance, or that of the Ninth Symphony, are attempts to take the tectonic element of the sonata form—an element that has ceased to be directly one with the musical flow—and to develop it out of that flow. The traditionally required eternal recurrence was to be legitimized as a result of dynamic execution. Eventually, in the historical unfoldment of this tendency, the invariants kept dissolving more and more; in essence, the history of great music over the past 200 years has been a critique of those very elements which complementarily claim absolute validity in popular music. In a sense, popular music constitutes the dregs of musical history.

Because it is so crudely simple, however, the standardization of that music should be interpreted not so much intramusically as sociologically. It aims at standardized reactions, and its success— notably its adherents' fierce aversion to anything different—proves that it has gained its end. It is not only the interested parties, the producers and distributors of pop music, who manipulate the way it will be heard; it is the music itself, so to speak, its immanent character. It sets up a system of conditioned reflexes in its victim, and the crux is not even the antithesis of primitivity and differentiation. Simplicity in itself is neither an asset nor a shortcoming. But in all music that deserves the name of art, every detail, even the simplest, would be itself; none would be arbitrarily interchangeable. Where traditional music does not meet this requirement it is not sufficient unto itself, not even if it carries the most famous signatures.

In a hit song, on the other hand, the schemata are so separated from the concrete course of the music that everything can be replaced by something else. More complex elements are sometimes needed to avoid a boredom that would scare off customers who flee from boredom to popular music; but not even those complexities stand for themselves. They are ornaments or cloaks covering an ever-sameness. Chained to the schema, a listener no sooner hears a deviation than he will dissolve it into his all-too familiar modes of ingrained reaction. The composition listens for the listener—something faintly comparable to the movie technique in which the social agency of the camera eye intervenes on the production side between the product and the moviegoer, anticipating the sensations he is to see with. Spontaneous, concentrated hearing, on the other hand, is not demanded and indeed scarcely tolerated by popular music, which proclaims the need for relaxation from the strenuous processes of labor as its own norm. One ought to listen effortlessly, perhaps with but half an ear; one famous American radio program was called "Easy Listening." Orientation is by listening models under which a man can automatically and unconsciously subsume whatever he comes across.

Unmistakable analogues of such premasticated material are the printed "digests." The passivity that has been furthered fits into the culture industry's entire system of progressive stultification. The stultifying effect does not issue directly from particular pieces; but for the fan—whose need for what is argued upon him may rise to the point of dull euphoria, a sorry relic of the old intoxication—for the fan the total system of popular music is a training course in a passivity that will probably spread to his thought and social conduct. The befogging effect which Nietzsche dreaded in Wagner's music has been taken up and socialized by the popular one. The subtly habit-forming effect contrasts oddly with the crudeness of the stimuli themselves. In that sense pop music is ideology, prior to all intentions that might perhaps be pursued with it, let alone with its silly lyrics. Research might poach on its preserve by analyzing the modes of conduct and the habitus of its addicts in other areas; the purely musical reactions to popular music itself are mostly too unspecific and too unarticulated for social psychology to obtain major results from them alone.

Yet the mode of turning out popular music as a mass product must not be too literally conceived in the image of industrial mass production. The forms of distribution are highly rationalized; so is the advertising, in which American broadcasters in particular spread the message of tangible industrial interests. But all this refers essentially to the sphere of circulation, not to that of production. However much the industrial division of labor may be recalled by features such as the dissection into minute components fitting without a break into the schema, or by the producers' division into those who have the alleged idea and others who formulate the song, into lyric writers and arrangers—for all that, the process remains one of craftsmanship, so to speak. Full-fledged rationalization, the composition of hits by musical computers, would be easily imaginable; Mozart was already toying with the idea. But until now we have not come that far.

This technological backwardness pays economic dividends. The nonsimultaneity of hits, the combination of sharp practice with the clumsiness of half-amateurish producing—these have a function, and what makes the function comprehensible is that popular music, being measured solely by its own social-psychological effect, is obliged on that effect's account to fulfill contradictory desiderata. On the one hand it must catch the listener's attention, must differ from other popular songs if it is to sell, to reach the listener at all. On the other hand it must not go beyond what audiences are used to, lest it repel them. It must remain unobtrusive, must not transcend that musical language which seems natural to the average listener envisaged by the producers—that is to say, the tonality of the Romanticist age, possibly enriched with contingencies of impressionistic or later derivation.

The difficulty facing the producer of pop music is that he must void the contradiction. He must write something impressive enough to be remembered and at the same time well-known enough to be banal. What helps here is the old-fashioned individualistic moment which in the production process is voluntarily or involuntarily spared. It corresponds as much to the need to be abruptly striking as to the need to hide the all-governing standardization, the ready-made aspect of form and feeling, from a listener who should always feel treated as if the mass product were meant for him alone. The means to that end, one of the constituents of popular music, is pseudo-individualization. In the cultural mass product it is a reminder of glorious spontaneity—also of freedom to choose in the marketplace, as needed—despite its own compliance with standardization. Pseudo-individualization is what fools us about predigestion. Extremes of it are the improvisations in commercial jazz, which jazz journalism feeds upon. They stress instantaneous invention even though the metric and harmonic schema keeps them in such narrow bounds that they in turn might be reduced to a minimum of basic forms. In fact, the chances are that most of what is served up as improvisation outside the innermost circles of jazz experts will have been rehearsed.

Pseudo-individualization does not extend to these offerings only.

31

It covers the whole field. Especially in the sphere of the harmonic and coloristic stimuli included in the planning of popular music—the pre-World War I Viennese operetta already had a sticky fondness for the harp—the rule is to create a semblance of immediacy and specificity backed by no more than the harmonizer's and arranger's routine. This routine should not be underrated. All in all, when talking about song hits we must beware of an apologetics of culture that would hardly be worth more than one of barbarism. Just as the standard forms of pop music are derived from traditional dances, those dances were frequently standardized long before commercial music started pandering to the ideal of mass production. The minuets of lesser seventeenth-century composers were as fatally alike as our pop songs.

On the other hand (if I may paraphrase a pretty line coined a generation ago by Willy Haas for literature) there is still some good bad music left today, along with all the bad good music. Under the pressures of the marketplace much genuine talent is absorbed by popular music and cannot be entirely crushed even there. Even in the thoroughly commercialized late phase primary ideas, beautifully arched melodies, pregnant rhythmic and harmonic turns will be encountered, particularly in America. But the spheres can only be defined from the extremes, not from the transitions, and besides, even the most gifted escapades within popular music are marred by considerations paid to the appointed guardians of salability. Boneheadedness is shrewdly calculated and revved up by highly qualified musicians, and there are many more of those throughout the realm of pop music than the serious one's sense of superiority likes to admit.

In America they are found chiefly among arrangers, but also among recording experts, band leaders, and other groups. Illiteracy, which remains the indispensable foundation, is presented to sound like the latest fad and, at the same time, if possible, like high culture—above all, however, to "sound well," in line with an ideal that is not easy to attain by any means. To get there, one must know his business. At times—as in the case of the Revellers, a vocal group famed in the twenties—there will be crass incongruities between the mediocre compositions and a reproduction that need not fear comparison with the practice of avant-garde chamber music. The preponderance of means over ends which holds sway throughout the culture industry is manifested in popular music as a waste of egregious interpreters on unworthy products. That so many who know better let themselves be thus misused is due, of course, to economic reasons; but their bad conscience creates a climate perfect for poisonous rancor. With cynical naiveté, yet not without a certain measure of awful justification, they tell themselves that they are holding the patent on the spirit of the times.

Jazz, in particular, advances this claim. An overwhelming portion of whatever the public regards as jazz ought to be classified as pseudo-individualization. Its basic idea, unchanged now for close to fifty years, is of that type. Even in its more sophisticated forms jazz is popular music, and only the bad German habit of turning any and everything into a pretentious *Weltanschauung* has clouded the issue here and installed jazz as the holy-unholy norm of what fancies itself in revolt against the norm of music. Within pop music, jazz has its unquestioned merits. Against the idiotic derivatives from the Johann Strauss-type operetta it taught technique, presence of mind, and the concentration which pop music had discarded, and it developed the faculties of tonal and rhythmical differentiation. The climate of jazz freed teenagers from the stuffily sentimental utility music of their parents. Jazz calls for criticism only when a timeless fashion, organized and multiplied by special interests, comes to misconceive itself as modern, if not indeed as an avant-garde. Jazz does not reflect whichever reactive forms of the epoch may have entered into it, nor does it lend them a free voice. What it does is duplicate them in humble agreement.

Some thirty years ago Winthrop Sargeant, one of the most reliable American experts, characterized jazz as a "get-together art for regular fellows"—a sportive acoustical occasion for normal citizens to gather at—and that is what it remains, now as before. "Jazz," Sargeant continues in his book, *Jazz, Hot and Hybrid* (New York, 1936), stresses a conformist regularity by submerging the individual consciousness in a kind of massive self-hypnosis. In jazz the individual will submit to society, and the individuals who participate in it are not only alike but virtually indistinguishable."

The social function of jazz coincides with its history, the history of a heresy that has been received into the mass culture. Certainly, jazz has the potential of a musical breakout from this culture on the part of those who were either refused admittance to it or annoyed by its mendacity. Time and again, however, jazz became a captive of the culture industry and thus of musical and social conformism; famed devices of its phases, such as "swing," "bebop," "cool jazz," are both advertising slogans and marks of that process of absorption. Popular music can no more be exploded from within, on its own premises and with its own habituated means, than its own sphere points beyond it.

As long as we interpret that music at all, according to its own musical and even psychological composition, we shall be too credulous in assuming that the criteria of autonomous musical production apply to popular music and its more or less exalted variants. Due to the preponderance of its commodity character over any esthetic one, the mechanisms of distribution carry at least as much weight as that which they distribute. Each single song hit is its own advertisement and a boost for its title, just as in American sheet music the phrases that repeat the title are usually set beneath the notes in capital letters. The whole entertainment music would scarcely have the scope and effect it has without the element Americans call "plugging." A song chosen for bestsellerdom will be drummed into the listeners' ears until they cannot help recognizing it and hence—as the psychologists of compositional advertising correctly figure—will love it. The institutions of "hit parades," "hit marts," and however else they may be styled, are prototypical: no telling any more which "hits" have really caught on with the public and are therefore offered to it as its favorites, and which owe their success to a presentation that merely acts as if the success were a fact. Yet for all this calculation, the undifferentiated material should not lure us into undifferentiated thought. To become a hit, a pop song must meet minimum requirements. It probably must show some characteristics of arising from "an idea," * a concept which in the higher music has long become problematical; but these original touches must be in realistic

---

* We do not have a word for the German *Einfall*. Literally it means something "falling into" one, i.e. occurring to or striking one; the only English phrase that conveys at least the manner of its happening is "stroke of genius." But it does not take genius to have an *Einfall*. Any number of them may strike in the most prosaic areas. The common expression we use when a German would say *"Mir fällt etwas ein"* is "I've got an idea!"—Transl.

proportion to the universally familiar. To a meaningful sociology of music, studying these structures, musically analyzing hits as well as polling audiences, should be a tempting challenge.

Knowledge of the social mechanisms that decide about selection, distribution, and effect—notably of the high-pressure advertising to which Douglas McDougald has devoted a special inquiry—may well lead us to conceive the effect of popular music as totally predetermined. We may come to regard hits as simply "made" by the mass media, with the listeners' taste carrying no weight at all. Yet this would be an oversimplification even under present conditions of concentrated culture-industrial power. For a song to become a hit, of course, its being broadcast and recorded is a necessary premise; the piece that has no chance to reach a large circle of listeners will hardly come to be the favorite of such a circle. But this necessary precondition does not suffice. To begin with, if it is to catch on, a popular song must generally conform to the rules prevailing at the moment. Mistakes in compositional technique matter little; automatically barred is any material in direct violation of current usage—above all, whatever belongs clearly to a fashion that has been ruled passé, or what employs substantially more modern means than customary. The normative modes, although they are certainly manipulated at first, tend nonetheless to turn into modes of audience reaction, and the audience will use them quickly and, as it were, spontaneously to measure what is forced upon it. It may be that in this insistence on the fashionable standards it fancies itself in possession of a remnant of free choice.

Nor is that all. Even in pop songs, in a music that can scarcely be counted as art, there is a specific quality very hard to describe but honored by listeners. The so-called "evergreens," hits that seem to defy aging and to outlast all fashions, testify to the existence of this quality; it would be worthwhile tracking down the story of such evergreens to see how far they are made by culture-industrial selection or have maintained themselves on their own, by means of traits that set them apart for certain periods, at least, from ephemeral products.

At first, of course, their indelibility which the culture industry exploits rests upon the primacy, throughout the sphere, of effect over matter. What vulgar empiricism takes for art suits the popular, vulgar art. In that empiricism art is conceived as a battery of tests, an agglomerate of stimuli that can be investigated only by observing and analyzing the reactions of human guinea pigs— whoever knows about the thing itself is deemed just a special case of the guinea-pig category—and in that case each hit is indeed an experimental setup in social psychology, a schema and possible trigger of projections, instinctual stirrings, and behaviors. Like levers, the evergreens mobilize private erotic associations in each individual. These will so readily yield to the general formula because they themselves, in their flowering period, were not so private after all—because it is only now, as sentimental memories, that they will merge with the individual's existence. The mechanism of the evergreens is once again synthetically set in motion by a particular, tirelessly cultivated species: by the type of hits which in America are classified as "nostalgia songs." They fake a longing for past, irrevocably lost experiences, dedicated to all those consumers who fancy that in memories of a fictitious past they will gain the life denied them.

And yet that specific quality of the evergreens—the basis, by the way, of popular music's stubborn claim to be the expression of its time—cannot be simply dismissed. We may look for it in the paradoxical feat of scoring, with wholly shopworn and platitudinous material, a musical and perhaps expressive hit on a specific and unmistakable target. In such products the idiom has become a second nature, permitting something like spontaneity, idea, immediacy. In America, the self-evident reification recoils at times, unforced, into a semblance of humanity and proximity—and not just into a semblance. Sociologically it may teach us a lesson about high and low music. Popular music shelters quality that was lost in the higher but had once been essential to it, a quality of the relatively independent, qualitatively different individual element in a totality. It has been pointed out by Ernst Krenek and others that the category of the idea, which is phenomenological rather than psychological, loses some of its dignity in the higher music; and it seems as though the lower unwittingly meant to make up for that. The few really good song hits are an indictment of what artistic music forfeited by making itself its own measure, without being able to make up the loss at will. I would suggest experiments to find criteria to determine, independently of plugging, whether a song will be a hit. A panel of musical experts who would have to be unaware of current ratings and altogether unfamiliar with the marketplace should listen to current hits and try to guess which are the most successful. My hypothesis is that they will largely guess right. They would then have to particularize what they consider the reasons, and the object of the final inquiry would take up the question whether unsuccessful songs do not lack this quality. Such a criterion might consist of plastic acoustical curves which nonetheless—as in the American evergreen "Deep Purple"—stay strictly within the approved idiom. But characteristic discoveries can be made in all possible musical dimensions. If commercialism requires the pop song composer to do the irreconcilable: to write, at the same time, what is universally known and what is memorable, i.e., different from everything else—then the qualitatively successful hits are probably the ones that have performed this squaring of the circle, and intensive analyses would have to describe this in detail.

The *qualitas occulta* of hits is a borderline value of advertising, in which they are embedded and which the greatest of them have turned into their own substance. People are ceaselessly wooed in behalf of what they crave anyway. A contributory factor may be their ambivalence: they not only balk at seriousness in music; they secretly resist their own favorites. Their resistance is discharged in the laughter with which the fans greet whatever they find dated. They are quick to perceive hits as "corny," as oldfashioned and cliché-ridden like the twenty- or thirty-year-old clothes in which the sex bombs of those days were packaged. That they are told this over and over is the reason behind all advertising: untiringly to rekindle the demand to which producers claim to be responding.

Even those can hardly fail to suspect consumers of harboring some doubt about their own enthusiasm. Hence the entire sphere, not just the single song hit, is ever more zealously seized by the advertising apparatus. The procedure follows the basic culture-industrial principle: affirmation of life as it is. Tautological tribute is paid to the socially dominant power concentrated in the industry. That this affirmative demeanor probably remains unconscious renders it socially hardly less harmful than the analogous one of the verbal media. It is only in the registering view of cultural administrations that popular music becomes an innocent discipline next to others, and with the same rights. Popular music is

37

objectively untrue and helps to maim the consciousness of those exposed to it, however hard the individual crippling effects may be to measure.

But that the mass phenomenon of popular music undermines the autonomy and independence of judgment—qualities which a society of free men would require—while a withdrawal of that music would presumably outrage the majorities of all nations as an undemocratic invasion of inalienable rights: this is a contradiction that goes back to the condition of society itself.

3

FUNCTION

The function of music in present-day society raises substantial questions. Music is considered an art among others; in the epoch of which we today are still conscious, at least, it has developed claims to esthetic autonomy. Even compositions of a more modest level want to be understood as works of art. But if it is true that the type of those who regard music as entertainment far outweighs the rest and cares little about the demands of esthetic autonomy, this means no less than that a quantitatively substantial part of our alleged cultural life has a social function basically different from the one it ought to have, according to its own meaning. It will not do to answer simply that its function *is* to entertain. How, one would have to inquire next, can people be entertained by something that will not reach their consciousness and their unconscious at all, or no longer as what it is? What does entertainment mean, then? What is the social significance of a phenomenon that in fact cannot get through to society at all?

Lest we summarily accuse the function of an absurdity that must not be veiled but will hardly exhaust it, certain things have to be borne in mind. First, the very lack of understanding which affects and rearranges all elements of music does carry over some of what those elements mean. And indeed, the listeners fail to perceive their own lack of understanding. They do understand scraps of the context of meaning. The idiom of tonality, for instance, which circumscribes the traditional stock of music consumed today, is identical with the worldwide musical consumers' language. People may fail to grasp what was said in that language, the specific content of the musical works, but they are familiar with the works' superficial connections insofar as the traditional idiom links them automatically. Splashing along with the idiomatic current substitutes for the performance of the thing itself and yet cannot be absolutely segregated—a sort of analogy with the relationship between communicative speech and the obligatory one of literary works of art and minted texts.

These elements too are in irreconcilable conflict and yet tied to each other. Specific values crystallized in the music—like the tone qualities that were to bring compositions to mind via the senses—are sensual stimulants themselves; they already have some of that culinary quality which only an extra-artistic consciousness will subsequently savor. The case of that element which nowadays, in lax usage, goes by the name of rhythm, or by that of melody is not much different. In the spirit of our time the sole remainder of the autonomous artistic language of music is a communicative language, and that does permit something like a social function. It is the remnant that is left of an art once the artistic element in it has dissolved. The reason why that remnant emerges so easily and resistlessly from art is that the art itself was late in achieving full autonomy, and that beside that autonomy it always dragged along heterogeneous moments such as the disciplinary function of medieval musical practice.

The function of music, following the social loss of the factor that made it great music, cannot be properly understood unless we admit to ourselves that its emphatic concept was never all there was to it. The extra-artistic side of its effect was always added. When social conditions have ceased, in the listeners' consciousness, to favor the constitution of the autonomy of music, that extra-artistic side of it necessarily comes to prevail again. The only reason why music's scattered members will fit into something like a second musical mass language is that the esthetic integration of its literally sensual, preartistic elements was always precarious—that throughout history, these elements lay waiting for a chance to elude the entelechy of the structure and to disintegrate themselves.

To ask about the function of music today, across society, would therefore mean to ask what the second musical language, the relic of the works of art in the household of the masses, is doing there. To begin with, music—the traditional works along with their accumulated cultural prestige—simply exists. The gravity of its existence preserves it even where it is not experienced at all, notably since the reigning ideology keeps the failure to experience it from becoming conscious. Crassly misunderstood works like the

Missa Solemnis can be performed and admired year in, year out.[1] It would be much too rationalistic to relate the present function of music directly to its effect, to the reactions of people exposed to it. The interests which take care to supply people with music, and the very weight of the given existing stock—these are too strong to be confronted everywhere with the actual demand; in music too, demand has come to be a pretext for the sphere of production.

When we speak of the irrationality of music, the phrase is ironically justified by the fact that the supply of music has its own irrational aspect—that it is due more to the wealth of piled-up goods than to that demand of the marketplace which is our favorite explanation. In sociology we know enough irrational institutions amid a society that has grown radically bourgeois. What cannot be directly derived from its function has a function anyway; society as it exists cannot unfold from its own principle but must amalgamate with precapitalist, archaic ones. If it were to realize its own principle without "noncapitalist" admixtures heterogeneous to it, it would be voiding itself. In a society that has been functionalized virtually through and through, totally ruled by the exchange principle, lack of function comes to be a secondary function. In the function of functionlessness, truth and ideology entwine. What results from it is the autonomy of the work of art itself: in the context of social effects, the man-made in-itself of a work that will not sell out to that context promises something that would exist without defacement by the universal profit. That something is nature.

At the same time, however, profit takes the functionless into its service and thereby degrades it to meaninglessness and irrelevancy. The exploitation of something useless in itself, something sealed and superfluous to the people on whom it is foisted—this is the ground of the fetishism that covers all cultural commodities, and the musical ones in particular. It is tuned to conformism. That a thing is loved simply because it exists is the consequence of obeying the extant, the inescapable; love alone can psychologically manage such obedience. Accepting what there is has become the strongest glue of reality, the replacement of ideologies as specific, perhaps even as theoretically justifiable, conceptions about what exists. The blind spot of unquestioning acceptance of a given thing, of something set in its place, is one of the invariants of bourgeois society. From Montesquieu onward that society has honored such given things with the title "historically evolved."

Corresponding to the abstract element of society's mere existence as a substitute for a transparent function is an equally abstract ideological role, that of distraction. It assists in the achievement of most of today's culture: in preventing people from reflecting on themselves and their world, and in persuading them at the same time that since this world provides such an abundance of enjoyable things it must be in good shape. Cultural life is said to be important and unintentionally made to seem more so by everyone who deals with it in any way, however critically—and that alleged importance sabotages our awareness of the essence. In the ideological function of film stars this is so plain to everyone that merely griping about it offers collective comfort; but the same phenomenon extends all the way to regions whose dignity is pronounced indubitable by an art religion that has decayed into a parody of itself. It goes all the way to the sites of Ninth Symphony performances.

Though not specifically musical, this ideological moment defines the space which music occupies: the space of possible chatter. It is hard to avoid observing how widespread is the faith that really unsolved and insoluble problems are solved by discussion; this explains why people flock to the ubiquitous panel sessions on culture. Akin to it is a fact which theoreticians should be the last to ignore: to many so-called culture carriers, talking and reading about music seems to be more important than music itself. Such malformations are symptoms of an ideologically normal condition, to wit, of music not being perceived as itself at all, in its truth and untruth, but solely as an indefinite and uncontrollable dispensation from dealing with truth and untruth. It is an inexhaustible occasion of irresponsible and inconsequential entertainment. Undaunted and without really noticing, countless multitudes devote a lot of time to something which to them is a sealed book.

Yet the mere existence of music, the historic force sedimented in it, and an enthralled humanity's imprisonment in institutions forced upon it—these alone would hardly explain the fixation of the masses, let alone the active demand. If something simply exists, without a raison d'être, and that is enough to console us for the fact that everything exists for something else, the comfort, function, the anonymous solace to the congregation of the lonely, ranks surely not lowest among the functions of music today. Its sound suggests a voice of the collective that will not quite forsake its compulsory members. At the same time, in the sort of extraesthetic shape it carefully presents to people, music regresses to older, prebourgeois forms—to forms, in fact, that may have preceded its evolution as an art. Whether those elements are still exerting their actual effect is difficult to determine; but certainly they are attested to music by ideology, and for those who react in the ideological realm this suffices to make them believe even against the witness of their own ears.

They consider music the purveyor of joy pure and simple, regardless of the fact that the developed art of music has long moved light-years away from the expression of a joy that became unattainable in reality. Even Schubert, the hero of their "Blossom Time," could ask whether there was such a thing as joyous music. They assume that whoever sings to himself is cheerful; that his head is carried high; that sound itself is always the negation of mourning, which is silent—whereas in fact any sound simultaneously expresses mourning in release. Primitive positivity, broken and negated a hundredfold by the art of music, reemerges in its function. Not for nothing is the consumers' favorite, that of the entertainment sphere, attuned to cheerfulness throughout, with minor keys a sparsely added seasoning.

This is not just the cliché of an existence whose pitifulness the biggest fool cannot deny. It is not meant to endow music with as much of that sadness as collective comfort will need for its foil. Instead, especially in calculated folk music of nationalist bent, the minor keys do something else, something which should some day be traced in principle. They bring the ancient shudder with them, as a dowry for activities whose rationality exorcises the shudder. They stand for goose-bumps and raised hair, as it were, as reactions to songs like the one of Roland's bow, to an accented "Rhine" in the song about the Watch on it, to fascist exhortations like "People: To Arms!" Feelings hoisted up to an irrational enthusiasm for one's own death are mechanically drilled by tried and tested means. Invariably it is archaic mechanisms that are steered and socialized in the entertainment sphere to its poorest and most nugatory aspect: permanent gaiety. The idea is to make those who identify with it believe that they too have so much fun.

Music is nonobjective and not unequivocally identifiable with any moments of the outside world. At the same time, being highly articulated and well-defined in itself, it is nonetheless commensurable, however indirectly, with the outside world of social reality. It is a language, but a language without concepts. Its definiteness fits it for a collective model of disciplined conduct; its conceptlessness guarantees that awkward questions about the goal of the discipline cannot even arise. But the quality of bringing solace, of intervening in the blind, mythical context of nature—this quality, attributed to music ever since the tales of Orpheus and Amphion, underlies its theological conception as the angels' tongue. Its aftereffects reached far into the autonomous art of music, not a few of whose demeanors were secularized versions of that conception. When the jejune life affirmation of wedding bells without any undertones recalling evil and death is all there is to it, the function of consumers' music has completed the secularization of that theological conception and has simultaneously converted it into its cynical counterpart: life on earth itself, life as it is, is equated with life without suffering—a doubly disconsolate equation since it is nothing but a repetitive circle precluding an eventual glimpse of something different.

It is precisely because it makes a mockery of what some day might be its true idea that the music of absolute affirmation is so infamous. It spreads a lie about what is; it shows the diabolical grimace of a transcendence that is in no way different from what it presumes to rise above. This, in principle, is its kind of function today, that of a class in the general classified ad section for the world—something the more necessary, the less inner confidence an enlightened mankind places in the positivity of what exists. Music is predestined for that function because it is not as easily nailed down as are crass falsifications of reality in films, for instance, or in magazine stories. Its ideology eludes unmasking by skeptics. A conscious will administers the distribution of the ideology, though scarcely the ideology itself. Rather, it is the objective reflection of a society that has no better argument for its perpetuation than the tautology of—to use its jargon—being "all right." Music as an ideology has its formula in a German metaphor that illustrates good cheer with a reference to music: "Heaven hangs full of fiddles." This is what has become of the angels' tongue, of its Platonic being-in-itself that had not come to be and would not pass away: the stimulus of groundless merriment on the part of those drenched with it.

But the merriment switched on by music is not simply the merriment of individuals at large. It is that of several, or of many, who substitute for the voice of the whole society by which the individual is outcast and yet gripped. The source of the sound, the font of the music, evokes preconscious reactions: that is where things are happening; that's where life goes on. The feebler the subjects' own sense of living, the stronger their happy illusion of attending what they tell themselves is other people's life. The din and to-do of entertainment music feigns exceptional gala states; the "We" that is set in all polyphonous music as the a priori of its meaning, the collective objectivity of the thing itself, turns into customer bait. As children will flock to whatever happens, the regressive types want to run after music; the most drastic proof of this function is the appeal of martial music, an effect far exceeding any political connotation. Thus the jukebox in an empty pub will blare in order to lure "suckers" with its false pretense of revelry in progress.

Music as a social function is akin to the "rip-off," a fraudulent promise of happiness which, instead of happiness, installs itself. Even in regressing to the unconscious, functional music grants a mere ersatz satisfaction to the target of its appeal. The first aim at intoxication on a grand scale were Wagner's works, in which Nietzsche discovered music as the ideology of the unconscious; and while they were pledged to a pessimism which in Schopenhauer was still socially ambiguous and therefore not just accidentally tempered by the late Wagner, the prescribed intoxication of the consumed music has nothing to do with Nirvana any more. That music, that dreary singsong of *"Trink, Brüderlein, trink!"* in the tradition of alcoholic bliss, maintains that everything is for the best if only grief and pain are shunned—as if this were up to the will, to a human will that keeps negating itself only by prescribing high jinks for itself. There is no help except from music. Its function is tailored to the demeanor of all those no one will talk to, of those who, as one says of the poor, have no communication. Music comes to be a comfort by the sheer redundancy of breaking the silence.

A more narrowly defined triumph is noisemaking. This suggests strength, power, and glory. Identification with it compensates for the universal defeat that is the law of each individual life. Just as poor old women shed tears at a wedding of strangers, the consumed music is the eternal strangers' wedding for all. At the same time it is disciplinary. It pretends to be irresistible, to leave us, as it were, without a mode of conduct other than chiming in. It does not tolerate sad sacks. Much of the consumers' music anticipates fanfares at victories yet unaccomplished, along with the applause. The garishly instrumented film titles which so often seem to resemble a barker's spiel: "Look here, everyone! What you will see is as grand, as radiant, as colorful as I am! Be grateful, clap your hands, and buy"—these set the pattern of the consumers' music even where the feats proclaimed by the shouting do not follow at all.

This music advertises itself at the same time, and its function changes along with the advertisements. It takes the place of the Utopia it promises. By circling people, by enveloping them—as inherent in the acoustical phenomenon—and turning them as listeners into participants, it contributes ideologically to the integration which modern society never tires of achieving in reality. It leaves no room for conceptual reflection between itself and the subject, and so it creates an illusion of immediacy in the totally mediated world, of proximity between strangers, of warmth for those who come to feel the chill of the unmitigated struggle of all against all. Most important among the functions of consumed music—which keeps evoking memories of a language of immediacy—may be that it eases men's suffering under the universal mediations, as if one were still living face to face in spite of it all. What the so-called "community music" does programmatically and intentionally is only so much more thoroughly accomplished by the music that is irresponsibly and unconsciously perceived. We can demonstrate this convincingly where reflection on the function of music becomes thematical and the music becomes a medium fitted into an overall plan: in motion pictures. A daily problem in their dramaturgical dispositions is which parts, which pictures, which dialogues should be musically "warmed up," as the jargon has it. This is probably the reason why the movies bother with a torrent of music that is not supposed to be attentively apperceived at all, only to be processed by the spectators' instincts.

What is added is not only warmth, however, but color. To replace black and white—which was unquestionably superior in many respects—in such great measure, the introduction of color film must have met a collective need. The qualities of the world of sense perception have become more and more gray, neutralized by the exchange relationship, the omnipresent equivalence. Where they are tolerated, colors have accordingly assumed the character of folderol, of the embarrassing monkeyshines witnessed at folk festivals in vacation countries. Music, due to its nonobjectiveness, can color the discolored world of things without being promptly suspected of romanticism, because the color is credited to its own nature; this, by the way, may explain some of the popular proclivity for orchestral as opposed to chamber music. But just as the line between inner and outer reality is not strictly drawn in the unconscious and preconscious strata reached by the consumers' music, the association with colorful tumult—as among precapitalist and extracapitalist peoples, for example—is probably not even crucial. Rather, what music colors is the desolation of the inner sense.

It is the decoration of empty time. The more the emphatic concept of experience, the sense of a temporal continuum, dissolves under the conditions of industrial production, and the more time decomposes into discontinuous, shocklike moments, the more nakedly and menacingly will the subjective consciousness come to feel itself at the mercy of the course of abstract, physical time. Even in the life of the individual this time has inexorably separated from that *temps durée* which Bergson still viewed as rescuing the living experience of time. Music calms the sense of it. Bergson knew why he contrasted his *temps espace* with permanence. Abstract time is really not time any more when it confronts the content of experience as something mechanical divided into static, immutable units; and its gloomy, unstructured character becomes the opposite of permanence, something spatial and narrow at the same time, like an infinitely long, dark hallway.

Whether the so-called "inner emptiness" is in fact the signature

47

of our time, as the jeremiads about modern mass man would have it, may well be impossible to determine. What similar phenomena existed in the past were so thoroughly administered by religious institutions that few traces remain, although *taedium vitae* is no twentieth-century invention. Yet if it really were as new as the eulogists of "close ties" desire, the blame would not rest on the masses but on the society that has made masses of them. The subject, deprived of a qualitative relation to the objective sphere by the form of its labor, is thus necessarily drained; Goethe and Hegel both knew that inner abundance is not due to isolation, not to a withdrawal from reality, but to its opposite—that subjective abundance itself is the transmuted form of an experienced objectivity.

We are not far from looking upon inner emptiness as the complement of internalization. There are indications of this in Protestant history. Yet if the void itself were that invariant which the ontologies of death would so much like to hypostasize against society, history has provided compensatory means to meet it. Once men have remedies, however poor, against boredom, they are no longer willing to put up with boredom; this contributes to the mass base of musical consumption. It demonstrates a disproportion between condition and potential, between the boredom to which men still are prey and the possible, if unsuccessful, arrangement of life in which boredom would vanish. Also hidden under the aspects of that mass base is the vague feeling that the road to real change has been cut off. Emptiness means less toil with continued unfreedom; we suffer of it in the measure of our frustrated possibilities. Our past condition was no better. The agony of toil has crushed the self-reflection that is required for the void to come about at all. In fact, the experience of the void is already an awareness, however blocked, of its opposite.

But people dread time, and so they invent compensatory metaphysics of time because they blame time for the fact that in the reified world they no longer feel really alive. This is what music talks them out of. It confirms the society it entertains. The color of the inner sense, the bright, detailed imagery of the flow of time, assures a man that within the monotony of universal comparability there is still something particular. The Chinese lanterns hung up in the individual's time by music are surrogates of that much-discussed meaning of his existence—of the meaning he vainly asks about whenever, exposed to abstract existence, he must ask about meaning at large. The only trouble is that the inner light itself has been sequestered by the very reifying power it illuminates. In fact, what dispels the sadness of ticking time from our psychological landscape is already neon light. The idea of great music, formally to draw the image of abundant time, of blessed permanence or, as Beethoven put it, of the glorious moment—this idea is parodied by functional music. That music also goes against time but does not penetrate it, does not on its own strength, and on the strength of temporality, condense that which would undo time. Instead, it parasitically clings to time and ornaments it. It "beats time," copying the chronometric beat, and in so doing "kills time," as the vulgar but entirely adequate phrase has it. Here too, and due to the very likeness, it is the perfect counterpart of what it might be.

Even the thought of a coloristic time may be too romantical. The function of music in the time-consciousness of a mankind in the clutches of concretism cannot be conceived abstractly enough. The form of labor in industrial mass production is virtually that of always repeating the same; ideally, nothing new occurs at all. But the modes of behavior that have evolved in the sphere of production, on the conveyor belt, are potentially—in a manner that has not yet been analyzed, by the way—spreading over all of society, including sectors where no work is performed directly in line with those schemata. With respect to a time thus choked off by iteration, the function of music is reduced to making believe that—as Beckett put it in *Endgame*—something is happening at all, that anything changes. Its ideology, in the most literal sense, is *ut aliquid fieri videatur*. By its purely abstract form of a temporal art, i.e., by the qualitative change of its successive moments, it brings about something like the *imago* of becoming, an idea which even the most wretched form of music cannot lose, and of which a consciousness that craves experience will not let go.

Music substitutes for the happening in which a man identified with music always thinks he has an active part, no matter how. And as such a substitute, in moments which popular consciousness equates with rhythm, music seems imaginatively to restore to the body some of the functions which in reality were taken from it by the machines—a kind of ersatz sphere of physical motion, in which the otherwise painfully unbridled motor energies of the young, in particular, are absorbed. In this respect the function of music today is not so very different from the self-evident and yet no less mysterious one of sports. In fact, the type of music listener with expertise on the level of physically measurable performance approximates that of the sports fan. Intensive studies of football habitués and music-addicted radio listeners might yield surprising analogies. One hypothesis on this aspect of consumed music would be that it reminds listeners—if it does not indeed con them into believing—that they have a body still, that even while consciously active in the rationalistic production process they and their bodies are not yet wholly separated. They owe this consolation to the same mechanical principle that alienates them from their bodies.

We may combine this thought with the psychoanalytical theory of music. According to that theory, music is a defense mechanism in the dynamic of drives. It is said to be directed against paranoia or persecution mania, the peril of the individual without relationships who has been alienated into an absolute monad and whose libidinous energy, the faculty of love, is devoured by his own ego. Yet the effect which consumed music has on such a man is probably less to repel these pathological symptoms than to neutralize or socialize them. The consumed music will not so much strengthen the lost relationship to what would differ from the individual as it will confirm the individual in himself, in his monadological seclusion, in the Fata Morgana of inward abundance. What it suggests to him, through the ritual of being present and the identification with social power as it paints his subjective course of time as meaningful, is this: that it is precisely in self-limitation, in entering into himself and departing from the hateful reality, that he will be in accord with all, accepted by and reconciled with all, and that that, ultimately, is the meaning. The deceptive moment that lies in great music too, the autarky of an inwardness split off from objectivity and practice and compensated in works of art by the truth content of their externalization in a structured objectivity—this moment, in functional music, is unreservedly transferred to ideology. It fulfills men in themselves, to train them for consent. It thereby serves the status quo, which could be changed only by people who, instead of confirming themselves and the world, would reflect critically on the world and on themselves.

Music, more than the other traditional arts, is suited for this function by several qualities without which it is scarcely thinkable. The anthropological difference between ear and eye fits in with the ideology of its historic role. The ear is passive. The eye is covered by a lid and must be opened; the ear is open and must not so much turn its attention toward stimuli as seek protection from them. The activity of the ear, its attentiveness, probably developed late, along with the strength of the ego; amid universally regressive tendencies, late ego traits will be the first to get lost. Deterioration of the faculty of musical synthesis, of the apperception of music as an esthetic context of meaning, goes with relapsing into such passivity. While the sense of smell weakened under the pressure of cultural taboos—or, among the masses, did not really unfold in the first place—the ear was the one sense organ to register stimuli without an effort. This set it apart from the permanent exertion of the other senses, which are coupled with the processes of labor because they are always laboring themselves.

Acoustical passivity turns into the opposite of work; listening, into a tolerated enclave amid the rationalized world of labor. While temporarily spared excessive demands within the totally socialized society, one remains respected as a person of culture even though cultural commodities may have been deprived of all meaning by that mode of behavior. The sense of hearing, archaic and lagging, as it were, behind the production process, furthers the delusion that the world itself is not yet wholly rationalized, that it still has room for the uncontrolled—for an irrationality that has no consequences for the demands of civilization and is therefore sanctioned by them. Another anthropological aid is the nonobjectiveness of the sense of hearing. The phenomena it transmits are not phenomena of things in extraesthetic experience. Hearing neither establishes a transparent relation to the world of things, a relation in which useful work is done, nor can it be controlled from the standpoint of this work and its desiderata. A mere undisturbed interior, which contributes so much to the establishment of an ideology of the unconscious, is already preformed in the sensual a priori of music. In a way, what turns music into a work of art equals its turning into a thing—a solidified text, quite simply. But in the mass function of radically reified music this very aspect disappears: the word *opus,* which recalls it, becomes an insult.

Today, however, the relation to reality is no more seriously severed by the function of hearing than by the artificial daydreams of the optical culture industry. For the musical phenomena are interlaced with intentions: of feelings, of motive impulses, of images which suddenly appear and disappear. Though not object-ified in the passive process of hearing, this pictorial world remains effective. It imperceptibly smuggles the contraband of external life into the domain of the imagination; it trains for the same performances, except that they have lost their concreteness; it forms dynamic schemata for the demands of the outside world. All by itself, before being sprayed on the workers at the conveyor belt, it is already a boost to their morale. Lively tunes are played for them as models of social virtue, of industry, activity, and indefati-gable readiness for team work. As soon as music is no longer synthesized it dissolves into imagery, and that imagery accords with the accepted norms.

Inexorably insistent on emotions, however, is a total constitution whose principle suffocates emotions, and whose lethal character would be revealed if the individual grew aware of it. It is true that some of the bodily functions which the individual has really lost are imaginatively returned to him by music. Yet this is but half the truth: in the mechanical rigor of their repetition, the functions copied by the rhythm are themselves identical with those of the production processes which robbed the individual of his original bodily functions. The function of music is ideological not only because it hoodwinks people with an irrationality that allegedly has no power over the discipline of their existence. It is ideological also because it makes that irrationality resemble the models of rational-ized labor. What people hope to escape from will not let them go. Their free time is spent dozing, merely reproducing their working energies; it is a time overshadowed by that reproduction. The consumed music indicates that there is no exit from the total immanence of society.

All this is a matter of ideology in the proper sense of the word, of a socially necessary and by no means always specially arranged appearance. European radio stations are more or less under public control, not directly dependent on commercial interests, but except for a lesser degree of skill, the entertainment music they pour out differs little from the American product fostered by a commercial broadcasting system which explicitly proclaims that ideology in the customers' name. Whoever compares it with old-style ideology will hesitate—because of its vagueness, albeit an inwardly most differentiated and definite vagueness—to talk of ideology at all. And yet we would be dead wrong to underestimate the ideological power of music for that reason. As the ideologies are made up less and less of concrete notions of society, as their specific content evaporates more and more, it will be so much easier for them to slide into forms of subjective reactions that are psychologically more deep-seated than manifest ideological contents and may therefore surpass their effect. Ideology is replaced by instructions for behavior. In the end it comes to be the *characteristica formalis* of the individual.

It is into this trend that music today fits its function: it trains the unconscious for conditioned reflexes. We hear a great deal of talk about the skepticism of the young and about their suspicions of ideologies. These categories surely miss the mark insofar as they confuse the hardboiled disillusionment of countless individuals with an undiminished awareness of the thing itself. The veil has not fallen. On the other hand, this much of the observed ideological loss is true: the ideologies keep thinning out. There is a polarization, with mere duplication of the extant, for the sake of its inevitability and power, on the one side and the arbitrarily devised, repeated, and revokable lie on the other. The predominant function of music corresponds to this residual ideology; indeed, its planned idiocy virtually tests what mankind will put up with, what threadbare, noncommittal intellectual contents can be imposed upon it. To this extent that function has today—entirely against its will—an aspect of enlightenment.

The well-meaning social educator, also the musician who takes his cause for a phenomenon of truth and not for mere ideology, will ask how to counteract this. The question is as justified as it is naive. If the function of music is really one with the ideological trend of society at large, it is inconceivable that its spirit, that of the institutional power as well as of the people themselves, would tolerate another public function of music. Innumerable mediations, those of economic interest above all, will be cited as irrefutable proof that it must be that way, once for all. In the extant framework this is hard to counter with any valid argument that is not ideological itself.

If one would obtain a concept of society through his own sensorium, he can use music to learn how—aided by God knows what intermediate mechanisms and often without any individual's ill will—the bad prevails even where it is faced with a concrete sense of the better. He can learn how impotent this consciousness will prove as long as it is not backed by more than mere cognition. All that he can do, without harboring any illusions about the outcome, is to say what he knows—and besides, wherever possible in the realm of musical disciplines, to work for a competent and cognitive relation to music in place of ideological consumption. To this consumption we can oppose no more than scattered models of a relation to music, and to a music that would be different.

4

CLASSES AND STRATA

If music really is ideology, not a phenomenon of truth—in other words, if the form in which it is experienced by a population befuddles their perception of social reality—one question that will necessarily arise concerns the relation of music to the social classes. Today the existence of classes is concealed by ideological appearances. We need not even think of vested interests calling for, and launching, ideologies. There is no shortage of such interests. But their subjective initiative, although it may be added, is secondary in comparison with the objectively benighting context. That context also creates the ideological appearance of music. In the exchange relationship, any adjustment to that which the World Spirit has made of men defrauds them at the same time. As a source of socially false consciousness, functioning music is entwined in social conflict, without the planners' intent or the consumers' knowledge.

Yet this is the cause of the central difficulties under which insights in musical sociology are laboring to this day. As long as it fails to encompass the concrete structure of society, that sociology remains mere social psychology and noncommittal. But the non-objective and nonconceptual character of music balks at tangible classifications and identifications between its various dimensions, on the one hand, and classes or strata on the other. This is just what the East's dogmatically frozen social theory profited by. The more puzzling the relation of music and specific classes, the more convenient its dispatch by labeling. All we need do is take the music consumed by the masses, willy-nilly, and equate it on the basis of its alleged closeness to the people with true music—regardless of the similarity between the alleged Socialist Realism of official Communist music and the dregs of the late Romanticist music from the capitalist countries of the fin de siècle. An equally simple measure is to seize the authority of famous music from the past for one's own authoritarian requirements. A stroke of the dictatorial pen coordinates it with the People's Democracy, and the same mindlessness governs the treatment of avant-garde musical art. From outside, heedless of its immanent composition, this is excoriated as decadent because of failure to serve as a social cement, and any recalcitrant individualists among composers are shown the knout with a mien of comradely solicitude.

Inquiries into the social distributions and preferences of musical consumption tell us little about the class aspect. The musical sociologist is faced with a choice between flat statements that apply the class concept to music—without any justification other than the current political aims of the powers that be—and a body of research that equates pure science with knowing whether middle-income urban housewives between the ages of 35 and 40 would rather hear Mozart or Tchaikovsky, and how they differ in this point from a statistically comparable group of peasant women. If anything at all has been surveyed here it is strata defined as subjectively characterized units. They must not be confused with the class as a theoretical-objective concept.

Nor would the origin, the social background of composers let us infer anything cogent about the class import of music. Such elements may play a part in music—can anyone perceive the sort of beery coziness which Richard Strauss exudes at the wrong moments, in Mycenae or in eighteenth-century nobility, without thinking of rich philistines?—but their definition tends to evaporate and to grow vague. In attempting a social interpretation of Strauss's effect in the era of his fame one would surely have a better right to associate him with words like *heavy industry, imperialism, grand bourgeoisie.* Conversely, there is not much modern music with more of a *haut monde* habitus than Ravel's, and he came out of the most cramped lower-middle-class circumstances. A differential analysis of family backgrounds is unproductive. Those of Mozart and Beethoven were similar; so, probably, were their milieus once Beethoven had moved to Vienna, rather better off than the materially insecure Austrian native; the age difference between them was no more than fourteen years. And yet Beethoven's social climate with its touch of Rousseau, Kant, Fichte, Hegel, is altogether incompatible with Mozart's.

We might cite cases that work better, but the chances are that the idea itself, the search for correspondences between class membership and a composer's social origin, involves an error in principle. The strongest argument against it is not even that in music the so-called social standpoint which an individual occupies is not directly translated into the tone language. To be considered first of all is whether, from the viewpoint of the producers' class membership, there has ever been anything other than bourgeois music—a problem, by the way, which affects the sociology of art far beyond music. In feudal and absolutist times mental labor was not too highly esteemed, and the ruling classes generally used to delegate such labor rather than perform it themselves. Even the products of medieval courts and chivalry would have to be further investigated to establish in what measure those poets and musicians really were representative of the classes to which, as knights, they formally belonged. On the other hand, the social status of the proletariat within bourgeois society served largely to impede artistic production by workers and workers' children. The realism taught by want is not as one with the free unfoldment of consciousness. Determining how all this stands in Russia would presuppose submitting the stratification over there to an analysis that would scarcely be tolerated.

The social odium which for thousands of years weighed especially on the arts that involve an artist's personal appearance, arts such as the theater, the dance, and music, has greatly limited the circle of persons from which those artists were recruited. Nor was the grand bourgeoisie apt to supply a great many musicians. Mendelssohn was a banker's son, but as a Jew, at least, an outsider in his own stratum; the slickness of his compositions has some of the excessive zeal of one who is not quite accepted. Except for Mendelssohn, Richard Strauss was probably the only famed composer born to wealth. Prince Gesualdo da Venosa, an outsider in every sense, defies modern sociological categories. Composers mostly arose from the petty bourgeois middle class or from their own guild: Bach, Mozart, Beethoven, Brahms grew up as musicians' children in modest circumstances, sometimes in stark poverty; even Strauss was the son of a hornist. Wagner came from the half-amateurish Bohemia to which his stepfather belonged.

Exaggerating a bit, all these might be called secularizations of the sphere of "wandering minstrels." For the most part the production of music was evidently handled by men who even before starting to compose belonged to the so-called "third persons," * assigned the practice of all art by bourgeois society. Handel would be a typical case; for all his fame in wealthy England he was denied bourgeois security and had "ups and downs" like Mozart. If we do in fact want to construe a link between the subjective origin of music and its social import, it is the concept of the third person, down to the dependency of servants, which may help to explain why music as a "service" to gentlefolk had so long unprotestingly complied with socially ordained ends. The brand of shame that once attached to vagabonds has turned into obedience to the purveyors of one's livelihood; in literature this held no such naked sway, at least. A marginal existence of protracted waiting for crumbs from the seignorial table, with no place in the regular bourgeois labor process—this was the specific social destiny of music under the aspect of its producers.

Until far into the nineteenth century—in other words, in a fully developed capitalist society—composers were anachronistically kept in this situation. Their work had long been marketed as a commodity, but under backward copyright laws it did not provide them with an adequate living even if the theaters got rich on it. This, above all, was Wagner's fate during his years in exile. Ernest Newman rightly points out the mendacity of the hue and cry at Wagner's extravagance and constant scrounging: for decades, bourgeois society rooked him out of the bourgeois profit which German opera houses were not ashamed to pocket from *Tannhäuser, Lohengrin*, and *The Flying Dutchman*. Among famed composers of the official musical culture, the first to make full capitalist use of their production were probably Puccini and Richard Strauss; of their predecessors, Rossini, Brahms, and Verdi became well-to-do, at least—Rossini thanks to the protection of the Rothschilds. Society controlled music by holding its composers on a tight and not so very golden leash; potential petitioner status never favors social opposition. That's why there is so much merry music.

Now let us turn to the sphere in which a social differentiation of music should most likely be notable, to the sphere of reception.

---

* A neologism referring to those who in seventeenth- or eighteenth-century German usage were addressed in the third person singular. —Transl.

Even there, a stringent link between the thing and its ideological function is hard to make out. Considering the unconscious and preconscious nature of musical effects upon most people, and the difficulty of accounting for those effects in words, their empirical study is hazardous. A few conclusions might be drawn if a random sample of listeners were asked to choose between crude statements ranging from "Like it very much" to "Don't like it at all," and even more if the listening habits of different social strata in regard to different radio programs were examined. Presumably we still lack data that would justify conclusive assertions, but a plausible hypothesis seems to be that the relation between types of music and social stratification corresponds more or less to the prevailing evaluation, the accumulated prestige of musical types and levels in the cultural climate. The result of standardized surveying mechanisms will inevitably be a rougher posing of this sort of problem, and such hypotheses too would therefore have to be simplified to the limit of their truth content—on the order of: highbrow music for the upper classes, middlebrow music for the middle class, and lowbrow music for those at the bottom of the social pyramid.

It is to be feared that empirical results would not much differ from this simplification. We would need only to have a blue-ribbon panel work out a kind of hierarchy of musical values—which, by the way, coincides not at all with authentic quality—to reencounter the experts' division in that of the listeners. Exclusively culture-conscious representatives of education and property would revel in the Ninth Symphony's appeal to mankind or wallow in the amorous plights of the highborn, as in *Der Rosenkavalier*, or else they would flock to Bayreuth. People from more modest income groups—who do, however, pride themselves on their bourgeois status and incline to what they consider culture—would respond to elevated entertainment, rather, to nineteenth-century operas and standard favorites such as the Arlésienne suites and the minuet from Mozart's Symphony No. 24 in E Flat Major, to Schubert's arrangements, to the intermezzo from *Cavalleria Rusticana*, and the like. Downward this would go on to a wretched infinity, via synthetic folk music complete with lederhosen, down to the hell of humor. In this schema, the few individuals not looking for entertainment would probably be distributed according to the ratio one might expect from their typological description.

59

For sociological cognition of music's relation to social classes such results would not be of much use—because of their superficiality, for one thing. They already are more reflective of the supply planned according to strata and offered for sale by the culture industry than they are indicative of any class significance of musical phenomena. It is even conceivable that the subjective leveling tendencies in the consumer sphere may by now have gone too far for that tripartition to come into drastic view. The gradations one might see in it are apt to resemble the high and low price ranges so carefully weighed by the automobile industry. There is probably no primary differentiation at all, only a secondary one according to "lines" offered to a consciousness that has been leveled in principle. The task of confirming or refuting this would oblige empirical researchers to go in for many complicated reflections and methodical inquiries.

The very simplest of these reflections shows how little an inventory of the stratification of consuming habits would contribute to insights into the context of music, ideology, and classes. Any assumption of a special affinity for ideologically kindred music in the conservatively class-conscious upper stratum, for instance, would in all likelihood be contradicted by the findings. Actually great music is apt to be preferred there, and that, as Hegel said, implies a sense of needs; what that music receives into its own formal constitution is the problematics, however sublimated, of realities which that stratum prefers to dodge. In this sense the music they appreciate upstairs is less ideological, not more, than the one they like downstairs. The ideological role which that music plays in privileged households is the role of their privilege and altogether different from its own truth content.

Empirical sociology has projected another, equally crude dichotomy: that today's upper stratum likes to interpret itself as idealistic while the lower boasts of its realism. Yet the purely hedonistic music consumed below stairs is surely not more realistic than the one valid above; it does even more to veil reality. If it occurred to an East German sociologist to speak of the extra-esthetic leaning which the uneducated feel to music as to something unintellectual, a mere sensual stimulus, and to describe this leaning as materialistic in nature and therefore compatible with Marxism, such a description would be a demagogic swindle. Even if we accepted the philistine hypothesis, it would remain true that such stimuli, even in entertainment music, are more apt to occur in the expensive product of skilled arrangers than in the cheap domain of mouth organ and zither clubs. Above all, music is indelibly a matter of the mind since even on its lowest level the sensual element cannot be literally savored like a leg of veal. It is precisely where the way of serving it is culinary that its preparation has been ideological from the start.

We can infer from this why a recourse to listening habits remains so fruitless for the relation of music and classes. The reception of music can turn it into something altogether different; indeed, it will presumably and regularly become different from what is currently believed to be its inalienable content. The musical effect comes to diverge from, if not to conflict with, the character of what has been consumed: this is what makes the analysis of effects so unfit to yield insights into the specific social sense of music.

An instructive model is Chopin. If a social bearing can without arbitrariness be attributed to any music at all, Chopin's music is aristocratic—in a pathos disdaining all prosaic sobriety, in a kind of luxury in suffering, also in the self-evident assumption of a homogeneous audience committed to good manners. Chopin's differentiated eroticism is conceivable only in turning one's back upon material practice, and so is his eclectic dread of banality amidst a traditionalism he does not sensationally violate anywhere. Seignorial, finally, is the habitus of an exuberance squandered. Corresponding to all this in Chopin's day was the social locus of his effect, and indeed, even as a pianist he would not so much appear on public concert stages as at the soirées of high society.

Yet this music, exclusive in both origin and attitude, has within a hundred years become exceedingly popular and ultimately, by way of one or two Hollywood hits, a mass item. Chopin's aristocratic side was the very one to invite socialization. Countless millions hum the melody of the Polonaise in A Flat Major, and when they strike that pose of a chosen one at the piano to tinkle out some of the less demanding Préludes or Nocturnes, we may assume that they are vaguely counting themselves with the elite. The role which Chopin, an important composer of great originality and an unmistakable tone, came to play in the musical household of the masses resembled the role Van Dyck or Gainsborough played in

61

their visual household—if indeed his ill-suited function was not that of a writer who acquaints his millions of customers with the alleged morals and mores of countesses. This is how much, and with respect to class relations in particular, a music's social function may diverge from the social meaning it embodies, even when the embodiment is as obvious as Chopin.

Without any extraneous attribution to an origin or an effective context, Chopin's music marks its social horizon. But the same applies less obviously, perhaps, to a great deal of music that can still be spontaneously grasped at all. If we listen to Beethoven and do not hear anything of the revolutionary bourgeoisie—not the echo of its slogans, the need to realize them, the cry for that totality in which reason and freedom are to have their warrant—we understand Beethoven no better than does one who cannot follow the purely musical content of his pieces, the inner history that happens to their themes. If so many dismiss that specifically social element as a mere additive of sociological interpretation, if they see the thing itself in the actual notes alone, this is not due to the music but to a neutralized consciousness. The musical experience has been insulated from the experience of the reality in which it finds itself—however polemically—and to which it responds. While compositorial analysis was learning to trace the most delicate ramifications of the facture, and while musicology was accounting at length for the biographical circumstances of composer and work, the method of deciphering the specific social characteristics of music has lagged pitifully and must be largely content with improvisations.

If we wished to catch up, to release the cognition of music from its inane isolation, it would be necessary to develop a physiognomics of the types of musical expression. Beethoven would have to remind us of the compositorial gestures of restiveness and refractoriness, of a handwriting in which good manners, conventions respected even in differentiation, are knocked aside, so to speak, by sforzati and dynamic jammings and abrupt piano continuations of crescendi. All this and far more deeply hidden things could be obtained from something I have occasionally called "Mahler's material theory of musical forms"; of these, however, we see hardly any rudiments. The scientific consciousness of music breaks asunder into blind technology and such poeticizing, childishly noncommittal exegeses as the ones of Beethoven by Schering. The rest is a matter of taste.

In thetical form a vast amount of music can be called by its social name; but until now such experiences have failed completely to be linked with the musically immanent facts, and that failure even serves as a pretext for arguing the most evident things out of existence. To hear the petty bourgeois in Lortzing, we do not need to know the texts; a medley from *Zar und Zimmermann* ringing from the bandstand at a summer resort will do. That Wagner has brought a decisive change in the pathos of bourgeois emancipation strikes us in his music, whether or not we reflect on Schopenhauer's pessimism. The leitmotif champion's abandonment of properly motive-thematic work, the triumph of compulsive repetition over the productive imagination of unfolding variations—these things tell us something about the resignation of a collective consciousness that can see nothing ahead any more. Wagner's tone denotes the social tendency of men to disavow the toil and stress of their own reason in favor of brutal and persuasive force, and to return from freedom to the disconsolate monotony of the cycle of nature. His is the very music in which expressive characters, technical procedures, and social significance are so fused that each one is legible in the other. The point of my own book on Wagner—if I may state it here in so many words—was to replace the sterile juxtaposition of music and social exegesis with at least a draft of models for the concrete unity of both.

Music is not ideology pure and simple; it is ideological only insofar as it is a false consciousness. Accordingly, a sociology of music would have to set in at the fissures and fractures of what happens in it, unless those are attributable merely to the subjective inadequacy of an individual composer. Musical sociology is social critique accomplished through that of art. Where music is intrinsically brittle, antinomical, but with the antinomies covered under a vocal facade rather than fought out, it is always ideological, itself imprisoned in the false consciousness. In interpretations moving within this horizon, sensibility of reaction must make up for any temporary, though perhaps not accidental, lack in methods capable of being handed down.

That Brahms—like the entire evolution since Schumann, even since Schubert—bears the mark of bourgeois society's individualistic phase is indisputable enough to have become a platitude. In Beethoven the category of totality still preserves a picture of the right society; in Brahms it fades increasingly into a self-sufficiently esthetic principle for the organization of private feelings. This is the academic side of Brahms. His music beats a mournful retreat to the individual, but as the individual is falsely absolutized over society Brahms's work too is surely part of a false consciousness—of one from which no modern art can escape without sacrificing itself. It would be barbarian and pedantic to elaborate that fatality into a verdict on the private person's music, and ultimately into one on all allegedly merely subjective music. In Brahms's case the private sphere as the substrate of expression does displace what might be called the substantial public character of music. But in his phase that public character itself was no longer substantial socially, no longer anything but ideology, and it retained a touch of this throughout bourgeois history. The artistic withdrawal from it is not only that flight which the dauntless progressives are so quick and pharisaical to damn. If music, and art as a whole, is resigned to its own social possibilities, if it fully develops them within itself, it ranks primarily—even in social truth content—above an art which out of an extraneous social will tries to exceed its dictated bounds and miscarries.

Music may also turn ideological when its social reflections make it take the standpoint of a consciousness that looks correct from without but conflicts with its own inner composition and its necessities, and thus with the things it can express. The social critique of class relations is not all the same with musical critique. Brahms's or Wagner's social topology devalues neither man. Brahms, in pensively and somehow worriedly taking the standpoint of the isolated, alienated, self-submerging private individual, negates negation. The great, encompassing problems of form are not simply cut off; Brahms transforms them, rather, preserving them in the question whether there can be a binding supra-personal formulation of the personal. Unconsciously posited in this is the moment of that privacy's social mediation. The objectification by form manifests the universal even in the private. Socially, in music, adequate presentation is everything; mere conviction is nothing. The higher critique, which must eventually name the element of untruth in the content of both Brahms and Wagner, extends to social bounds of artistic objectification, but it does not dictate norms of what music must be.

Nietzsche, who had more flair than anyone for the social aspects of music, forfeited his main chance when he let the wishful image of Antiquity induce him to equate critique of content too directly with esthetic critique. There is, of course, no separating the two. The ideological side of Brahms also turns musically wrong when the standpoint of the subject's pure being-for-itself keeps compromising with the traditional collective formal language of music, which is not that subject's language any more. The fiber and the form of Brahms's music already point in different directions. But music, in the unchanged split society, is not therefore allowed to wave conviction's magic wand so as to surrogate a supra-individual position. It must be incomparably less reserved than Brahms in yielding to that individualization of the lyrical subject if, without lying, it wants to perceive there something that is more than individual. The manner in which art corrects a socially false consciousness is not collective adjustment; rather, it is an act of carrying that consciousness so far that it will shed all appearance. Another way to put it would be that the question whether or not music is ideology is settled at the centers of its technical complexion.

In our time, with music directly involved in social struggles by partisan propaganda and totalitarian measures, judgments about the class significance of musical phenomena are doubly precarious. The stamp which political movements put upon musical ones has often nothing to do with the music and its content. We know what music the Nazis denounced as "cultural bolshevism" and—with the cheapest equivocations between a fissured-looking score and alleged social implications—christened "subversive"; it was the same music which the Eastern bloc ideology indicts for bourgeois decadence. The former found it politically too far left; the latter rails at "rightist deviationism." Conversely, actual differences in social content do slip through the meshes of political frames of reference, sociological as much as compositorial.

Stravinsky and Hindemith are equally undesirable to the totalitarian regimes. My first major piece of writing about musical sociology was an essay *"Zur gesellschaftlichen Lage der Musik"* ("On the Social Position of Music") that appeared in the periodical

Zeitschrift für Sozialforschung in 1932, just before the outbreak of fascism. There I called Stravinsky's music "grand bourgeois," and Hindemith's, "petty bourgeois." But this distinction was not merely based upon unweighable and uncontrollable impressions. Stravinsky's neoclassicism—whose explication, by the way, would require an exegesis of the whole neoclassicist movement about 1920—was not meant literally; rather, the turns from the so-called preclassic past were handled with a self-pointing, self-estranging license. Underscoring this license were fractures and intentional trespasses against the traditional tonal idiom and the familiar appearance of its rationality. No respecter of the sanctity of the individual, .Stravinsky stood above himself, so to speak. His irrational objectivism recalls games of chance or the posture of men whose power lets them ignore rules of the game. He paid no more attention to the tonal rules than to those of the marketplace, though the facade was left standing in both places. His sovereignty and his freedom combined with cynicism in regard to his own self-decreed order. All this is as grand bourgeois as the supremacy of taste, which in the end, simultaneously blind and selective, decides alone what is or is not to be done.

By Hindemith, on the other hand, who for decades aped Stravinsky with conscientious craftsmanship, the great gambler is deprived of his savor. The classicistic formulas are taken literally, sought to be fused with the traditional language—with Reger's, little by little—and trimmed into a system of humbly serious bustle. It finally converges not only with musical academicism but with the dauntless positivity of quiet souls. Having found himself, Hindemith follows some tried and true models in ruing the excesses of his youth. "Systems are for little people," says Heinrich Regius in his *Dämmerung.*[1] "The great have intuition; they bet on whatever numbers come to mind. The larger a man's capital, the better the chance of new intuitions making up for those that failed. It cannot happen to the rich that they stop playing because their money runs out, or that as they walk out of the door they hear the very number coming up that they could no longer bet on. The intuitions of the rich are more trustworthy than the laborious calculations of the poor—calculations that always fail because they cannot be thoroughly tested." This physiognomics fits the difference between Stravinsky and Hindemith; with such categories the class significance of contemporary music might perhaps be handled. Confirmation comes, moreover, from the intellectual ambience of the two composers, from their choice of texts, from their slogans. Stravinsky, heading an elegant *cénacle,* would issue the latest watchwords and be noncommittally aware of his top position, like the haute couture. Hindemith plied an archaicizing guildsman's humility, composing "to measure" halfway through the twentieth century.

But things are not always so plausible in musical sociology. The literary and theoretical self-comprehension of the Schönberg school lags far behind the thoroughly critical content of its music. It would not only be easy to uncover petty bourgeois elements in its treasury of associative conceptions; the very ideal of that music, its *terminus ad quem,* was traditionalist and tied to the bourgeois faith in authority and culture. For all its expressionism, the dramaturgy of the stage composer Schönberg was Wagnerian all the way to *Moses und Aron.* Even Webern was still guided by a traditional, affirmative concept of music: there are radical departures from bourgeois culture in his oeuvre, but he himself was as unaware of them as Schönberg could not understand why his merry opera *Von heute auf morgen* did not score a hit with the public. I take it that all this is not entirely irrelevant to the social content of the matter either. But the truth about it, like any truth, is fragile. There can be no inquiring after it whatsoever until the sociology of contemporary music has been emancipated from all outwardly disposing classifications.

There have been very few attempts to imbue music itself, the compositorial habitus, with something like class significance. Aside from a couple of Russian composers soon after the Revolution, men whose names have long been buried under battle and victory symphonies, those attempts include some of Hanns Eisler's works, mainly workers' choruses from the late twenties and early thirties. There a genuine compositorial imagination and considerable technical skill entered the service of expressive characters, of purely musical phrasings which in themselves, prior to any extramusical program and content, show a distinct kind of sharp and pointed aggressiveness. This music achieved an exceedingly close union with the agitational texts; at times it rang directly, concretely polemical. It was art seeking to occupy its class position by its

67

behavior, a procedure analogous to that of George Grosz, who placed his graphic artistry at the service of unmerciful social critique. Today, of course, such music is no longer written in the East. Finding out whether those workers' choruses can still be performed there at all might be worth one's while. The musical handwriting of Weill, in any case—once brought into the same force field by his collaboration with Brecht—no longer had anything in common with that acuity; this music could effortlessly turn away from the goals it had used to excite itself for a time.

Even in such cases there remains an element of undefinability. If music can harangue, it is nonetheless doubtful what for, and what against. Kurt Weill's music made him seem a leftist social critic in the prefascist years; in the Third Reich he found apocryphal successors who would at least rearrange his musical dramaturgy and much of Brecht's epic theater so as to fit the collectivism of Hitler's dictatorship. As a matter of principle, instead of searching for the musical expression of class standpoints one will do better so to conceive the relation of music to the classes that any music will present the picture of antagonistic society as a whole—and will do it less in the language it speaks than in its inner structural composition. One criterion of the truth of music is whether greasepaint is found to cover up the antagonism that extends to its relations with the audience—thus involving it in the more hopeless esthetic contradictions—or whether the antagonistic experience is faced in the music's own structure.

Intramusical tensions are the unconscious phenomena of social tensions. Ever since the industrial revolution all of music has been suffering from the unreconciled state of the universal and the particular, from the chasm between their traditional, encompassing forms and the specific musical occurrences within those forms. It was this that eventually compelled the cancellation of the schemata—in other words, the new music. In that music the social tendency itself turns into sound. The divergence of general and individual interests is musically admitted, whereas the official ideology teaches the harmony of both. Authentic music, like probably any authentic art, is as much a cryptogram of the unreconciled antithesis between individual fate and human destiny as it is a presentation of the bonds, however questionable, that tie the antagonistic individual interests into a whole, and as it is finally a presentation of the hope for real reconcilement. The elements of stratification touching the several musics are secondary in comparison.

Music has something to do with classes insofar as it reflects the class relationship in toto. The standpoints which the musical idiom occupies in the process remain epiphenomena as opposed to that phenomenon of the essence. The purer and more unalloyed its grasp of the antagonism and the more profound its representation, the less ideological the music and the more correct its posture as objective consciousness. An objection to the effect that representation itself is reconcilement already, and is thus ideological, would touch upon the wound of art in general. Yet representation does justice to reality insofar as the organized and differentiated totality, the totality from which representation derives its idea, attests that through all sacrifice and all distress the life of mankind goes on.

In the exuberance of the nascent bourgeois era this was expressed in the humor of Haydn, who smiled at the world's course as an estranged bustle while affirming it with that same smile. It is by the anti-ideological resolution of conflicts, by a cognitive behavior without an inkling of the object of its cognition, that great music takes a stand in social struggles: by enlightenment, not by aligning itself, as one likes to call that, with an ideology. The very content of its manifest ideological positions is historically vulnerable; Beethoven's pathos of humanity, meant critically on the spot, can be debased into a ritual celebration of the status quo. This change of functions gave Beethoven his position as a classic, from which he ought to be rescued.

He who would socially decipher the central content of music cannot use too delicate a touch. It is by force or on occasion only that antagonistic moments will be musically identifiable in Mozart, whose music so clearly echoes the passage from enlightened late absolutism to the bourgeoisie, a transition deeply akin to Goethe. Rather, his social aspect is the force with which his music returns to itself, the detachment from empiricism. The menacingly looming power of unleashed economics is sedimented in his form as follows: as though afraid of getting lost at any touch, the form keeps the degraded life at arm's length, yet without feigning a content other than the one it can humanely fulfill by its own means, i.e., without romanticism.

Of all the tasks awaiting us in the social interpretation of music, that of Mozart would be the most difficult and the most urgent. But if one finds the social complexion of music in its own interior, not simply in its effective links with society, he will not rely on any social adjustment, of whichever kind, to take him past whatever is false consciousness in music. Such adjustments merely add to the general fungibility, and thus to the social ills. What is unattainable for music of the utmost integrity might solely be hoped for from a better organized society, not from customer service. The end of music as an ideology will have to await the end of antagonistic society.

Although in 1962 I would no longer phrase the constellation of music and classes in the same terms as thirty years ago, I would still stand by a few lines I wrote then, in that essay for *Zeitschrift für Sozialforschung*. They read as follows:

Here and now, music can do nothing else but represent, in its own structure, the social antinomies which also bear the guilt of its isolation. It will be the better, the more deeply it can make its forms lend shape to the power of those contradictions, and to the need to overcome them socially—the more purely the antinomies of its own formal language will express the calamities of the social condition and call for change in the cipher script of suffering. It does not behoove music to stare at society in helpless horror; its social function will be more exactly fulfilled if the social problems contained in it, in the inmost cells of its technique, are presented in its own material and according to its own formal laws. The task of music as an art comes thus to be a kind of analogue to that of social theory.[2]

5

OPERA

What I say here about opera is not intended as a draft, however rudimentary, of a sociology of opera.[1] Instead, I would like this model to jolt us out of a habit of thought that is the exemplary embodiment of the dubiousness of unreflected observations on musical sociology: the assumption that the esthetic state of musical forms and structures will always harmonize with their social function. As a matter of fact, the reception of structures can move all the way to a full break with their social origin and meaning. We cannot, as the community-loving cliché of popular sociology would have it, judge the quality of certain music according to whether or not it is widely accepted here and now, or accepted at all; neither should we moralize about the social function even of lesser music as long as people have that music forced on them by powerful authorities and by the nature of society itself, and as long as they live under conditions in which they need that music for their so-called relaxation. The position of opera in present-day musical life allows divergences between the esthetic substance and its social fate to be studied concretely.

Neither from the musical nor from the esthetic point of view can we avoid the impression that the operatic form is obsolete. During the geat depression of the late twenties and early thirties, when people talked about a crisis of operas as about the crisis of everything else, they did not hesitate to connect the reluctance of composers to write more operas or music dramas à la Wagner and Strauss with the general strike of the economically hard-pressed audience. And they were right. What thirty years ago induced the judgment that opera was passé was not mere surfeit with the world of its forms, including products of such late dramatic music as Schreker's, which in view of musical developments rang dated even at the time they were in vogue. The dawning insight, rather, was that in style, in substance, and in attitude the opera had nothing to do any more with the people it had to appeal to if its outwardly pretentious form was to justify the prodigal extravagance required.

Even in those days the public was no longer up to the feats of antirationalism and antirealism which the stylization of opera demands. To a human intellect trained to watch at the movies for the authenticity of each uniform and telephone set, the improbabilities served up in each opera, even if the hero was a machinist, could not but appear absurd. Opera seemed exiled along with such specialties as the ballet of the balletomaniacs—the ballet which to opera was never extraneous, and crucial traits of which, like the musically accompanied gestures, remained traits of opera even after Wagner had driven the danced inserts off to the nether world. When the entire current operatic repertoire in America dwindled to hardly more than fifteen titles including Donizetti's *Lucia di Lammermoor*, the petrifaction was confirmed.

Its crassest symptom was the public's hostility to modern music in opera. *Der Rosenkavalier* was and remained the last work of the species to become broadly popular while superficially, at least, satisfying the standard of compositorial means set in the years of its origin. Not even Strauss's extraordinary prestige sufficed to win similar success for any of his later operas, for the dramaturgically ingenious *Ariadne auf Naxos* or for his personal favorite, *Die Frau ohne Schatten*. In fact, *Der Rosenkavalier* already marks the beginning of Strauss's decline. The well-known lapses in his treatment of the text are mere visible manifestations of evils within the music. He showed not much real understanding for Hofmannsthal's poetic work, and for all the merits of his theatrically effective conduct of the action he coarsened it immensely. But what kind of theatrical chef d'oeuvre is one that composes past its own theme? It was not due to incompetence on Strauss's part. He was thinking of the public, of the success which even then was not to be had unless one curbed one's own productive powers. Not only the final duet is a concession; the whole *Rosenkavalier* capitulates. It is not by chance that the name Lehár appears in the correspondence preceding this exquisite comedy for music.

Strauss can hardly have deluded himself about the failure of his two most important works for the stage—*Salome* and *Elektra*—to find an echo. His reaction was not *"Quand même";* it was to give in. Whatever part of the blame may be laid on his complaisant mentality, which his own genius had disavowed for several years: Strauss's decision—and it cannot have been less than a decision— was surely affected by the innervation of an absurdity, an opera without an audience. For the work's own curves necessarily encompass something like the emotional movement of a listening multitude. Yet all that Strauss wrote for the stage after *Ariadne*, all that tacitly obeyed the secret instrument of surrender, was thereby subjected to the compulsion to make decent copies of that one and final instant of success. Thus Strauss turned to stone, like the emperor in *Die Frau ohne Schatten*. His adjustment to the public only cost him more of the public's favor. In catchiness, the strips of music avidly accompanying the action could not compete with the movie sound track which, willy-nilly, they so often recall.

On the other hand, whatever counts among things written for the musical stage since about 1910 withdraws from the canon of opera and music drama as though pulled away by a magnet. The two short stage works of the expressionist Schönberg last less than a half hour each—in itself a disclaimer of the obligations tradition- ally assumed by a sumptuous evening at the theater—and their subtitles are *Monodrama* and *A Play with Music*. In the first a woman sings alone, without the dramatic antithesis of other voices; the external action is rudimentary. In the other, only scattered sounds are sung at all; few words are spoken. *Die glückliche Hand* as a whole is an act of silent expressionism; its formal law, that of an abruptly startling picture series, had not much in common with the rules of pantomime either. The audience was shown no consideration and no prospect of the normal repertoire. Both were spurned from the outset. Even when Schönberg tried for effect, in his comic opera *Von heute auf morgen*, it was—to his credit— denied him by the complexity and dark potency of his music, despite all points and allusions. The antinomy of opera and audience became a triumph of composition over opera.

Stravinsky, if we disregard his early *Rossignol*, also shunned opera and the music drama as passé. Only his ability to tie up with the Russian ballet tradition smoothed his public relations. But the crux, the listener's identification with chanted emotions, was severed. Stravinsky's contributions to the demolition of musical theater were hardly less than those of *Erwartung* and *Die glückliche Hand*. In *L'histoire du soldat*, the narrator of the action is separated

73

from its mimical presentation; in *Renard*, the actors part with their own song. The mechanism of identification is as bluntly challenged as by the subsequent theories of Brecht. Stravinsky's late work, *The Rake's Progress*, scarcely gave him back to opera. It is a pastiche, a disassembling imitation of unbelieved conventions, as distant from them as his most advanced ballets, devoid of effects on the naive.

The operas of Alban Berg, *Wozzeck* in particular, are literally the exceptions that prove the rule. The contact between them and the audience rests on the moment to which they gave permanence; it cannot be interpreted simply as actualizing the entire species. That *Wozzeck,* was so lucky on stage could be credited first of all to the choice of a text—a fact made much of by the envious. But the music demands so much of the listener, was felt at the world premiere in 1925 to be so excessive, that the text alone—which could be more conveniently experienced on the legitimate stage—would not have sufficed to overwhelm a restive audience. What people sensed was the constellation between lyrics and music, that peculiarly indicative moment in the music's relation to the topic. Besides, the social effect and authority of any music is by no means directly equal to the understanding it has found. It is conceivable that in the case of *Wozzeck*—as at the performances of the two acts from Schönberg's Moses opera twenty-five years later—neither the details nor their structural connection were fully understood, but that the phenomenon fashioned by the compositorial force conveyed that force to an audience whose ears would have been unable to account for it in the particular.

This opens a perspective in which the primarily undeniable divergence of new music and society no longer appears as an absolute. The stringency of a structure that is not quite transparent to the audience enables quality to transcend the realm of assured comprehension. This agrees with the fact that the entire question of the comprehensibility of works is newly posed in the light of the latest artistic developments. An observation that is hard to check, of course, has shown that there are different levels in the reception of music as well: one on which the applause gives unburdened, rather noncommittal thanks for having kindly adjusted to what is wanted, and another, which confirms the rank of works even though communication remains desultory. The latter type of success has something brittle and prickly about it. Today its nonexistence is inconceivable as soon as the thing itself, even when speaking against society, speaks for it, for its objectively shrouded needs. The public is not aware of such differentiations. But it would be unfair and inappropriate to say that therefore it cannot be latently differentiated. In their heart of hearts even the obdurate know what is true and what is not. As though explosively, works of high quality uncover this unconscious knowledge that has lain buried under ideologies and consumer habits.

Büchner's drama *Wozzeck* is a work of the highest rank, incomparably superior to all the texts or, as Pfitzner maliciously put it, all the "literature libretti" ever set to music. Its choice as a text came long after K. F. Franzos rediscovered the manuscript, but at the very time when major performances started the play on its commanding rise above all the dramatic wastepaper approved in nineteenth-century Germany. The composition was a monument at the same time, a reminder of a rescue operation in the philosophy of history. But the scenes themselves, which Berg admirably arranged for music, accommodated the music as if destined for it. The drama occurs on several levels, so to speak: from the language of a paranoiac's clinical psychology it distills an objective world of images, and where the mad fantasies recoil into the escaped poetic word they take shelter in a void. The void awaits the music that leaves the psychological layer beneath. Berg recognized and occupied it with unfailing assurance.

Wozzeck is a music drama starting out from the impulses of the main characters, with which the music empathizes; but simultaneously it points beyond the form it kindled for a last time, with a poetry already far in the past. It did this by clinging to the words more faithfully than had ever been done. The indescribable concretion of its pursuit of the poetic curlicues helps to achieve that differentiation and multiformity which then, in turn, lends to the composition an autonomous structure alien to the music drama of times past. Because, crudely put, there is no turn in the entire score without its strict literary reference, the outcome is not operaticized literature but a musical structure freed in its every last note, progressively articulated, and eloquent at the same time. It was probably the very premise of the reception of *Wozzeck* that it fulfills and dissolves as one. Utter consistency with tradition is revealed as something qualitatively different from tradition.

Wozzeck is no traditionalistically warmed-up opera, but neither does it miss its audience by features which, measured by the ideal of what is meaningful in a musical drama, might have been resented as experimental.

In *Lulu*, Berg carried his intentions farther. As in Frank Wedekind's intentional horror dramas the style of the nineties becomes surrealistic and imaginary in circus acts, so does the music here too transcend the accommodated species. Like Schönberg's *Moses und Aron*, in which a similar tension between stylistic principles of music drama and oratorio prevails, *Lulu* remained unfinished. That agrees perfectly with the history of the operatic genre. The point of indifference between irreconcilables, the point marked by *Wozzeck*, could hardly be occupied twice. That *Moses und Aron* was not finished may have been due to doubts about the operatic form which suddenly beset Schönberg after a period of immense compositorial tension; the conclusion of *Lulu* was stalled by a prohibitively protracted production period. In the present situation every intellectually decisive thing is evidently doomed to remain a fragment.

The verdict on the operatic form was carried out in the infinity of the production process. It sabotaged the product. When Berg declared emphatically that nothing had been farther from his mind than the thought of reforming the opera he was saying more than he may have intended: he was saying that the history of the form was not to be turned around any more, not even by his magnificent oeuvre. Its merit is precisely that it was wrested from the formal impossibility, just as the achievement of Karl Kraus—akin to Berg's in many respects—would be inconceivable without the disaster of language.

The difficulties encountered by Schönberg and Berg, like the fissures in the artificial rock massif of Stravinsky's *Oedipus Rex*, are not merely individual in kind. They reveal the immanent formal crisis. It has been registered by all composers who count even in the generation of those three, let alone the next; whatever goes on writing operas as if nothing had happened, possibly even proud of its own naiveté, is subaltern from the outset. If it succeeds, its success sounds hollow and ephemeral. After Berg, resistance to the operatic imitation of states of mind became universal. Self-conscious producers no longer found a general denominator for the demand of autonomy for a music that wants to be itself and imageless, and for the desideration of opera that music must be similar to language and the image of something else. The line of the servant in Hofmannsthal's prelude to *Ariadne*, about the "language of passion tied to the wrong object," comes to be the verdict on opera, which gets its first taste of irony from that glittering work.

All the idiosyncrasies which avant-garde composers have against operaticism become explicable from this center. They feel ashamed of a pathos boasting of a dignified subjectivity which the world of total subjective impotence no longer accords to any individual. They are skeptical of the grandiose in grand opera, which is ideological prior to any particular content, and of the intoxication with power. They disdain the representative aspect in a deformed and imageless society that has nothing to represent any more. Benjamin's word about the decay of the aura suits opera more exactly than almost any other form. Music in which dramatic events are a priori doused in atmosphere and exalted is aura pure and simple. And where that character is abruptly abandoned, the combination of music and action becomes illegitimate.

The antagonism between the disenchanted world and a form that is illusionary to the core and remains illusionary even where it borrows from so-called realistic trends—this antagonism seems too great ever to grow fruitful. It would be futile if producers, perceiving the problems of a straightlined progress of musical drama today, were to go back to older forms of opera. Those forms were not victims of a mere change in style, not of what since Riegl has been called an "altered artistic volition," but of their own insufficiency. What Wagner wrote against them applies now as it did then. Escape to presubjective objectivity would be a noncommittal, subjective arrangement and therefore untrue. The price infallibly paid for it would be the impoverishment of music, the essential element of opera. Rescue attempts born of a stylistic will, including those of temporarily powerful public suggestiveness, reduce musical representation to the point of abolishing it.

Opera was not, as one might well have thought, made dubious only in the interior of works and in the stirrings of avant-garde compositorial taste. The permanent crisis of opera has since become manifest as a crisis of the presentability of operas. Directors are incessantly forced to choose between being dustily tedious or feebly contemporary—mostly a third rehash of tendencies in painting and sculpture—and awkwardly trying to invigorate older works by dragged-in ideas of direction. Motivating them is fear for tried and true but threadbare classics like *Die Fledermaus* or *Der Zigeunerbaron*, where the idiocy of the action can no longer be hushed up. Yet the opera director toils in vain with Lohengrin's swan and with Samiel of *Der Freischütz*. For what he is seeking to actualize needs those props not just substantially but in its intellectual composition. Elimination of the props will not admit him to the Elysian fields of realism but plunge him into arts-and-crafts. Modernism suffocates modernity. The baroque and allegorical elements of the operatic form, once linked profoundly with its origin and content,[2] have lost their nimbus. They stick out baldly, helplessly, at times ridiculously, prey to jokes like the one told about virtually every tenor who ever sang Lohengrin: "What time does the next swan leave?"

One might expect that hearing people sing as if that were natural, and seeing them act the way it was done on stage a hundred years ago, would be unbearable to the present generation. Why the young do not all flee from opera takes more explaining than it would if they did. All the vicissitudes of modern operatic direction are due to the same cause: the director must try to do justice to modes of reaction which he may be presupposing as self-evident, but in so doing he clashes with the form itself, the principle of which calls for empirical persons to be stylized into song. Singers sufficient for bel canto, or even for a more recent author like Wagner, have become rarities.

The causes ought to be explored. One of them is probably aversion to a long and materially unprofitable training period. Where a singer with such qualifications is discovered he will be promptly lured away by the financially strongest institutions. Germany's operatic culture rested on the repertoire of its large and medium-sized provincial theaters, but now these theaters are hard put to furnish what was the primary basis of that culture: reliable ensembles with distinct features, used to performing together. For more exacting leads they must depend on borrowing singers who will spend more time in the air than at rehearsal; for the minor parts one makes do with what is at hand. German opera thus turns more and more into a tour de force by a few conductors who literally stretch the physical limits of their strength to whip a few top performances out of the shaky ensemble. These conductors had to develop faculties undreamed of in the opera activities of old, and in the process they themselves became stars like the guest singers, working in positions of responsibility in many places at once. Their best performances have to be quickly turned over to aspiring "comers" under whose baton, most of the time, little remains of the deceptive glamour.

While the organizational form of nineteenth-century opera, that of repertory theater, is doggedly maintained in German-speaking countries, the artistic potential of operatic offerings gravitates toward the seasonal. It is not by accident that the great festivals of Bayreuth, Salzburg, or Vienna are gradually coming to be the only occasions where halfway decent performances are heard at all. Often the best opera nights from various cities can be enjoyed there, exhibited according to a novel selection process, like record feats in sports. This too is a symptom of some radical damage that has been done in the relation of opera to society, however loath each side may be to admit it.

On grounds which are social themselves, and among which full employment during our long-lived prosperity must not be forgotten, the public that wants opera no longer gets adequate reproductions, and applauds just the same. One of the strangest contradictions to be observed at the moment is that despite a continuing shortage of good musicians, not in the field of opera alone, those looking for employment—the residents of West Berlin, for instance, who gave up their jobs in East Berlin after August 13, 1961—often find it hard to get. In the musical marketplace the vaunted law of supply and demand functions only imperfectly; it is breached the more, evidently, the farther one gets from the economic infrastructure, from the practical economy.

A visible sign of the social aspect of the opera crisis is that the new German opera houses, those built after 1945 to replace the gutted ones, look so often like movie theaters, lacking the boxes that were one of the characteristic emblems of the opera theaters of old. The architectural form of these houses contradicts most of what is performed there. What remains in doubt is whether today's society has even retained the capacity for that *acte de présence* that took place at the opera in the heyday of nineteenth-century liberalism. In those days people were still clinging so conservatively to absolutist ways that the proscenium above the stage, where privileged spectators could watch or receive acquaintances at will, was preserved in some Parisian theaters until about 1914. Such secularizations of a courtly style had something fictional about them, a kind of self-dramatization, as did all the monumental and decorative forms of the bourgeois world. In opera, at any rate, a self-assured bourgeoisie could celebrate and enjoy itself for a long time. On the musical stage the symbols of its power and material ascent combined with the rituals of the fading, but arch-bourgeois, idea of liberated nature. As everyone knows, however, society after World War II is ideologically far too leveled to dare have its cultural privilege so crassly demonstrated to the masses. Today there is hardly any real old-line society like that economic backer of operas in which it found itself intellectually reflected, and the new luxury class eschews ostentation. Despite the economic flowering of the period, the individual's sense of impotence, if not indeed his fear of a potential conflict with the masses, is far too deeply ingrained.

It was therefore not just the evolution of music which so far outran the operatic stage and its audience that any contact, even a possibly kindling friction, with new ideas came to be rare and exceptional. The social conditions, and thus the style and content, of traditional opera were so far removed from the theatergoers' consciousness that there is every reason to doubt the continued existence of any such thing as an operatic experience. The esthetic conventions it rests upon, perhaps even the measure of sublimation it presupposes, can hardly be expected of broad listening strata. But the charms which opera had for the masses in the nineteenth century and earlier, in the Venetian, Neapolitan, and Hamburg performances of the seventeenth—the decorous pomp, the imposing spectacle, the intoxicating color and sensuous allure—all this had long since wandered off to motion pictures. The film has materially outbid the opera, while intellectually underbidding it so far that nothing from its fund could keep it competitive.

Besides, one may suspect that the very perspective of the self-emancipating bourgeoisie in opera, the glorification of the individual rising against the spell of order—a motive shared by Don Giovanni and Siegfried, and by Leonore and Salome—that this motive no longer finds an echo. It may be flatly rejected by those who have forsworn individuality or have no idea of it any more. *Carmen, Aïda,* and *La Traviata* once meant humanity, the protest of passion against conventional congealment, and there music represented nature itself, as it were. As the sound of immediacy, today's operagoers presumably do not even recall that any longer. There is no chance any more of identifying with the ostracized "kept woman" whose type has long since died out, nor with the opera gypsies who keep vegetating as costume party outfits. In short, a kind of chasm has opened between opera itself and present-day society, including those members it delegates to serve as an opera audience.

But in this chasm opera has made itself at home, if only until notice is given to the contrary. It offers the paradigm of a form that is incessantly consumed although it has not merely lost its intellectual topicality but, in all likelihood, can no longer be adequately understood at all. Not only at a profane sanctum like the Vienna Opera will nonsubscribers and others without preference find it difficult even to buy a ticket,[3] but at plain German provincial theaters as well. In Vienna about 1920, fanatics lined up on the eve of star performances, ready to stay awake all night in order to grab a ticket, perhaps, in the morning. True, the old contact between the public and its operatic favorites is not so close any more, but one may still hear young men in the lobby use the tender diminutive and the possessive pronoun "my" in speaking of the tenor with the radiantly beautiful voice. The applause at opening nights is frenetic, albeit suspiciously regular; hardly anything is ever criticized by the enthusiasts.

All this is explicable only if we start from the assumption that opera is no longer received as what it is, or was, but as something altogether different. Its popularity has departed from expertise. To its adherents it radiates some of the old seriousness, and of the old dignity of great art. Even so, it will submit to their taste—to a taste which is neither able nor willing to give that dignity its due, and which therefore builds its own bomb shelter out of the rubble of the nineteenth century. The force that ties men to opera is the memory of something they cannot possibly remember: of the legendary Golden Age of the bourgeoisie, to which the Iron Age alone lends a glamour it never possessed. The medium of this unreal memory is

81

the familiarity of specific melodies or, in Wagner's case, of drummed-in leitmotifs.

The consumption of operas comes to be largely recognition, not unlike that of song hits, except that the recognition scarcely occurs with the same exactitude as that of the hits. Few listeners will be able to sing *"L'amour est enfant de Bohême"* from beginning to end. They are more likely to react to a signal—"Ah, that's the *Habañera"*—and to be glad they noticed. The conduct of today's opera habitué is retrospective. He guards the cultural assets as possessions. His creed is a line to be voiced in a local dialect: "Still a damn good old opera, isn't it?" The prestige comes from the period when opera was still counted with the more pretentious forms. It attaches to the names of Mozart, Beethoven, Wagner, also that of Verdi. But it is linked with the possibility of a deconcentrated mode of conception that feeds on habit and maintains a state of universal semi-education.[4] Opera, more than any other form, represents traditional bourgeois culture to those who simultaneously fail to take part in that culture.

Exceedingly symptomatic of the present social situation in opera is the role of subscription. Presumably it covers a far larger percentage of operagoers than in the past; a comparison would be worthwhile. This accords with looking on the present social state of opera as the reception of something that is not understood. Informed about the season program only vaguely, if at all, the subscriber signs a blank check. He does not control the choice of offerings according to the old laws of the market. The hypothesis that to the bulk of present subscribers "that" one hears opera matters more than "what" and "how" is hardly an exaggeration. The want has emancipated itself from the concrete form of what is wanted. This tendency extends to all organized culture consumption; it is particularly striking in the book clubs. The steering is done either by the organization heads or by the institutions whose customers make up the organizations. A number of operas is supplied with the rest, possibly unwanted by the customers, but certainly not resisted by them either. Much of this could probably be checked out by research among opera listeners. It would have to be very shrewdly designed, of course; direct questions would yield little.

Due to the share of organizations in the opera audience, the picture of its social reception today is apt to be rather blurred. One might predict that the regular operagoers will prove to be essentially recruited from neither intellectuals nor grand bourgeois. A disproportionately large segment will probably be elderly—among women, above all, according to what is known so far; though in their youth opera was already shaken, they expect it to bring back something of those days. Another part will come from a better situated petty bourgeoisie—by no means *nouveau riche* only. These hope by attending the opera to give a convenient demonstration of culture to themselves and others. Remaining as a kind of invariant, for the time being, is the romantic youth of both sexes; with the growing attraction of the teenager ideal they are apt to dwindle. Subjectively the main function is that opera awakens a sense of belonging to a fictitious status of the past. Its present reception obeys a mechanism of futile identification. It is frequented by an elite that is no elite.[5]

Hatred of things modern—much more virulent in the opera audience than in that of the drama—combines with obstinacy in praising the good old days. The opera is one of the stopgaps in the world of resurrected culture, a filler of holes blasted by the mind. That operatic activities rattle on unchanged even though literally nothing in them fits any more, this fact is drastic testimony to the noncommittal, somehow accidental character assumed by the cultural superstructure. The official life of opera can teach us more about society than about a species of art that is outliving itself and will hardly survive the next blow.

From the side of art the condition is unalterable. The hopeless level of most novelties that reach the operatic stage today is enforced by the conditions of social reception. If composers do not begin by abandoning all hope to be included in the repertoire, they are inevitably forced into concessions like the ones of the few hit operas in which the specters of Strauss or Puccini are warmed up and anachronisms are confused with redblooded theater—unless preference is accorded to the standpoint of composer-directors who write background music and hang on to topics which in literature have already "arrived." Today even the better-intentioned no sooner think of dealing "realistically" with the theater than their music succumbs to fatal moderation and dilution. Social controls strip the result of just the punching power by which restive listeners might be won over. This is not to say that great compositorial talents with radically new dramaturgic ideas may not have some chance to conquer the opera houses. But the difficulties are extraordinary, and thus far not one of the young generation's foremost talents seems to have written anything that could compare with the best instrumental and electronic music of recent years.

The upshot of such reflections on opera for the sociology of music would be this: unless it wants to be mired down in the most superficial kind of fact-finding, that sociology must not be content to study simple dependency relations between society and music, or the complex of problems of compositorial autonomy, the quest of independence of social determinants. The sociology of music has its proper object only when it focuses on the antagonisms which today are really crucial for the relationships of music and society. It must pay enough attention to a state of facts which until now has been little noted: to the inadequacy of the esthetic object and its reception. The abstract category of alienation, one that has been automated in the meantime, no longer suffices. We must reckon with the social consumption of that which society has alienated. As a pure "being for" something else, a consumer commodity that has public value because of moments which to the thing itself were not essential at all, it also became something other than itself. No one would deny that the esthetic forms change with history, but society's relation to forms already molded and established is also historic throughout. To this day, however, the dynamic of this relation is that of a permanent decay of the forms within the social consciousness that preserves them.

6

CHAMBER MUSIC

In searching for the sociological aspect of chamber music I start out neither from the type of work—whose boundaries fade into one another—nor from the listeners, but from the players. By chamber music I mean essentially those products of the sonata epoch, from Haydn down to Schönberg and Webern, that are characterized by the principle of discontinuous work. The inner character, the tissue of this type of music is constituted by its distribution among several musicians. In its initial import, at any rate, it is dedicated at least as much to the players as to an audience whom the composer seems at times scarcely to have considered. This is what distinguishes chamber music (in which category the bulk of nineteenth-century song production may be included) from the ecclesiastically defined effective circle of sacred art—whose cast may also be small—as well as from the vague and broad realm occupied by the public of orchestras and virtuosos. The question is what that means socially.

Surely presupposed is expertise. A dedication to the players as shown in the very gist of chamber music means reckoning with persons who in performing their own parts will be aware of the whole and will adjust their performance to its function in the whole. When the Kolisch Quartet, with chamber music already at a late stage, used only scores, not parts, at rehearsal and played all works, including the most difficult contemporary ones, by heart, this was the consummation of an intent implied from the outset in the chamber-musical relation of note text and player. Anyone who presents chamber music correctly is reproducing the composition once more, as something that becomes, and simultaneously constitutes its ideal audience, one that shares in its most secret quiver. To this extent the authentic chamber music type concerned itself with uniting music and audience, no matter in how limited a social realm.

The two had been withdrawing from each other ever since

bourgeois music achieved full autonomy. Chamber music was the refuge of a balance of art and reception which society denied elsewhere. It strikes the balance by dispensing with that element of publicity which is as much a part of the idea of bourgeois democracy as the property distinctions and educational privileges of this democracy run counter to it. What makes such a homogeneous model space possible is the state of relative security enjoyed by individual, economically independent citizens, by entrepreneurs and, in particular, by well-to-do members of the so-called free professions. Obviously there is a relation between the flowering of chamber music and the peak period of liberalism. Chamber music is specific to an epoch in which the private sphere, as one of leisure, has vigorously parted from the public-professional sphere. Yet neither are the two embarked on irreconcilably divergent courses nor is leisure commandeered, as in the modern concept of "rest and recreation," to become a parody of freedom. Great chamber music could come into being, could be played and understood, as long as the private sphere had a measure of substantiality, albeit one already fragile.

Time and again, and not without reason, the action of those who play chamber music has been likened to a contest or a conversation. The scores take care of that: the work with themes and motifs, the alternation of voices, their mutual emergence, the whole dynamics in the structure of chamber music has an agonistical touch. The process represented by every composition in itself actively carries out antitheses—openly at first, and not without irony in the cases of Haydn and Mozart, but later on concealed in strict technique. The players are so evidently in a sort of competition that the thought of the competitive mechanism of bourgeois society cannot be dismissed; the very gestures of the purely musical performance are like the visible social ones.

And yet they are not alike. For nowhere does the Kantian definition of art as purposeless efficacy, a definition formulated at the outset of bourgeois emancipation, fit its object more precisely than in chamber music. In the first works of the species, works not yet aiming at extremes, there is often a bustle as if the four instruments of the string quartet were engaged in some socially useful labor; and yet what they do is merely an impotent and innocuous copy of such labor, a production process without a final product. In chamber music the sole product would be the process itself. The reason is that in a twofold sense the players, after all, are merely playing. In fact, that production process is objectified in the structure which they simply repeat: in the composition. The activity has turned into pure doing, a doing that has escaped from self-preservation. What seems to be the players' primary function has long been done by the thing, and they only get it back, so to speak, from the thing.

The relation of social purposes is sublimated into a purposeless esthetic in-itself. To this extent even great chamber music has to pay tribute to the primacy of the thing; its native hour coincides with the abolition of the figured bass, and thus of the modest remnants of improvisation, the irrational spontaneity of players. Art and play are in accord: chamber music is an instant. It almost seems like a miracle that its period lasted so long. Yet that spiritualization of a nonetheless unmistakably social event shapes that event's own phenomenon, the contest. For the chamber-music contest is a negative one and thus a critique of the real one. The first step in playing chamber music well is to learn not to thrust oneself forward but to step back. What makes a whole is not boastful self-assertion on the several parts—that would produce a barbarian chaos—but self-limiting reflection.

If great bourgeois art transcends its own society by remembering and revising the functions of feudal elements victimized by progress, chamber music—as the corrective of the bumptious bourgeois who stands on what is his—practices courtesy. Down to Webern's gesture of extended silences, the social virtue of politeness helped to bring about that spiritualization of music which occurred in chamber music and presumably nowhere else. Great chamber musicians aware of the mystery of the species tend to listen so much to each other that they only mark their own parts. Heralded as a consequence of their practice is the silence, the passage of music into soundless reading, the vanishing point of all musical spiritualization. The most likely analogon to the chamber musician's behavior is the ideal of fair play in the English sports of old. The spiritualization of competition, its transposition into the realm of the imagination, anticipates a state of things in which competition would be cured of aggression and evil. Ultimately it anticipates the state of labor as play.

Whoever behaves like that is conceived as someone exempt from compulsory labor, i.e., as an amateur. The early string quartets of Viennese classicism, even the last three which Mozart wrote for the king of Prussia, were meant for nonprofessional musicians. Today it has become difficult to envision amateurs able to cope with such technical demands. To grasp the pathos of that amateur idea one must recall a motif of German idealism that emerged in Fichte, but especially in Hölderlin and Hegel: the contradiction between human destiny, between Hölderlin's "divine right" of man, and man's heteronomous role in making a bourgeois living. The sick Hölderlin played the flute, by the way, and some of the spirit of chamber music can be felt throughout his lyric poetry.

The private chamber musicians were noblemen who did not need to pursue a bourgeois occupation or, later, men who refused to regard their bourgeois occupation as the measure of their existence. They sought the best part of that existence outside their working hours—although molded so strongly by those hours that even where they had a narrow realm of freedom the working period could not be ignored. This constellation may explain the specific features of a chamber musician. Reserved for his private life was an occupation which, lest it remain ridiculous bungling, required full qualifications—what would today be called professional standards. The chamber music lover who is up to his task might as well be a professional. Even the most recent past does not lack instances of amateurs turning into concert performers.

That physicians tend to love chamber music and have a talent for it may well be explained as a protest against a profession that makes unusual demands on the intellectual who takes it up. It calls for sacrifices of a kind otherwise required of manual laborers only, for touching nauseating things and being on call, not master of one's own time. The musical sublimation in chamber music makes up for this. It would be the mental activity a doctor feels deprived of. The price is that it does not intervene in reality, that it does not help—for which Tolstoy, fully aware of its esthetic dignity, rebuked chamber music in the work named after one of its great items.

Finally, the relation of chamber music to German idealism—as the erection of an edifice in which human destiny is to be consummated—may also show in the fact that chamber music in the emphatic sense of the term has been confined to the German-

Austrian region. I hope one will not suspect me of nationalism when I say that the world-famous quarters of Debussy and Ravel, masterworks in their way, are not really covered by that emphatic concept. This may have to do with the fact that the French composers' works themselves were not written until a phase in which the concept was shaken. The feeling behind their quartets is essentially coloristic; they are artfully paradoxical transpositions of colors from the orchestra palette, or from the piano, to the four string soloists. Their formal law is the static juxtaposition of tone levels. They lack what was the vital element of chamber music, the work with themes and motifs or its echo, that which Schönberg called "developing variation": the dialectical spirit of a self-engendering, self-negating, but then, most of the time, newly self-confirming whole. In such a spirit even the utmost chamber-musical intimacy clings to its relation to social reality, from which it withdraws as though in horror. Great philosophy and chamber music are deeply entwined in the structure of speculative thinking. Schönberg, the chamber musician par excellence, has long been accused of speculativeness. Chamber music probably has always had some of the esotericism of the systems of identity. In it, as in Hegel, all the world's qualitative abundance has turned inward.

It therefore invites definition as the music of inwardness. But the idea of inwardness hardly covers the historic-social phenomenon. Not in vain has chamber music come to be the instrument of cozily reactionary apologias for the species, advanced by those who would resist technological civilization by clutching their music as if it protected them from external, commercial and—in their language—decadent activities. These activities are not transcended by a chamber music lover striving for provincial conservation or restoration of stages that are passé, economically as well as esthetically. A book published after World War II was called *Das Stillvergnügte Streichquartett (The Serenely Cheerful String Quartet)*. Great chamber music has nothing to do with such ideologically misbegotten inwardness. The substrate of that ideology is a concretion which in fact is most abstract: the individual as pure being for itself. But chamber music, by its very structure, is objective. By no means does the alienated subject's expression exhaust it. It comes to be that expression only at the end, in a polemically extreme posture that is least agreeable to the serenely cheerful. Previously, however, it unrolled the unpictorial picture of an antagonistically progressing whole insofar as the experience of privacy is still commensurable with that whole.

Such a recurrence of lost objectivity in a subjectively limited realm defined the social as well as the metaphysical nature of chamber music. A more apt description of it than the fustily self-righteous word *inwardness* is the bourgeois home, in which chamber music was essentially located by its sound volume. In that home, as in chamber music, no provision is made for any difference between player and listener. There are seemingly trivial figures without which the domestic chamber music practice of the nineteenth and early twentieth century is nonetheless unthinkable, figures like the one who turns the pages of the piano score, a listener who precisely follows the musical course. These figures are social *imagines* of chamber music. Like that music, the old-style bourgeois interior wished on its own to be the world once again.

There, of course, a contradiction took shape from the outset. What was relegated to the private sphere, by its locale as well as by the executors, transcended that sphere by its content, by its visualization of the whole. A lack of consideration for broad effectiveness, included in the principle of such privacy, served by way of that content to spur the autonomous unfoldment of the music itself. This was bound to shatter its social scene and the circle of players. The species of musical intimacy was not even fully established before it ceased to feel at home in its home. Of the definitive form of the six quartets of opus 18, his first work indicating sovereign control over the compositorial means, Beethoven said that not until then had he learned the right way to write quartets. The remark deserves special attention because there really was no model for that opus; its procedure has little to do with even the great quartets Mozart dedicated to Haydn. Beethoven deduced the criteria of the true string quartet from the immanent requirements of the species, not from traditional models.

Yet that very exaltation of the production of chamber music over its archetypes—still very young in those days—is apt to have prevented an adequate interpretation by amateurs, and thereby, as a matter of principle, their performance in private homes. Professional musicians were economically dependent on a larger audience, and thus on the concert form. It probably was not much different with those Mozart quartets, whose very dedication to a great composer attests the composition's primacy over the act of music-making. They are works of a sort of which Mozart left a few in almost every species of composition, works which were meant to be something like paradigmata of true composing, protests against the jumble of commissioned items and the restrictions in technique and imagination which that jumble imposed on a genius.

In chamber music we can accordingly speak rather early of an antagonism between productive forces and productive conditions —and not as a disproportion extraneous to production, one between its form and its reception, but as an artistically immanent one. This contradiction carried farther, bursting the last assured locale of musical reception, but it resulted in the evolution of the species and in its grandeur. Without harmonistic-total fictions it was appropriate to the internally antagonistic state of a society organized along the lines of the *principium individuationis,* and at the same time it surpassed its assimilation to that society by what it said. In the pure pursuit of its own formal law it critically honed itself against the activities of the music market and against the society they complied with.

This contradiction too has found a visible *imago* in the small auditorium. There used to be small concert halls in palaces; now, in response to bourgeois needs, they were planned in the large concert houses that were built for symphonic productions. The atmosphere and the acoustics of these rooms were still more or less in keeping with the intimacy of chamber music, but they already served to make it public and adjust it to market conditions. The small auditorium—I owe my own acquaintance with the whole traditional quartet literature, with Beethoven above all, to the Rosé Quartet concerts in the acoustically ideal auditorium of the Frankfurt concert hall building—was the site of a truce between music and society. It would not be surprising if after the disastrous bombings of World War II such small auditoriums had not been rebuilt anywhere, or only at a few places.

The chamber-musical truce between art and society did not last. The social contract was cancelled, with the result that small auditoriums really have no place any more in the bourgeois world. If they are built for art's sake—not to satisfy real purposive needs of a palace, as under feudalism—they stand in the shadow of a

91

paradox. The bourgeois idea of a hall is inseparable from associations with a political mass meeting or at least a parliamentary body; it always implies thoughts of monumentality. Chamber music and the rise of capitalism did not agree. The tendency of chamber music, which once upon a time created an ephemeral concordance of all participants, was the first of all musical types to dissociate itself from its reception. It was precisely in that domain that the new music began evolving. Schönberg's crucial innovations would not have been possible if he had not turned away from the ostentatious symphonic poems of his age and chose the obligatory Brahmsian quartet structure for his model.

The musical form that was designed for the large auditorium is the symphony. One must not underestimate the well-known fact that the symphony's architectonic schemata coincided with the ones of chamber music, and that both the Brahms and the Bruckner schools kept using them when the conception of symphonic poetry had broken away. This conception rebelled much earlier, but much less radically, than the literatures of chamber music and piano solo, where productive critique grasped the canonized forms in their fiber, then, all the way into their smallest elements. The Mannheim School in the prehistory of Viennese classicism did not strictly draw the line between symphony and chamber music, and it always remained unstable. The chamber-musical features in the first movement of Brahms's Fourth Symphony are as indubitable as the symphonic traits in his piano sonatas—already noted in Schumann's famed review—let alone in the first movement of Beethoven's Quartet in F Minor, op. 95. The sonata type must have been particularly well suited to the presentation of a dynamic subjectively mediated totality.

The idea of such a totality—as one of the music itself, not of its relation to the recipients—was drawn from the social ground that carried it, and for that reason it maintained its primacy over the more drastic but secondary difference between public and private spheres. This difference itself could not claim to be fully substantial since the musical public was no agora, no true community in the sense of direct democracy, but an association of individuals who on festive symphonic occasions might subjectively shed their sense of isolation without jarring its base. The contents of symphonic and chamber music had much in common: the dialectics between particulars and entirety, the nascent synthesis of contradictory interests. At times the choice of one medium or the other seemed almost arbitrary. Also responsible for the structural similarities of symphonics and chamber music was surely the fact that, after a long prehistory, the polished sonata structure and its associated types offered the security of universal familiarity and at the same time left ample room for spontaneous musical impulses. They were available, selected, and tested for craftsmanship.

The force of gravity of extant forms is an essential element in the sociology of arts, including music: but by itself it would not have sufficed to forge a structural tie to the same formal premises for types as spatially different, in both a literal and a metaphorical sense, as symphonics and chamber music. As Paul Bekker spoke of the community-forming power which always had an ideological touch—since the humankind that took shape before a symphony, even if it was Beethoven's Ninth, remained esthetic and never reached into real social existence—so was the microcosm of chamber music also aimed at integration but dispensed with the decorative and representative facade of expansive sound. Even so, Bekker was right to reject the formalistic definition of the symphony as a sonata for orchestra.

Schönberg stubbornly disputed this in conversation, pointing to the prevalence of the sonata in each species to justify his insistence on that immediate identity. Guiding him was an apologetic will that would brook no fractures and contradictions, not even stylistic ones, in the sacrosanct great masters' work; now and then he even denied differences in rank within the several composers' oeuvre. The difference between symphony and chamber music is nonetheless beyond question. What illuminates the contradictory nature of the musical consciousness is that precisely in Schönberg's own oeuvre the handwriting of the orchestral works deviates completely from that of the chamber music. On the occasion of his *Variations for Orchestra*, op. 31, he himself discussed the problem that arose with the twelve-tone technique's first application to a large orchestral apparatus, when the sound material forced him to go far beyond the polyphonous combinations he had previously dared with the new technique.

To be sure, the previous difference between the sonata of chamber music and the symphonic sonata was the exact opposite of the difference that dominated in the sonata form's age of crisis. In principle, Beethoven's symphonies are simpler than chamber music despite their substantially more lavish apparatus, and this very simplicity showed what effects the many listeners had in the interior of the formal edifice. It was not a matter of adjusting to the market, of course; at most, perhaps, it had to do with Beethoven's intent to "strike fire in a man's soul.' Objectively, his symphonies were orations to mankind, designed by a demonstration of the law of their life, to bring men to an unconscious consciousness of the unity otherwise hidden in the individual's diffuse existence. Chamber music and symphonics were complementary. The first, largely dispensing with pathos in gesture and ideology, helped to express the self-emancipating status of the bourgeois spirit without as yet directly addressing society. The symphony took the consequence, declaring the idea of totality for an esthetic nullity as soon as it ceased to communicate with the real totality.

In exchange, however, the symphony developed a decorative as well as a primitive element which spurred the subject to productive criticism. Humanity does not bluster. This may have been what Haydn felt, one of the greatest geniuses among the masters, when he ridiculed young Beethoven as "The Grand Mogul." In so drastic a way as could hardly be surpassed in theory, the incompatibility of similar species is the precipitation of the incompatibility of universal and particular in a developed bourgeois society. In a Beethoven symphony the detail work, the latent wealth of interior forms and figures, is eclipsed by the rhythmic-metrical striking force; throughout, the symphonies want to be heard simply in their temporal course and organization, with the vertical, the simultaneity, the sound level, left wholly unbroken. The one exception remained the wealth of motifs in the first movement of the "Eroica"—which in certain respects, of course, is the highest peak of Beethoven's symphonics as a whole.

It would be inexact, however, to call Beethoven's chamber music polyphonous, and the symphonies, homophonous. Polyphony and homophony alternate in the quartets too; in the last ones, homophony tends to a bald unison at the expense of the very ideal of harmony reigning in the highly classicist symphonies, as in the Fifth and the Seventh. But how little Beethoven's symphonics and his chamber music are one is evident from the most superficial comparison of the Ninth with the last quartets, or even with the last piano sonatas. Compared with those, the Ninth is backward-looking, takes its bearings from the classicist symphony type of the middle period, and denies admission to the dissociative tendencies of the late style proper. This is hardly independent of the intentions of one who addressed his audiences as "Friends" and proposed to join them in chanting "more pleasant tones."

People who think they are musical take it for granted that chamber music is the highest musical species. This convention certainly serves largely for elitist self-affirmation; the limited circle of persons permits the inference that matters reserved for those must be better than what the *misera plebs* enjoys. The proximity of such feelings to fatal claims of cultural leadership is as plain as the untruth of that ideology of musical education. That traditional chamber music outranks great symphonics merely because it manages without drums and trumpets and employs less suasion than does symphonics—this is not convincing. Time and again the important and resistant composers from Haydn to Webern have reached out for the symphony or its derivatives. For all of them knew what price chamber music had to pay for sheltering a subjectivity that needs to surrogate no public and stays unimperiled with itself, as it were: a moment of privacy in the negative sense, of petty bourgeois happiness in hiding, of a simplicity that is more than merely imperiled by resigned idyllicism. The chamber music of the romanticist composers makes this obvious, for all its radiant beauty, and even Brahms—whose chamber works start to objectify themselves emphatically by constructive consolidation out of their own substance—shows traces of it still, now in arid sobriety, now in a tone borrowed from Victorian chromolithographs. If music springs from the split and dubious condition of the whole, if it cannot transcend that condition, it is socially necessary —even where its ambitions do not go beyond what seems attainable—that this limitation will limit the music itself unless it expresses the suffering under the condition. The quality of works of art is the revenge of the false social condition, no matter what position they take in regard to it.

On the other hand that glorification of chamber music is true also, just as its adepts do surpass other listeners in expertise. But this precedence is no more one of the much-cited inner values than it is one of the specific chamber works over comparable symphonic ones. Rather, its place is in the musical language, in a higher degree of mastery of the material. Reducing the sound volume as well as renouncing broader gesticulative effects permits shaping the structure of chamber music all the way into its inmost cells, into the smallest differences. This is why the idea of the new music ripened in chamber music. What the new music took up as its task, the integration of the horizontal and the vertical, was anticipatorily sensed in chamber music.

Brahms reached the principle of universal thematic work as early as in his Piano Quintet. And in Beethoven's last quartets it was the rejection of monumentality that allowed an interior structure to be thoroughly shaped in each single moment, a structure that was incompatible with the al fresco manner of the symphony. What favored such composing was the medium of chamber music with its independently forthcoming and yet mutually qualifying parts. As resistance to expansiveness and decor, chamber music was essentially critical, "unemotional" and, in Beethoven's last stage, anti-ideological. It took this to establish the superiority of chamber music. Socially it owes itself to the limitation of means insofar as that permits it to be autonomous by being ascetical toward appearance. It extends from the dimension of mere sound to a handwriting organized so that all contexts and interrelations are justified in compositorial reality, that they are composed progressively, not left standing on the musical facade.

Even back in classicism it was this progressive organization that permitted chamber music to deviate more profoundly from the schemata than symphonics could. Not only Beethoven's last quartets are irregularly structured; as Erwin Ratz has emphasized, so are quartet movements from the middle period, like the great second movement of op. 59, No. 1, and the slow movement from op. 95. It is thereby, not by an especially bold leading of the parts, that they marked the first radical emancipation of music; pieces of this type would be unthinkable in any Beethoven symphony. The consequence of all this is paradoxical. Outwardly, chamber music aims less at integration—at the illusionary integration of the audience—than does symphonics; but from within, through the tight and finely woven net of thematic relations, it is more integral, more inwardly unanimous and at the same time, by virtue of continued individuation, more free, less authoritarian, and less violent. What it lost in encompassing appearance by its retreat to the private sphere has been regained by a commitment that was severed and windowless, so to speak. For almost a century this has benefited chamber music even in reception.

The new music emerged from the great chamber music of a style specifically marked by Viennese classicism. That Schönberg's roots lay in the polyphony of the string quartet has never been doubted. The qualitative leap occurred in his first two quartets. In the First, which was still tonal, the work with themes and motifs came to be omnipresent. The results were an expanded harmonics and a counterpoint of undreamed-of density. Next, in the Second Quartet, the whole process was visibly carried through, from a tonality extremely tensed by independent chromatic side-steps to free atonality. Socially this meant canceling the accord with the audience. The consequence of the chamber music principle of totally finishing the structure was to stop paying any attention to the listeners' receptivity, however unwilling Schönberg—naive all his life about social relations—was to take this into account.

The first scandals of the new music erupted after his quartets in D minor and F sharp minor, although what happened there was really nothing but a pervading of Brahms's call for panthematic procedure with Wagner's harmonic innovations. Only, both trends were reinforced as by an inductor: the harmonics became more abrupt, now that even the sharpest dissonance was vindicated by the leading of the parts, by the autonomy of working with motifs and themes, and the movements of this work came to be infinitely less hampered in the widened tonal domain than they had been in Brahms's conservative harmonics.

However, in the dialectical synthesis of means of composition drawn from the two hostile late nineteenth-century schools, the social dichotomy of musical interior and musical public dissolved as well. The requirements of Schönberg's chamber music could not be reconciled any more with *Hausmusik,* with the ambience of domesticity. They were as explosive in content as in technique. They obliged chamber music to make its definitive move to the concert hall. Conversely, their mere existence was a disavowal of the decorative-lapidary character of public music. To a music driving beyond intimacy, they brought as its heritage a wealth of compositorial procedures that had been able to thrive only under this protective cover.

Central under this aspect is the invention of a form: the chamber symphony, from which all chamber orchestra structures are descended to this day. The first impulse which moved Schönberg to this conception—an extremely daring one in point of sound, by the way, and still very difficult to realize—was probably the simple fact that the polyphony emancipated in the first Quartet could no longer get along with the accustomed four parts of the quartet structure. Once wholly unleashed, polyphony required a greater multiplicity of parts, and indeed, Schönberg's dosage of polyphony was always going to depend on the available apparatus—a procedure contrary to the tendency of classicist Viennese symphonics. In the grand execution of real polyphony the chamber symphony surpasses everything since the Middle Ages, even Bach, while the Second Quartet rather limits the polyphony again, in favor of harmonic events.

Combined with this in the First Chamber Symphony, however, is a trend to the outside. As Webern put it, the piece is impetuous and mobile in character. It has been said that Schönberg mistakenly expected this very work to make a big hit with the public. Of the secret social impulses behind the new music, the wish to liquify the congealed, reified antithesis to the now truly externalized public music, to the program music of Strauss, was surely not the weakest. Uninhibited expression, usually associated with artistic esotericism, implies a desire to be heard. What was later, in expressionism—with which the younger Schönberg has much in common—called "the cry" is not only incommunicable as a renunciation of the well-worn linguistic articulations of meaning; it is also, objectively, a desperate attempt to reach those who do not hear any more. On this ground, too, the thesis of the new music's self-sufficient asociality—far too stubbornly upheld to this day—needs revision. Its first manifestations would be better understood as a publication without publicity. Not the least irritant in the new music was that it did not simply retire, like chamber music, but turned its impervious armor against the people it seemed to dislike. From the outset, it was not just introverted but an attack on the concurrence of the extroverts.

What was heralded in Schönberg's First Chamber Symphony has

since been achieved: the end of chamber music as a kind of composing centered around the string quartet. Since Schönberg's Fourth Quartet (1936) virtually no more high-ranking string quartets have been written. Webern's approximately simultaneous opus 28 (1937–38) sounds a little as if his and his teacher's native species had been forsaken by its living spirit; the rigor of the exposition in the first movement denies whatever gains chamber music had made earlier, as recently as in Webern's own masterful String Trio. It may be part of the same context that while the most famous chamber music work by Berg, his *Lyrical Suite*, makes do with the means of the string quartet, its course resembles that of a "latent opera" or, more drastically put, of program music such as *Verklärte Nacht*. At the peak of the bourgeois era chamber music was the counter-pole of opera. Opera, though objectively undermined, found and keeps finding its audience; chamber music, far more adequate to the objective form of society, found it less and less, for that reason. The two complement each other. In Berg the types begin to float, to oscillate as if the self-sufficient ideal of chamber music had faded for him as much as, conversely, he would trust opera only if it had been truly progressively composed.

In any case, the string quartet and everything related to it has been vanishing for the past fifteen years. What has been heard until now of Boulez's *Livre à Quatuor* is not equal to *Marteau sans maître*—a work conceived later and perhaps to be deemed a descendant of Schönberg's idea of the chamber orchestra, especially of *Pierrot lunaire*. The reason for the decline of the string quartet, or for the composers' allergy to it, is primarily technological. If they include the dimension of color in the construction— something that began precisely in Schönberg's first two quartets, of course, although retreating in the Third and Fourth behind an all but defensive congruence with the material of the pure quartet structure in its normal form—they are balking at the relative homogeneity of that form, at its want of timbres. Above all, however, the chamber music tradition as the domain of proceeding with themes and motifs is denied by serial music-making where the motif is spurned as material and recourse is had to the single tone and its parameters. It is hard to prophesy whether this is a permanent phenomenon; whether the repressed means of chamber music will not be reactualized as composers grow more critical of the serial mode of proceeding. Stockhausen's increasing interest in the tone material of the solo piano speaks for it.

In the crisis of chamber music the immanently compositorial history of the species coincides in turn with the change in social conditions. We can state determinants on altogether different levels of abstraction, ranging from the general social tendency to most tangible circumstances. Primarily, the crisis of chamber music recalls the crisis of the individual, in the sign of which that music stood. The premises of autonomy and independence, extending all the way into the compositorial ramifications of chamber music, have been weakened; the solid order of property, in whose favored groups so fragile an activity as chamber music could feel sheltered, is a thing of the past. One need only visualize the role of the white-collar worker as a social type increasingly taking the place of what used to be called the middle class. White-collar workers are not stay-at-homes; a whole cultural supply has been tailored to fit them; their free time is not leisure but an overt or covert object of institutional regulation, and the white-collar culture has spread beyond the occupational group, without reaching a fixed limit. The monotony of mechanized labor, including office work, presumably requires other correlates than the time-consuming, demanding, and difficult work of playing quartets or trios, and the models of modern life as the culture industry supplies them stigmatize such serious and uncomfortable occupations in their naive victims' eyes. They must bear the odium of being "old-fashioned," like an unrenovated guest house as compared with a plastic, neon-lit diner. Whatever seeks to flee from the damaged inwardness strives toward bustle and gadget.[1] The progressive and regressive sides of this entwine. Reflections of it fall on the act of composing. Discontent with the possible sound combinations of all traditional chamber music is often paired with a desperate dread of intellectualization: it pretends to a cultural accomplishment that no one believes any more. Where production dries up, though, reproductive cultivation will scarcely survive. Even in the stratum in which it used to thrive, it has—we are told time and again—become an exception. This has been much deplored, and it would be up to empirical research to test the thesis and then to uncover and to weigh the causes.

The quantitative decline of chamber music is a thesis which one man repeats after the other, and of course it is difficult to check.

Comparable figures for the past are lacking, and old-style music lovers are the very ones who may balk at statistical questionnaires tailored for the consumers of the mass media. It is conceivable that the number of those who make music in private has declined only proportionally, not absolutely; probably one could determine this only indirectly, notably by questioning private music teachers and comparing their number, on the basis of membership lists of professional organizations, with that of thirty years ago. The chances are that the change is qualitative rather than quantitative, that the import of domestic music-making for the life of music in general has waned since the peak period of liberalism. Today the girl who plays Chopin is as untypical as are four amateurs joining to form a string quartet. The answer to the question whether there is less private singing than formerly is not so self-evident as might be suggested by the fact that we are hardly ever asked to private musical soirées any more.

One of the tasks of an empirical sociology of music would be the pointed posing of problems in order to test opinions that have become common property as expressions of a prevailing cultural ideology. Against this, one may well be free to say that the trend to administrative organization, at least to an unofficial one, has largely swept private music-making in Germany, to use the jargon of the administered world; it probably was by this tendency of musical life that the resentment listener type was institutionally bred at all. The ambition to immerse oneself, the quest for a specific musical quality and a developed individual performance—all this yields to compact adjustment and blithe going-along. Compared with the joy of a chamber music player who is suddenly struck by the beauty of a particular work, the relation to the thing itself often acquires an abstract touch; the man who is over-whelmed by Beethoven's Ghost Trio or by the slow movement of op. 59, No. 1, is replaced by rather indiscriminating "friends of old music"—and in pre-Bachian music, after all, the qualitative differences are indeed either problematic or hard to perceive today. What in the private practice of chamber music used to be the basis of good and adequate listening—taste—deteriorates and takes on a bad odor. It certainly was not the highest category of musical experience, but it was one that we need so as to rise above it.

The decline of domestic musical instruction may have contributed to that of chamber music. The inflation after World War I put private lessons by qualified teachers beyond the reach of the more modest middle class; but even the boom of the fifties did not bring them back, according to unsystematic observations, although piano purchases, at least, have recently increased. It seems plausible to blame the mass media; but those do spread a knowledge of the literature and would be as apt to win new converts to domestic chamber music as to relieve others of the effort of playing. In all likelihood it will be the listener's mentality—mediated in turn by society as a whole—that is more responsible. The influence of the mass media should probably be sought, rather, in the sphere of what German social psychologists call *Reizüberflutung*, a "deluge of stimuli." That radio addicts have been weaned of personal musical activity may matter less than that whatever they might play strikes them as too monochromatic, too modest in comparison with the cheap deluxe sounds offered by the loudspeakers.

The decay of the cultural interior—or its lack, in some countries —coincides with hunger for more coarsely sensual stimuli. Their absence is forgotten only by those who experience music from the outset as a matter of the mind, and precisely that is prevented by its preparation as a consumer commodity. This reduces the potential of chamber-music activity. At stake everywhere are forms of collective reaction; it therefore does little good to preach great chamber music to individuals. One should be content if they get to know chamber music literature at all, to see what they do themselves out of. Circumstances hardly permit them to appropriate it, and again it is something on the surface that stands for the core. People today rush to marry into apartments with small rooms, low ceilings, and thin walls, apartments in which a string quartet would be impossible simply on acoustical grounds, while the blues pulsing out of the loudspeaker can be tuned down at will and is less irksome to the neighbors—who are accustomed to it—than Beethoven's great Trio in B Major would be. Besides, for this one would lack the grand piano that costs more than the stereo and has no room in the minidwelling. But its replacement, the upright, is no instrument for chamber music.

Chamber music remains possible, not as maintenance of a tradition that has long been moth-eaten, but only as an art for experts, something quite useless and lost that must be known to be useless if it is not to decay into home decoration. It would have no defense against the charge of *l'art pour l'art*. But that principle itself has changed in a period in which all agree on denouncing it as a relic of neoromanticism and Art Nouveau. In a society in which all things intellectual have become consumer goods, the trend of history has doomed the precarious haven of that future possibility which is precluded by the universal sway of the reality principle. Whatever has a function is replaceable; irreplaceable is only what is good for nothing. The social function of chamber music is to be functionless. Even this function, of course, is no longer performed by traditional chamber music.

7

CONDUCTOR AND ORCHESTRA
Aspects of Social Psychology[1]

Reflecting on the conductor, the orchestra, and the relation between the two is not only justified by the social relevance of their role in musical life. The main reason for such reflection is that conductor and orchestra in themselves constitute a kind of microcosm in which social tensions recur and can be concretely studied—something comparable, for example, to a community or municipality as a sociological research object permitting extrapolations on society, which is never tangible as such. This is not a matter of formal sociological group relations independent of a specific social content, however much some observations on conductors and orchestras may look like special cases of a universal group sociology. A separate discussion of the social characters of conductor and orchestra, of their function in today's society and of the ensuing esthetic problems, could not be anything but arbitrary. All intraesthetic distortions of the music-making of orchestras under their leaders are symptoms of some social wrong.

Among musicians it is hardly in dispute that the public prestige of conductors far exceeds the contributions which most of them make to the reproduction of music. At the least, their prestige and their actual artistic work point in different directions. A conductor does not owe his fame to his ability to interpret scores, or certainly not to this ability alone. He is an imago, the imago of power, visibly embodied in his prominent figure and striking gestures. Elias Canetti has pointed out this element,[2] which in music is by no means limited to the conductor. The virtuoso—a pianist of Liszt's type, for instance—shows similar traits. In identifying with him, fantasies of power are acted out with impunity because they cannot be nailed down as such. On the occasion of a celebrated salon piece by Rachmaninoff I once drew attention to this context and suggested naming it the "Nero complex." [3] Besides, the conductor demonstrates his leadership role visibly: the orchestra really must play the way he commands. Being purely esthetic, this imago has something contagious and at the same time nugatory about it: the tyrant's manner sets off a crescendo, not a war, and the coercion he exercises rests on an agreement. But what serves unreal ends appears as if it were real, and the conductor acts as if he were creating the work here and now. This is what poisons his every factual achievement. Impressed by his medicine-man gestures, the listener thinks it takes just such an attitude to make the players give their artistic best—a best that will be taken for something like the setting of a physical record. But the quality of the performance, the aspect of conducting faced by the orchestra, is largely separate from the one that beguiles the audience. Relative to the audience a conductor has, a priori, a propagandistic and demagogical touch. One is reminded of the old joke about the lady at a concert who asks the expert in the next seat please to let her know as soon as Nikisch starts spellbinding.

This is how much the social rating of things musical differs from their own structure. Feats which a delight in fascination credits to the conductor are sometimes not performed by him at all. A wealthy family in a large German city once had a deranged son who imagined that he was a brilliant conductor. To cure him, the family hired the best orchestra and arranged for the youth to conduct it in Beethoven's Fifth. Although he was a miserable layman, the performance turned out no worse than any other current one; the orchestra, which could have played the work with its eyes closed, simply ignored the dilettante's false entrances. Thus he found his delusion confirmed. Of related significance were the experiments of American social psychologists who had their test subjects listen to mislabeled records, with Toscanini performances bearing the name of an unknown backwoods conductor, and vice versa. The reactions turned out to correspond to the label—either because the listeners could not distinguish between the performance qualities or because the differences were incomparably less than the official musical ideology would have it.

The conductor acts as though he were taming the orchestra, but his real target is the audience—a trick not unknown to political demagogues. The substitution satisfies the sadomasochistic need if, and for as long as, no other leaders are at hand for hailing. Experiments with conductorless orchestras were made in the first years of the Russian Revolution, and however naive those may have been in a purely musical sense, they were merely calling the conductor figure to account for permanent debts incurred in social psychology. The conductor symbolizes dominance even in his attire: it is that of the master class and of the whip-wielding ringmaster in a circus—also that of headwaiters, of course, a fact bound to flatter the audience. "What a gentleman—and here he is at our service!" may register in the unconscious. At the same time this lordliness is moved into the distance of esthetic space, permitting the bandmaster to be equipped with magic qualities that could never stand the test of reality. Equipped, in other words, with the medicine man's gift of fascination.

This too retains some phenomenal support in the conductor's need, under present conditions, to develop certain suggestive faculties if any of his intentions are to be conveyed at all. That in so doing he seems to feel committed to the cause alone, unconcerned with the audience and indeed turning his back on it—this fact lends him that loveless detachment from his devotees which Freud, in *Mass Psychology and Ego Analysis*, named among the constituents of the leader imago. The segregation of the esthetic is turned back into the ritual that spawned it. The exaggeration, the fanaticism that bursts forth as needed, the exhibition of an allegedly purely introverted passion—all of this recalls the demeanor of leaders trumpeting their own unselfishness. The histrionics at the podium are easy to credit with the dictatorial capacity for frothing at the mouth at will. It is astonishing that the Nazis did not persecute conductors as they did soothsayers, for competing with their own charisma.

This is not to say that the conductor's activity lacks artistic justification and necessity. All modern music bears the mark of integrating a diversity. The idea is not as immutable, of course, as its familiarity would suggest; the relentless polyphonous combinations of as recent a movement as the Florentine *ars nova* do not seem wholly subject to the unity of simultaneity, and if today the groups influenced by John Cage renounce the compositorial integral, this also indicates a resurgence of something which the procedures of European art music and their rational control of nature managed to hold down but never to eliminate. But as soon as music features many parts—whether it is really polyphonous or homophonous with "discontinuous work"—and aspires to unify the diversity, it must be guided by a unified consciousness that will first achieve the integration in the mind and then will realize or at least supervise it. Even small ensembles cannot do without the like, for all their members' comradely understanding. Proper performances by a string quartet call for an authority that will decide controversies and will differentiate as well as coordinate the individual feats of players in accord with the idea of the whole. In most cases this is the job of the first violin.

Yet the chamber music ensemble, like any other, is laboring under a profound contradiction. Ensembles are parables of a productive diversity which spontaneously brings forth the whole, and they wait for this diversity to produce itself on its own. Esthetically, however, the act of synthesis can only be performed by one individual, and the diversity—in itself an esthetic semblance—is thus reduced to a semblance once again. Each member of a good string quartet really must be a first-rate soloist, and yet he must not be a soloist. The typical squabbles which fatally limit the duration of string quartets are not based only on the financial conditions but on an antinomy: quartet playing calls as much for autonomous activity by the individuals as for their heteronomous subordination to an individual will that represents a kind of *volonté generale*. Appearing in such conflicts, purely intramusically, are social conflicts. The principle of unity which immigrated into music from society outside, as a trait of authoritarian rule, and immanently conferred its stringency on music—this principle continues to exert repression in the musical-esthetic context. The social thorn keeps growing in the midst of art.

The music acts as if each man were playing for himself and thus the whole were emerging; but in fact the whole emerges from one guiding, equalizing center which in turn negates the individual spontaneities. The need for such coordination is strengthened, of course, in the orchestra, where a "social void" is formed by the mere fact that each of the many performers cannot possibly pay as much attention to the others as they would be able to in a chamber group. Besides, in traditional orchestral literature the accompanying individual parts are not always so articulated that their unguided execution would by itself assure a meaningful whole. The orchestral apparatus is as much alienated from itself—for no member can ever precisely hear all that happens simultaneously around him—as from the unity of the music due to be played. This is conjured up by the alienated institution of the conductor whose relation to the orchestra, the musical as well as the social relation, prolongs the estrangement. These problems return to society, as it were, what society submerged as a dark mystery in integral ensemble music. The conductor's sins reveal some of the negativity of great music as such, some of its striking violence.

These sins are not mere deformations. They result from the conductor's situation: else they could hardly be so regularly observed. They are, of course, always reinforced by the extramusical temptation to capture the audience. Since music needs the conductor—while he, the outstanding individual, is at the same time the opposite of what seeks to be polyphonous—and since, in prevailing musical activities, integration under a single will always remains precarious, he must compensate by developing qualities alien to his work, qualities which easily degenerate into charlatanism. Without an irrational surplus of personal authority it would hardly be possible to wrest unity, let alone a mental image, from a body of sound segregated from its immediate musical conception. Found in preestablished harmony with such irrationality are social needs, notably that of personalization,[4] the ideological compounding of objective functions in a visible individual. This trend is the shadow that accompanies the real progress of social alienation.

The conductor's figure comes to be the one that acts directly on the audience; at the same time his own music-making too is necessarily estranged from the audience, since he himself is not playing. He thus becomes an actor who plays a musician, and precisely that conflicts with a proper performance. By no means only strangers to music are affected by these histrionics. There is a famous remark by the adolescent Richard Wagner: "You don't want to be an emperor or king, but to stand like a conductor." [5] Immanent to the structure of important compositions from Wagner to Mahler, perhaps even to Richard Strauss, is the model of the conductor surveying and holding sway; it is partly responsible for the "as if" character of much late romanticist music. On the other hand, the *kapellmeister's* importance in the late nineteenth century rose in proportion with the complexity of works. The invective "bandmaster music," aimed at the lack of originality in so many pretentious pieces, brands as individual failure what is a far more objective state of facts that should be grasped in terms of musical sociology. During the economic flowering of the sphere merchandising the conductor, the musical mediator pure and simple, also moved into the focal point of interest; but because the true decision-making power was no more in his hands than it had been in those of his economic archetype, he always had a deceptive admixture about him.

Besides, someone who will not be terrorized by the ideology of genuineness in the realm of esthetic semblance ought once to explore the principles governing the affinity of histrionics and music; it certainly is not the symptom of decay as which it was misconceived by Nietzsche. Rather, what it manifests in the mimetic impulse is the unity of the arts of an era. As precapitalist periods made not much social distinction between the two vagrants, the juggler and the musician, so it is likely that now, in the same families, acting and musical talents continue to alternate and often directly to coincide. In a sociological deciphering of music its definition as a mimetic preserve should not be neglected; the vernacular, in which the word "play" is used to define the mime's work as well as the instrumentalist's, recalls that kinship. It especially predestines music for an "ideology of the unconscious."

It also helps to understand why orchestras are not less responsive to conductors' qualities which at first, as emotional and irrational, one would consider bound to repel the craftsmanlike rationality of the people who produce the sounds. The orchestra respects the conductor as the expert, the man who can ride the refractory horse, and if he can do that he will instantly look like the opposite of a social lion. But his competence in his field must be complemented by his qualities outside that field. A circus director can ride too. The sheer esthetic purity of one who possesses no such qualities at all makes him drop out of all art and become a philistine music employee—just as, to paraphrase Horkheimer, a top physician must have a touch of charlatanism, a surplus of imagination over scientific rationality with its division of labor. Where taste has expunged the last trace of the green covered wagon, music will no longer stir. Orchestras expect a conductor to know the score by heart and to hear every false note or hint of imprecision, but they also expect that with one move of his hand, without reflection, he can hold the orchestra together, can make it play correctly and, if possible, can draw his notion of the music from it—leaving aside the question whether suggestive faculties ever suffice for that or just create the illusion.

Orchestras do put up affective resistance to every intermediary, however, to whatever is neither technique nor direct transmission. The talking *kapellmeister* becomes suspect as one who cannot drastically concretize what he means; also as one whose chatter prolongs the detested rehearsals. Aversion to talk is something orchestra musicians have inherited from manual laborers. They fear the practice of deceit by the intellectual who has mastered the verbiage they lack. Archaic, unconscious mechanisms may have a part in this. Hypnotists keep silent; if they do speak, it is to issue commands. They do not explain; any rational word would break the spell of transmission. It would no sooner effectuate communication than the person given a command would potentially become an independent subject, while the narcissistic loneliness on which so much of the commander's own authority depends would dissolve. It is as if the subject's masochism were resisting modes of conduct that would impair the superior's traditional role. If he violates the taboos attached to that role in the prehistory of his archetypes, the violation is rationalized and registered as his factual incompetence. The anti-intellectualism of orchestras is one of closely linked collectives whose consciousness is limited at the same time. Similarly, actors feel suspicious of the dramaturgist's* Ph.D.

The orchestra's attitude toward the conductor is ambivalent. All set for a brilliant performance, its members want him to hold them on a tight rein, but at the same time they distrust him as a parasite who need not bow or blow an instrument and gives himself airs at the expense of those who do play. The Hegelian dialectic of master and servant is here repeated in miniature. The superior knowledge that qualifies the conductor for direction removes him from the sensual immediacy of the production process. It is rare for both to

---

* *Dramaturg*, a literary advisor usually on the staff of German theaters. —Transl.

go together. He who knows how all of it should be can seldom realize it physically; for too long have the two functions been historically separated. There are reasons why, in judging a conductor, orchestra musicians will see first what he can do in terms of sound; this faculty will then be often overestimated in comparison with the structurally intellectual ones.

Concretistically, orchestra musicians are averse to all things musical that are not tangible and controllable. Their skepticism— "There's no fooling old pros like us"—grows in world-famous bodies to be a vast, sabotage-happy arrogance that is both justified and unjustified. Justified against the spirit as prattle, against an esthetic reflection that does not enter into the thing but besmears it; unjustified, because it is a posture that has music swear by its sensual facade and defames that which makes it music. For its structural elements cannot all be sensualized in entrance and stroke techniques but would require explication of a kind which in advanced chamber music practice is self-understood. The orchestra musician's social background—usually a petty bourgeois one without educational premises that might make his work self-understood—serves to reinforce the psychological ambivalence, but its roots extend to the objective situation also. Conductors might be helped to self-critique by that ambivalence. But the conclusion which many tacitly draw from the ever-threatening latent conflict is unconditional adjustment to the spirit of the orchestra. Instead of learning, they want to be liked. The price has to be paid by music.

A description of the conduct of orchestra musicians would amount to a phenomenology of recalcitrance. The primary factor is unwillingness to submit. It must be especially violent in those who because of the material and form of their work feel themselves as artists and thus as free men. But since submission to the person is a technological demand of the matter, since in the conductor personal and material authority are murkily intertwined, the original resistance must fabricate justifications. They exist in abundance. To observe how conductors, after successful performances, will try to bring the orchestra to its feet is to sense two things: an awkwardly eager attempt to outwardly rectify the misshapen relationship, and an enduring recalcitrance that ignores such rectification because the basic relationship remains unchanged.

111

But recalcitrants are ready to submit where they feel strength. The orchestra musician's social psychology is that of the Oedipal character, vacillating between rebelling and cringing. Resistance to authority has shifted: what used to be rebellion, and may still feel as such, attaches itself to those elements of authority which tend to ridicule it as not authoritarian enough. From my student days I remember a musician who moved on from the orchestra to become a famous soloist. In his rebellious phase it delighted him to paint a mustache on Beethoven's death mask, but I prophesied to our common teacher that some day the rebel would become an arch-reactionary. He did not disappoint my expectations.

Significant for the habitus of recalcitrance are all the anecdotes emanating from orchestras, anecdotes which gleefully charge modern composers of the most varied schools with having failed to notice that some wind instrument had intentionally missed a transposition and played the wrong part. The truth of these tales is doubtful; beyond doubt is what they reveal about the spirit of orchestras. The Oedipal character tends to be anti-modern; it wants fathers to be more right than sons. The act of sabotage, the intentional misplay, is thus selecting its object in modern music, a field where the stronger authority, that of *communis opinio,* will back it from the start. Authorities get theirs, of course, but only the unconfirmed: they are put down as bunglers. The stories are traced back to far too many sources to believe in the humorous experiment's success; besides, the orchestral sound of a complex work is so surprising to someone who hears it for the first time, the composer included—intensity makes it so different from even the most exact imagination—that mistakes in hearing, if they occur, mean little. The reliability of outward hearing is by no means bound to harmonize with the exactitude of the inner conception.

The sadistic humor of the orchestra musicians takes us to conjectures about musicians' jokes at large. The profession obviously goes with jocularity, with a leaning to practical jokes, dirty jokes, and, above all, puns. That all this will thrive less in bourgeois occupations proper, where the prohibitions have greater force, is obvious, but even among artists and intellectuals—for whom society makes allowances, so to speak—the musicians presumably hold the record. The domain of their humor extends from the striking *mot* to the inane or grossly indecent. The tendency may depend on introversion, the a priori of musical behavior. The libido is turned inward, psychoanalytically speaking, but in the imageless space of music it is denied many sublimations.

Now and then those jokes gush far beyond the manifest intellectual faculties of the respective musicians. Their verbal associations have to do with the language character of music; they take revenge on a language that remains a mystery to those who speak it. The higher the musical spiritualization, the lower sometimes the jokes—as in Mozart's letters to his little Augsburg cousin. Wagner's jokes also may have been embarrassing; Nietzsche resented them. The orchestra musician's rancor takes refuge in the pun. In the orchestral score of a piece which, sadly enough, was called *Fanal*, the title was changed to *Banal*. For *Pli selon pli* by Boulez, Parisians invented a subtitle, *L'après-midi d'un vibraphone*, which contained everything: the homage to Mallarmé, the Debussyist sweetness of sound, the favoring of that instrument, the great length, and above all, the fact that technology has scattered the neoromanticist-vitalistic fauns of 1890. Many jokes of this genre originated with music coaches, the in-between types of the orchestral hierarchy. Bandmasters, who often have something of the orchestra musician's makeup, also produce them. They are jokes in a kind of emcee vein, transitions between the spirit of musicians and that of actors.

The collective mentality of orchestra musicians—which is not that of all those individuals, of course—is caused initially, in the sphere of ego psychology, by disappointment with their trade. Many of them, certainly most of the fiddlers, started out with other goals in mind; this has probably changed only today, when even young musicians have union protection and receive realistically high pay for their services. The threat to music posed by its immediate integration in society is strikingly apparent in the social institution which protects the orchestras from social exploitation: in the musicians' union. Union contracts, limitations of working hours, agreements against unfair practices—under present forms of organization these will unavoidably depress the artistic level. What they objectify is the recalcitrance of that percussionist who sat through a Wagner opera in the orchestra room, playing cards, rushed into the pit for his triangle stroke, and went on with the game as though the music interfered with his business.

Workmen's protection laws are a necessity for artists under the profit system, but at the same time they restrict the possibility of something being determined by its own quality rather than by the abstract working time required to produce it. This possibility is inalienable in music, and anyone choosing music as a profession would have to realize it. He would thus be in revolt against the activities of self-preservation even if not conscious of it at all. He would take up a sterile art for a living, would try from the outset to outfox the rationalized society. In German generational novels from about the turn of the century, boys caught in the scholastic machinery look for a counter-world in music; their prototype is Hanno Buddenbrook. But society takes its toll. It reserves recognition and a comfortable income to an infinitesimal minority of individuals, most of them with exceptional technical gifts; even among those it has for decades rewarded only the ones somewhat arbitrarily chosen by monopolistic institutes such as the largest concert agencies, subsidiaries of the radio and recording industry.

The stars represent exceptions that confirm two things: that useful work is given precedence, and that the establishment has nothing against the intellect if only the intellect deigns to go by the rules of the competitive system or its successors. The majority, however, is cold-shouldered by the commanders of musical life. The truth that average performance is no esthetic criterion, that it conflicts with the very concept of art, becomes an ideology. Musicians who had striven for an absolute, however dimly, are all but inevitably broken in punishment, by a society that will add up their insufficiencies. Social psychology, considering itself superior to the resentments of the orchestra musician, is simultaneously limited for that reason: it misconceives the justice of those resentments. The orchestra musicians get a visible demonstration of what secretly—as Freud well knew—permeates bourgeois civilization: the sacrifices which it exacts from its members, the sacrifices they make either for a cause or for their own self-preservation, are made in vain; at least, the equivalent remains accidental. Sacrifices are as irrational as in mythology.

What an orchestra musician has to do—they call it "going on duty"—is altogether disproportionate, in terms of musical-intellectual significance and of individual satisfaction, to the Utopia which everyone once yearned for. The routine performance, the triteness or low quality of most of the individual performances vanishing in a tutti, finally the often merely fictitious superiority of the conductor—all that brings about surfeit: "I just hate music." The positivism of orchestra musicians who hold on to what can be controlled: to beautifully sounding chords, to precise entrances, to the ability to beat more complex rhythms in comprehensible fashion—this positivism not only reflects their concretism. Such moments are the epitome of what they think they are realizing, the last refuges of their one-time love of the cause. Humbled, it survives exclusively as expert dogmatism.

Their anti-intellectualism—which, by the way, they share with all the collectives whose mutual identification integrates them against the individual—also has an element of truth: the succinct and irrefutable experience of the intellect's usurpatory side under the prevailing social circumstances of production. To make up for it, they sometimes take up hobbies such as fanatical reading or compulsive collecting. The sole remainder of what music originally touched them with, of the dream that things should be different, is good will as soon as that otherness is encountered in the form of technical competence, and the good will that no otherness should any longer exist. When orchestra musicians, instead of enthusing like culture consumers, sullenly and gruffly stick to quarter notes and sixteenth notes, they on their part are honoring music itself, the realm in which no intellect that has not become a configuration of notes can be objectively valid. The Utopia that used to refer to music includes dregs of the absurd, the muddied, the deformed; it spurns the normal. The dregs come in sight as mementos of the permanent defeat.

Orchestra musicians have about them something of Kafka's *Hunger Artist* or of those tightrope walkers who for meager pay learn the most foolhardy tricks for the tricks' own sake. Their senselessness holds up the mirror of protest to a meaning which in itself is nothing but a self-perpetuating bustle. Great works of nineteenth-century letters have saved that image without express reference to the orchestra: Grillparzer in his incomparable novella about the poor fiddler; Balzac in the two friends Pons and Schmucke, socially maimed eccentrics who perish by the infamies of normal society. Such eccentric characters show better than do representative statistics what is happening to music in society.

115

While philosophical idealism was doomed, some of its truth remains in the vernacular that confers the title of idealist on one who for a socially condemned whim's sake will spurn the role that awaits him. The defects of his abasement embody what would be higher, and yet they harm the art which he kept faith with, at the cost of his own fall.

The musical result of the relation between conductor and orchestra is an antimusical compromise. The measure of coarsening can only be compared with that of a dramatic text on stage; even the much-extolled precision is rarely worth noting. Orchestras do not much care for composers who conduct—because of their lack of routine, which in point of fact would be an advantage—but in the crucial point, having experienced the matter from within, composers are not infrequently superior to the alleged experts in the experts' own domain, as was Anton von Webern in conducting Mozart, Schubert, Bruckner, Mahler. Of Webern there exist neither records nor tapes, evidently for the simple reason that he was not socially stamped as a great conductor. Richard Strauss was often bored with conducting and presumably with all music; but when he wanted to, he could achieve extraordinary performances because he approached compositions with a composer's eye. So did Stravinsky even in his old age.

Despite his seignorial habitus, Strauss got along well with orchestras in the sense of what Americans call intelligence—which is a kind of technological solidarity, Veblen's "instinct of workmanship." He impressed them as someone who had risen from the ranks, who always was as ready to play cards with good players from the orchestra as with his board chairmen. The orchestra as an "in-group" reacts to a certain noningratiating kind of solidarity, united against musical authorities outside its immediate practice, especially against critics. But the vaunted collegiality among musicians—by no means merely those in the orchestra—can quickly recoil into hatred or intrigue. Among competitors, mutual strangers who are alike only in their type of work, that collegiality becomes a substitute for friendship, branded with the stigma of untruth. Yet this extremely dubious esprit de corps, akin to the syndrome of obedience to authority, occasionally glues the productive association of conductors and orchestras together.

Not even as so-called "bodies of sound" are the orchestras as homogeneous as the collective of colleagues makes one believe. Their present form is the musical residue of anarchic commodity production—in this sense, too, a microcosm of society. The customary equipment was not developed consciously and according to plan, not as an adequate medium of compositorial imagination, but in a sort of natural growth process. To be sure, the unusable, uncouth, or grotesque was Darwinistically expurgated, but the result remained accidental and irrational enough. The most striking defects—the lack of a balanced continuum of tone colors, or of really adequate bass woodwinds—have time and again brought futile complaints from composers. The harp can still not avail itself of fully chromatic possibilities. Such innovative attempts as Strauss's introduction of the Heckelphone, his institution of a third violin part in *Elektra*, or the unaccustomed combination in Schönberg's op. 22 had no consequences for the orchestral structure; not even the contrabass clarinet won wide acceptance, nor did the marvelous bass trumpet from Wagner's *Ring*.

There is a glaring discrepancy between the requirements of composition and the archaic inventory of the orchestras, an inventory defined by social conventions and extremely shy of innovations—not to mention the reactionary modes of playing. The chamber orchestra's emancipation from the large one is not only based on compositorial reasons, such as aversion to the auratic infinity of the string tutti and a need for distinct parts to polyphonous ends. The orchestra has failed in principle to satisfy the coloristic needs. Small ensembles adhere to them far more closely. Even as a brittle totality the orchestra is a microcosm of society, paralyzed by the dead weight of what, after all, turned out this way and not otherwise. Today's orchestras are still like the skyline of Manhattan, imposing and fissured as one.[6]

8

MUSICAL LIFE

We know that Richard Wagner's concept of Bayreuth was not simply that of a place for exemplary performances of his works. His aim was a cultural reformation. Houston Stewart Chamberlain, one of the harbingers of Nazi ideology, found a lucky formula with which to introduce himself to Cosima: he was, he said, a Bayreuthian, not a Wagnerian. Wagner looked to the "total work of art" to further his notion of a regenerated German people: a fascist-type national community. Amidst the existing society, the view of the total work of art was to unite men from all strata, men linked by the idea of the German race. They were to form a kind of elite beyond class distinctions; the distinctions themselves remained untouched.

But there was something of an Art Nouveau chimera about the thought of so real a power of art—and indeed, what Wagner still expected from the spirit was then pursued by Hitler with his realpolitik. The social reality of Bayreuth already made a mockery of the national community concept. Not one of the populist impulses which the disenchanted revolutionary of 1848 nursed into his old age would take effect. Gathering in Bayreuth was that international set which the Teutonic nationalist could not but despise. Invitations to Haus Wahnfried went to persons of name, rank, and property, to people who belonged, to nobles and notables. Left for the descendants of the Meistersinger were free tickets, at best.

Emerging visibly, however, were the members of the Wagner societies: beer-drinking, sausage-eating philistines whose appearance so shocked Nietzsche, people who felt little of the Bayreuth idea, however problematic it might be, who were drawn by nothing but a hullabaloo in which Nietzsche quickly recognized the faithful echo of the post-1870 German Reich. The conglomerate of upper class and philistinism disavowed the Wagnerian notion of the

German people as pure retrospective self-aggrandizement. Even if something of the kind had still existed, it could not have been achieved by organizing dramatic festivals. The composition of the audiences was determined by stark economics: by considerations of potential "angels" or the sphere they came from, as well as of the organized petty bourgeois whose mites added up.

Nietzsche's experiences in the year 1876 offer us several lessons in the sociology of musical life. First an empirical one: under finance capitalism, the community-forming power that manifests itself in the gestures of so much music does not go beyond the esthetic reception of that music; it does not change the world. And secondly: even forms of musical life that are believed to be above the capitalist marketplace remain tied to it, and to its underlying social structure. The life of music is not a life for music. The Wagnerian renaissance of the Greek theater did not change that either. To this day, except in the domain of the mass media, participation in musical life depends essentially on material conditions—not just on the potential listeners' direct ability to pay, but on their position in the social hierarchy. This is entangled in privilege, and thus in ideology. Sometimes it has as much to do with the idea of art as does the potbellied, bullnecked after-dinner speaker with *Tristan und Isolde*. Music is realized in musical life, but that life conflicts with music.

Erich Doflein has described the present musical situation in pluralistic terms, as a juxtaposition of divergent functions of which one often negates the other, and whose diversity would have dissolved the real or imagined unity of periods which—in Riegl's sense—had style. Descriptively, as an inventory of the facts, this is correct, but not structurally and dynamically. There is no peaceable social atlas of musical life, no more than there is one of society. Intramusically the sectors of that life do not have equal rights. If our conciliatory kindness goes so far as to accord the same right to a backwoods zither player as to one who listens with understanding to a complex piece from Bach's late period or one by a modern composer, it not only suppresses qualitative differences but the music's own claim to be true.

If those works by Bach, or any works of great music, are true, they will objectively, by their very content, refuse to tolerate others which are not at home in Hölderlin's "land of the high, more serious genius." If the zither player and Bach have the same right, if individual taste is the only criterion, great music is deprived of the only thing that makes it great and valid. Degraded to a consumer commodity for the demanding, it forfeits precisely what those demands might refer to. Yet pluralism is no more tenable sociologically than it is musically. The juxtaposition of various forms of music and musical practice is the opposite of reconciled diversity. The hierarchic system of offering cultural goods does people out of those goods. As for the human qualities which predestine one man for zither-playing and the other for listening to Bach, even these are not natural but based on social conditions. What strikes the inventory-taker's eye like a colorful wealth of musical phenomena is above all a function of socially determined educational privilege. If there is no longer a road from one musical sphere to the other—something Doflein admits—this is the phenomenon of a fractured total condition that can no more be settled by the artist's will than by mere pedagogics or by dictatorial fiat. It sears stigmata into every musical phenomenon.

Even the purest and most consistent efforts, those of the musical avant-garde, run the risk of merely playing to themselves. They are exposed to that peril, which they can do nothing about, by their necessary renunciation of society. Neutralization and a loss of tension on the radical moderns' part are not due to their asociality but have been socially forced upon them: ears balk when they hear what would concern them. The lack of an art's relation to things outside it, to the part of it that is not art itself, threatens its inner composition, while the social will that vows to cure it does inalienable damage to the best of it: to its independence, its consistency, its integrity. As an extensive quality, of course, the life of music will heed none of that. The principle which governs that life, crudely and with limitations, is that whatever is supplied as quality should be adapted to the social and material status of the recipients, whether they are individuals or groups. Only where this principle is violated can music come into its own, along with the audience.

Not in its official life, though. Elements of this are the public concerts, mainly the ones given by established music societies, and the opera houses, both seasonal and repertory. The borderlines with other musical domains are blurred; it is idle to argue whether such concert series as *"Neues Werk,"* of *"Musica viva"* or *"Reihe"*—all analogues of modern art exhibits that have "arrived"—should or should not be counted with official musical life. On the other hand, many church concerts and public offerings by chamber orchestras and song circles pass imperceptibly into activities which in Germany are covered by the name "youth and folk music"—and those activities, in which the separation of interpreter and audience posited by great musical art is not recognized, arouse feelings of opposition to official musical life, above all to the traditional symphony and solo concerts.

Generally counted with that life are the forms of musical practice that have come down to us from the nineteenth century. They presuppose a contemplative audience. *D'accord* with culture as a matter of principle, those forms pose no problem for themselves as cultural institutions. Their aim is to administer accumulated treasures. Few steps beyond the repertoire from Bach to the moderate moderns of the nineteenth and early twentieth century are taken on both sides. Where such steps do occur, the sole point is to replenish the all-too small and exhausted field of standard works: or else a couple of radical novelties are played once, halfheartedly and with a sympathetic wink at the unsympathetic audience, in order to avoid being called reactionary and at the same time slyly to prove that the moderns' failure to find a public was not the fault of the institutions—which gave them their chance—but that of the works themselves. It is significant that most performances of serious modern works in official musical life are inadequate, that adequate ones originate almost exclusively with avant-garde groups.

The official life of music is divided into international and local sectors, with tangible differences in level. International musical life has its focal points in metropolitan New York or London, in historic centers such as Vienna, or in festival towns like Bayreuth, Salzburg, Edinburgh and Glyndebourne. If what goes on there is no longer the preserve of the old high society, it is that of the most affluent strata to which this musical life is a chance to celebrate meeting the relics of the previous society. Research into the percentage of both groups would be fertile, notably since the oft-repeated claim that there is no high society any more sounds much too purposive to be simply believed; it is part of the signature

121

of our time that exclusiveness is as ashamed of itself as wealth hesitates to display the uninhabited opulence of nineteenth-century Paris or the Riviera. Another reason why official musical life survives so stubbornly may be that it permits some ostentation without exposing the audience—stamped as cultured, after all, by its very presence in Salzburg—to reproaches for high living and showing off.

The programs probably are not much different from those around 1920. Perhaps the approved supply continues to shrink; the most frequently repeated works, great symphonics in particular, will surely wear away further. This necessarily causes a shift in interest, to their reproduction; if an ever-sameness attracts attention at all, it will not be by what is presented, but by how it is presented. The tendency goes with the cult of instrumental music, of the brilliant feat, with the cult that was inherited from the age of absolutism and that favored the star and virtuoso system throughout the whole bourgeois era. Ever-sameness is the very thing one likes to chide as an excrescence of our time; the culture critics' faith in culture is not rich in motives. The principle of ostentation is simultaneously the one of music-making itself; the virtuoso, whether of the baton, the voice, or the solo instrument, reflects the glamour of the audience in his own glamour. Moreover, by achieving what in the marketplace is called a record performance he celebrates the enhancement of technological-industrial productive forces; unconsciously, criteria of material practice are transferred to art.

Yet the role of famed conductors or stupendous virtuosi is by no means the only one that matters. Certain sacrosanct instances of what Americans informally and precisely call "sacred cows" carry just as much weight. Elderly ladies who know how to end their program at the piano with the mien of seeresses, like some divine service, are fanatically hailed even for the most impeachable interpretations. Unconscious conventions of this sort work back upon the interpreters. Musical life does not favor structural interpretation. In practice, even by its own standards, the idolatry of anything "first-class"—a caricature of esthetic quality—leads to absurd misproportions. In New York's Metropolitan Opera, for example, the singing stars' exorbitant fees left so little for conductors and orchestra that the overall level of performance used to lag piteously behind the quality of the singers. But this seems gradually to have been brought into balance, probably helped by the influx of able European conductors and instrumentalists during the Hitler era; things which the bourgeois music culture itself has long deplored can usually be coped with. Now as in times past, however, the international life of music hampers the formation of firm traditions. Artists are rounded up like acts for a monstrous circus. Performances are illusionary apotheoses. What is sensually pleasing and takes an errorless, undisturbed course comes to replace a meaningful presentation. Such a presentation would require the only wealth denied by the plentiful activity: time to waste.

The current objections to official musical life are evoked by many of its aspects. They refer to a commercialization that regards the cause it plugs with such high-pressure salesmanship as a mere pretext for naked material interests and power needs of the music tycoons. They refer to effects that are often far removed from genuine understanding. Finally, they refer to actual musical defects in a system whose social circumstances aim toward a technicolor-style perfectionism to which the powers that be, enthralled by Toscanini, are largely kowtowing anyway. All these arguments, in which the avant-garde regrettably concurs with the pharisaical elite of inwardness, and which were integrated into the official life of music—all these arguments call for a heretical reminder that this life, by virtue of the economic means concentrated in it, will in many respects always be superior to the oppositionist trends.

Trends that rebel against the establishment will rarely meet its standards. Whoever follows the Hollywood movie output would like to prefer the unpretentious, frankly or cynically mass-market-oriented strips classed as "B" or "C" pictures over the highfalutin "A" pictures equipped with false psychology and other elaborate intellectual garbage. But when you see the "C" Western a little later, its loveless, ready-made inanities will make it even more unbearable, if possible, than the award winner with the multimillion-dollar budget. The same is true of international official musical life, in which musical Hollywood ideals are teleologically inherent: there the other, the deviate, as well as the one that simply did not get so far, will be eclipsed by the very undisturbed perfection which in its turn strangulates the spirit of the music.

If, for example, an exceptional conductor is lured from a more modest place of work—where, so one feels, he would be able to make decent music of his own choice—by an offer from international musical life, causing him to stay is difficult not only because of the higher salary or prestige connected with the international positions. Such a conductor can rightly point out that his chances to be effective will be much more far-reaching, and that the artistic means he will have at his disposal in the international centers greatly surpass the ones available outside that sphere. Music is not only fettered by the economy, but at the same time, within limits, the economic premises also turn into esthetic qualities. If the conductor stresses that on the international site the brasses play more exactly and produce a more beautiful sound; that the chorus of strings radiates more amplitude and warmth; that an orchestra made up of virtuosi lets you work more fruitfully, that is to say, more in keeping with your own conception than an apparatus where elementary technical questions, the musicians' functioning in a pre-artistic sense, absorb an undue measure of vigor and energy—all this is perfectly true.

A lady once said that the world one is not bored in is not half as boring as the picture of it drawn by those who failed to get in. The same is true of the official life of music. We tend to mistrust matadors because of their totalitarian artistic ambitions as well as because of their culture-conservative mentality; and yet, once risen to the top rung of command, most of them prove to be well-qualified in many ways and far better musicians than the good musicians would like. Some years ago, I let myself be persuaded to attend the performance of a work on which the oppositionists think they hold a monopoly—conducted, by the way, by one of their pet aversions. The performance was not only far above the multifarious crimes committed by some of modernism's inadequate friends among conductors; it was meaningful down to the last detail, so thorough a piece of work and conscious music-making that Webern himself as interpreter would have had no need to feel ashamed.

Criticism of official musical life is often coupled with resentment caused by economic weakness. One of the contradictions of musical life is this: its bad side, the commodity character, is most concentrated in the very sphere which absorbs so much productive vigor that the uncorrupted part, the part that is true in itself, will also be made susceptible by a reduced power of realization, a lack of precision, a sensual threadbareness. The crassest symptom of this could be found among the vocalists. In the years between the two wars, beautiful voices and sovereign singers were confiscated for the official musical life and its stationary programs, while the hazardous moderns remained the preserve of interpreters who either had no voice at all or had lost it. Proud of their mostly nonexistent musical intelligence, these people smelled out any chance to get their names into the papers, but the cause they championed with so much alleged heroism was only hurt by their howling.

In terms of the sociology of music it will be permissible to state the facts somewhat more generally, as follows: by concurring with the real social tendency and its power, the official life of music drives any divergent productive force and legitimate critique into a sectarian and severed stance that weakens the objectively legitimate. Analogously, the groups which in themselves stand for the strict and most advanced form of political theory, the ones which are "right" to swim against the mainstream of a centrism that has the apparatus at its disposal—those groups often turn into impotent minorities, decried as heretics and belied in practice, despite their being theoretically right. Insights to which Hegel came in his maturity are similarly concretized in phenomena of the sociology of music. But Hegel's siding with the stronger, with the one who gains the day, must not—unless we equate victor and world spirit—tempt us to deny the truth of dissent; and neither are we to relax our intransigence in criticizing the official life of music.

The wealth of disposable means is not a blessing. All cultural riches stay false as long as the material ones are monopolized. The slick, glossy quality which performances at the international centers all but inevitably assume, the quality whereby they mean to condemn everything else as provincial, turns against the "consciousness of needs" and the immanent labor of works that are defined in themselves as a process and miss their meaning if presented as pure results. The work of art always attacks the law of the marketplace, and the polish of whatever that law unreservedly honors will expunge the freshness of becoming. The work has ceased to step out of qualities measurable with compasses, out into the realm of incomprehension. Yet it suffices unto its own concept

125

only insofar as its course does not wholly exhaust it, insofar as it reaches something that has not been shaped ahead of time, insofar as it transcends itself. And thereby hangs the part of culture that is more than a social network. Entering least of all into the internality of performances are the so-called natural qualities, the beautiful voices, for example, which the official life of music cultivates. They are a facade trying with more or less luck to hide the cellophane character. Nature is the favorite disguise of essential conventionality; it is honored only in a phenomenon so thoroughly kneaded that it will no longer be self-understood.

The audience of international musical life is homogeneous in well-versed naiveté. A culture that shuns no expense, and whose advertising machinery drills this into mankind, will be unquestioningly relished as what it pretends to be; fetishistically, second nature appears as the first. Culinary merits always furnish solid justification for agreement. The listening habits are probably less conservative than attuned to the technological standard. Occasionally, as in Bayreuth, specific ideological elements are added; chances are, however, that precisely there the racial ideology has been eliminated since World War II, as far as the texts permit—and those, to my knowledge, have not yet been retouched. It is not so much specific contents that make the international life of music seem reactionary than its unquestioned relation to culture and to the world in which it thrives.

According to the rules of that world things are in good order. Those who pay the piper call the tune. In case of conflict, the practicing artists—experts inserted between the economic powers and the demands of the cause—must obey orders; they probably can also be kicked out whenever the economic powers feel like it, and if it were only because their suits look ill-fitting. In both the international and the local domain the class character is maintained by the wealth of those who have the final word. Yet the more purely a society is organized according to the exchange principle, the less will the organizers listen to the spokesmen of an autonomous culture and the less relevant will expertise be for the guidance of musical life. America is marked by figures which the opposition there calls "culture vultures"; elderly ladies with too much time on their hands and not much knowledge, who plunge into culture as an ersatz satisfaction, with a kind of rage, and

126

confuse their zeal and their contributions with expert authority. On occasion, murky crosscurrents connect the culture vultures with artists who let themselves be pampered by them. It would be unworldly to regard musicians and their financiers as simple opposites. In the first, dependency and the legitimate pursuit of happiness are still furthering traits of the "third-person" type. Yet the immediacy of the artist's relation to his cause makes it as hard, if not painful, for him to see through the type's social function—as to know what art really is. The spell of the official musical life is reinforced through the consciousness of artists and through their unconscious.

Representative character, oligarchic control, a "cultural lag" with respect to modern music—this is what the international centers of musical life have in common with the major local ones. But as the latter grow increasingly provincial, some typical differences may become apparent and be reinforced. The oligarchy here is less one of financial power than one of traditionalist notables, although the two groups frequently merge. Program policy is not so much set by the market as by an expressly conservative mentality; practitioners of avant-garde music are systematically excluded; the most popular are celebrities wreathed in a nimbus of "the good old days," in Germany not seldom priestesses of pseudo-inwardness. The audience is still largely recruited from the patriciate, from families that have been local residents for generations, and habitués feel as if they belonged to that stratum. Such norms are not rigid, however, and perhaps, *sauf imprévu,* they will be softened in time.

Advantages of the system are certain critical faculties developed by the long-schooled audience, and the standard of well-practiced orchestras or ensembles which sometimes spend decades under the same conductor's baton. The disadvantage is stagnation, both in spirit and in the humdrum orthodoxy of reproduction. The ideal of these local institutions is solidity. Taste becomes a defensive weapon, also against such older composers as Mahler, who do not harmonize with categories of taste. Before the program gets to pieces that are unusual, if not downright radical, the guardians of the Grail like to leave the premises; that is why such pieces will conclude the concert, however absurd this may be. Cleanliness and clarity are rightly stressed and pains are taken at rehearsals, but with a tendency to resist the power of imagination, without which music cannot be unlocked. The counterpart of international glamour is local boredom. It is from an older bourgeois life, notably from the code of honor observed in merchant cities, that the category of solidity was borrowed and transferred to art; small, musically very tradition-bound countries such as Switzerland and Holland would lend themselves especially well to its study.

Because in the large local centers there is still some unity between musical life and upper-class social life, conceptions from the second pass into the first in toto. For music this is hardly a lucky break. True, the norm of solidity preserves an element which since the triumph of the neo-German school * has often vanished from musical life otherwise: precise, responsible reproduction irrespective of effects. The fanatical performance practice of the extreme moderns was the very one to receive and transform this element. Without the fermentation they contributed, however, artistic solidity becomes a prosaic sobriety incompatible with the whole idea of art. The taboos perpetuated by the norm of solidity choke off the free, spontaneous reproduction required by the cause in whose service solidity stands. The concise name for it is academicism; only seldom can an official local musical life rise above it.

A significant phenomenon in larger cities may be the second orchestra, which takes the growth of the listening masses into account, the democratic need that is balked by the notables system. The concerts of the second orchestras are cheaper and more accessible than the official philharmonic ones, also more favorably disposed toward modern music; often less well attended, because they lack the elitist aura. The greater liberality that distinguishes the concerts of this type from the academic-philharmonic ones is not infrequently marred by what the official musical life chides as third-rate performances. Each institution sins in its own way: one by obduracy and cultural arrogance, the other by indifference, noncommittal offerings, and an audience lacking the faculty to discriminate—a lack which in turn will affect the level.

---

* Adorno's definition of the term is given later, in Chapter 10 (p. 170), as "Wagner's . . . school which also included such differently-minded composers as Bruckner, Strauss, Mahler, even the early Schönberg . . ." —Transl.

Quantitatively, as far as numbers of listeners are concerned, the mass media far surpass the official musical life, in some countries probably so far that live concert attendance becomes insignificant. This may establish a new quality for people's relation to music. It becomes noticeable, meanwhile, in production, including the so-called serious one. Music is no longer exceptional, as at feudal and absolutist festivities and in the bourgeois concert; rather, it has achieved an ubiquity that makes it part of everyday life. The great festivals seem to be more the synthetic antithesis than a real contradiction of that everyday character. Surviving in the traditional music we are offered, however, as well as in much that has been newly composed, are qualities such as gravity, edification, joy—qualities based on the premise of exceptionality and containing it within themselves. Whatever great music turned out well to this day has been inseparable from that premise; wherever men dispense with it, music resigns its own claim. Content with a craftsmanship that is available at any time, it regresses to mediocrity.

Yet in present musical life those qualities assume a touch of fiction beyond all traditional esthetic appearance. Part of the fatality of this life is that the exception will be practiced as a rule. Musical phenomena which deny the artistic side of art, which assimilate it to a practical or at least sporting activity such as jazz, attest to more than lack of the strength to keep empirical existence at the distance which music, once upon a time, would set as soon as it rang out. They also reveal the mendacity of a condition that ignores Hölderlin's line: "For never, henceforth, is the sacred fit for use." Recalcitrance is the answer of the young to the unfit attempts to adapt exalted music to that bustle which has in fact swallowed it in the meantime. They avoid the contradiction, dodging into the bad identity of banal situation and banal music. But at least they denounce the contradiction.

The mass media take a hand in broadening the official musical life, by affiliating the second orchestra with radio, for example, whose financial means can subsidize that orchestra and greatly improve it. And yet, if you talk in Europe of musical life, without much reflection, what you have directly in mind will scarcely be the mass media[1] even though they alone provide millions with the opportunity to come to know music of lasting import at all. The reason is the "built-in structure" of radio, which has been pointed out time and again and is not apt to be greatly modified by request concerts either. Nor, in this dimension, should one overestimate the differences within the totally reified musical activity; the average philharmonic listener will hardly exert more influence on the programs of his society—the core of which remains identical year in, year out anyway—than the man who chooses the program he likes in his living room. Whether today one's immediate presence at performances will still assure a more vivid relation to music than will the mass media—this would have to be investigated in very carefully planned, qualitatively accentuated researches.

In any case, American studies have shown what probably applies universally: that the musical taste of men who came to music via live performances is better, by rough standards, than the taste of those who hear it exclusively through the mass media. One research problem that remains here is whether the differences actually come from the sources of the musical impressions or from the fact that in America the audiences of so-called "live music" are a select group from the start, a group that brings more with it, thanks to family and social status. It is conceivable that the decisive factor in musical experience is not whether one has it in front of the radio or at a concert hall, but that the very choice between radio and concert hall depends on the structure of the musical experience. This much is likely to remain true, however: the passive and effortless stance of the radio audience does not favor structural listening. Listening preferences can be researched, of course, but generally they will correspond to the official cultural standards— again with differences which more or less reflect the social stratum.

Letters from the audience are of dubious value for sociological cognition, as the American *Radio Research* found out long ago. Writers of such letters are a group with specific characteristics, frequently narcissists who want to prove that they amount to something, or grumblers, or even blatant paranoiacs. Violent nationalism and anti-modern wrath are not rare. A striking gesture is aggressive cultural outrage, couched in such opening phrases as "I at any rate" and coupled with a reminder of the many valuable individuals with whom the protester knows himself to be in accord, and whose potential power serves him as a threat. Compared with this minority which delights in negation while professing positivity, the less articulate majority is ready—within limits—to consume what it is offered, particularly as long as the program selectors grant it some breadth and variety.

The wealth of programs exacted by the need for music to keep broadcast times ceaselessly filled will give most listeners their money's worth anyway. The programs are a priori made up in analogy to the presumptive makeup of the audience; which is the egg and which the chicken is hard to tell now, after forty years of institutionalized broadcasting. The situation of the program directors necessitates thorough examination, disposition, and supervision. Under the dictate of a demand that is quantitatively all out of proportion with the one once satisfied by a compositorial production to which it remains qualitatively attuned, musical literature is transformed into a cultural warehouse, a place for confined rummaging. This serves, against the planners' stated will, to reinforce the prevailing fetish character of music. Supposedly to correct it, a mass of bad and mediocre stuff from the past is dug up. Even the reduction of the standard works to a small number obeys a fatal necessity: many of those are really the better pieces.

Quantitatively—as radio executives could prove in reply to reactionary denunciations—broadcasts of avant-garde concerts carry virtually no weight in comparison with the tame ones. They fill an infinitesimal fraction of broadcast time; the commissioning of compositions also is extremely limited. Still, this aspect of radio is of great qualitative importance. However modest such assistance may be, without it the only production that remains objectively worth noting would be the prey of marketplace and consumer ideology, doomed to die out. Expert promotion in the mass media attests to modern music some of the relevance it is denied by the market, or by the pseudo-market. Sociologically we note a peculiar change of functions. In the nineteenth century and as late as the twentieth—in other words, at the high tide of liberalism—free institutions were more progressive than the ones steered by public officials; but today, under the conditions of monopolistic mass consumption, the allegedly free market serves to strangulate what may be stirring. Public or semiprivate institutions, on the other hand, use whatever margin of independence they can retain to become refuges of the advanced and uncomfortable in art, with all the fertile paradoxes this entails. Similarly, in American academic life, state universities display a freer spirit than the ones maintained by the private economy. It is easy to see why this very side of the mass media furnishes pretexts to those who in tried and tested fashion employ formal democratic rules to sabotage democracy.

In general, outrage at the alleged mass era has become an article for mass consumption, fit for inciting the masses against politically democratic forms. Thus it grew to be a habit to hold the mass media responsible for the decay of musical education. Their home delivery system relieved listeners of any need for personal activity. Since it did not literally produce what it was hearing, the audience was said to be barred from inwardly experiencing the works. This sounds convincing enough, and the verdict seems confirmed by our observation of men who do not feel well without background music, who need it to work but neutralize it at the same time by banishment to the background.

Meanwhile, however, suspicions are raised by the mechanization of the argument against mechanization. Equating musicality as an active performance with practical, personal music-making is too simple. We are both right and wrong when we lament the decay of domestic music-making. To play chamber music, no matter how awkwardly, was certainly the humus of musicality in the grand style; it was how Schönberg, almost without noticing it, became a composer. But on the other hand, when the performances which one can hear by radio surpass what is attainable for the domestic amateur, such music-making in the home becomes superfluous—and that is bound to erode its objective substance. The advocates of a revival of home music forget that once authentic interpretations are available on records and in broadcasts—thus far, of course, they are rare exceptions in both media—that home music no longer has a point, then; that it becomes a private repetition of acts which, thanks to the social division of labor, can be better and more meaningfully performed in other ways. They are no longer legitimate as taking up an otherwise unattainable cause; they are degraded to inadequate doing purely for the doing's sake, and for the doer's.

Worth thinking about, at least, would be whether the concept of doing is not all too literally borrowed from what we call practical life, if not indeed from romantic handicraft idols of concrete labor close to its material. For all the truth of the philosophical insight that there is no true relation to anything in the world which has not been actively experienced, and that the standstill of supposedly pure contemplation makes us miss what we think we have secured as its object, such active experience must not be confused with physical production. The process of internalization, to which great music as a self-deliverance from the external world of objects owes its very origin, is not revocable in the concept of musical practice either, if that practice itself is not to regress to primitive and obsolete stages. The active experience of music does not consist in tinkling or fiddling but in an imagination that does justice to the matter. It consists in listening so that the works to which it passively yields will in turn come to be by such yielding. If the music of the mass media delivers us from physical exertion, the liberated energy might benefit an intellectual, sublimated activity.

One question that may remain unsettled is the pedagogical one whether such sublimation requires a measure of prior physical training in music-making, which it would then depart from; but in no case must blind practice become an end in itself. What continues to vegetate in the inwardly ones' standard jeremiads about the mass media is always some of that fatal work ethic that dreads nothing more than a world in which hard, alienated labor would be superfluous, and that seeks to perpetuate such labor by the pedagogic steering of culture, among other ways. An artistic activity that insists on external, morally rationalized toil contradicts the very idea of art, whose detachment from the social practice of self-preservation implies a promissory note on a toil-free state of affairs. Full employment is not a norm of art, whatever truths or half-truths may—always presumptuously—be uttered under present circumstances about men's not knowing what to do with their alleged surplus leisure.

If broadcast music were to take the consequences of this as well as of the critique of the experience actually lost by the transformation of works of art into consumer goods, it would have to start a systematic training course in active imagination and to do its part in teaching the mass audience to listen adequately, i.e., structurally —in a way corresponding, perhaps, to the "good listener" type. I might also put it this way: the social-pedagogic contribution of the musical mass media should consist in teaching their listeners truly to "read" music, to enable them to appropriate musical texts in silence, in pure imagination—a task far less difficult than people's awe of the professional as a medicine man leads them to imagine. The mass media might thus really counteract that illiteracy toward which—as an acquired second one—the objective spirit of our whole epoch is heading.

The other musical mass medium, the phonograph record, is closer to the listener, due to several of its qualities. It is not tied to given programs but at the listener's disposal; the catalogs leave a greater freedom of choice; besides, a record allows frequent repetition and can thus acquaint us more thoroughly with a work than the broadcast, which is mostly a one-time thing. For the first time in music, the record form permits something analogous to collecting in the fine arts, notably in graphics; and we know how much collecting, the esthetic object's mediation by literal possession, has contributed to incorporation, to the understanding of the thing itself. The same result can be expected of records, which technically have now been vastly perfected, especially since LP recording broke the time barrier that limited older discs to short pieces and often to genre music, excluding the great symphonic forms and making records the musical counterpart of bric-à-brac.

In principle, the medium of the record would enable us today to make all of musical literature available to all those willing to hear, and this potential abolition of educational privilege in music should socially outweigh the disadvantages which hoarding records as a hobby of an audience of consumers involves under present conditions. The question what mass reproduction does to music itself, to its own content, need not detain us here.[2] Yet records have to pay their social dues in the form of material selection and also of quality of reproduction. Program policy must be sales-oriented, far more so than in radio. The principle governing choices is largely that of prominence, of great works that have "arrived" and of "name" interpreters; the record output mirrors the official life of music in its most conventional form.

Thus the phonograph record, which might accomplish a productive change in musical consciousness, reproduces every dubious side of current judgment. One would need a catalog of what is missing; to this day, for instance, only a small part of Schönberg's oeuvre is accessible in Germany. Furthermore, the acquisition of discs is inhibited by international barriers. Large numbers of important recordings of modern works exist in America only, and endless time may pass before they will be sold in Germany at all. In America, on the other hand, record sales are ruthlessly determined by the current demand for popular music. Outside of New York it could quite recently happen that a record shop would refuse to order a serious modern disc because ordering a single one did not pay; such manners are now spreading round the globe. Few phenomena show as drastically as this how the social circumstances of production sabotage musical culture; one yardstick of the rise of barbarism—again not in music alone—is the number of relevant works of the mind currently unobtainable, for all the talk of mass consumption.

Nor does the selection of modern performances to be recorded meet any standard of desirability—in part, no doubt, to keep costs down. Thus the first recordings of Berg operas were caricatures bound to reinforce the social prejudice against things modern. In older works too one can note such defects. The bulk of the obtainable Mahler records is altogether inadequate in performance and often in purely technical quality; of the Third Symphony there is no halfway satisfying disc at all. Still, some of these defects will probably be overcome like childhood diseases once the great new music is established somewhat on the order of its counterpart in painting. Then the collector's ambition to own the best records will likely spur production. For the time being the motto "only the best" bars the good. That under the heading of cultural obligations all sorts of things are added to the current sellers, including many superfluous, warmed-up pieces, is a matter of course. What is wrested from commercialism remains disfigured by commercial interests. Their very desire to demonstrate a sense of higher things is an obeisance to the reified consciousness.

The mutual hostility and irrelation of the branches of musical life is an index of social antagonism. An observation I once made as an academic teacher has never been forgotten. I had to attest students' attendance at my lectures on esthetics to auditors or those who were registered for credit. If I asked one of them, "Are you a musician?" I would be told in the gently protesting tones of someone not wanting to dirty his hands with music or to face unpleasant professional demands: "No, I'm in musicology." The realm of musicology usurps laws of its own, laws that will have nothing to do with mere music. In that realm music is a means, a pedagogic means, not an end. The road from one sphere to the other is virtually cut, and the unity of music is negated with subaltern arrogance. This continues all the way into the interrelations of the modern schools.

The onetime battles between movements have degenerated into a sterile divergence. Kurt Weill once told me that today he recognized only two possibilities of composing: twelve-tone music and his own. He did not doubt that both could exist side by side, did not consider that what he rather summarily called "twelve-tone music" rests on a critique of tonality, however processed. Once we are offered a choice between fixed styles, musical life has disintegrated already. The word "twelve-tone music" is a product of reified nomenclature, no indication of the thing. At the top formal level of contemporary production, including the Vienna School, it is only a part, and in the final analysis not even the weightiest part, that employs the procedure of composing in twelve tones solely related to each other—this was how Schönberg put it—and what is brought together under that slogan is thus not a particular species of music but a technical procedure, a rationalization, as it were, of what took shape in the dynamics of the musical language. A layman will be hard put to distinguish between free atonal compositions and twelve-tone compositions, say from Webern's middle period.

And yet the undifferentiated term "twelve-tone music" has been popularized for everything that is not tonal, a formula for receiving the unreceived. Analogously, while "electronics" is a term that subsumes the most unsynonymous, from a strict construction built on premises of electronic sound to the mere coloristic inclusion of sounds that have been electronically produced, the phrase has become customary for most of what sounds astronautic to the audience. Such seemingly indifferent questions of nomenclature are precipitations of the tendency to use automatically triggered cover concepts to withdraw the matter from living experience and, positively or negatively, to settle it. We dispose over the extant instead of following the specific. When someone says "twelve-tone music" and "electronics," the turn of mind is potentially the same as speaking of "the Russian" or "the American." Clichés such as these subsume irreconcilables and falsify them by adoption for communication's sake.

The phenomena are indeed irreconcilable. Embodied in the plurality of the musical languages that exist today and in the types of musical life, especially in its calcified educational levels, are different historic stages, one of which excludes the other while the antagonistic society compels them to be simultaneous. It is only in socially particular realms that the forces of musical production can freely evolve; in others they are dammed back, even psychologically. No qualitative wealth of possibilities is realized in diversity; rather, most of them exist only because they could not keep up with others. What decides, instead of the materially obligatory quality of musical ideals, schools, compositorial figures, and types of musical life, is the state of universal incompatibility as it is given at the moment, anarchically attained and maintained by its own gravity alone, without anyone even raising the question of being just to the divergent. The life of music has but the appearance of a life. Music was hollowed out by its social integration. The seriousness which entertainment music spurns has been entirely removed by integration. The extreme forms to which the normal consumer of musical life objects are socially desperate efforts to maintain or restore that seriousness; to this extent its radicalism is conservative. But the life of music, the epitome of a production of cultural commodities graduated according to the appraisal of customers—that life disavows what is really said by every tone that rings out and strives beyond the bustle in which musical life integrates it.

9

PUBLIC OPINION AND CRITICS

The question of music's relation to public opinion cuts across that of its function in present society. What is thought, said, and written about music, what views of it people express, does indeed often differ with its real function, with the actual effect it has on people's lives, on their consciousness and on their unconscious. Yet this function enters into opinion, whether in adequate or in distorted form, and conversely, opinion works back on the function and may even shape it. The factual role of music takes a good deal of its bearings from the reigning ideology. If we were to isolate the pure immediacy of our collective musical experience from public opinion we would be ignoring the power of socialization, the reified consciousness; one need but recall the mass swoonings at the appearance of certain pop singers—a reality, but one which depends on publicity drives, on a fabricated opinion. In view of such interaction my own remarks about music and public opinion are no more than supplementary.

In the usual view—a rather dubious one which the results of psychoanalysis have greatly restricted—music is tied to a special gift. We hear that one must be "musical" to understand it, although there are no analogous requirements for poetry or painting. The sources of this view should be explored. It certainly registers part of the specific difference between the arts, of the difference that comes to be invisible by their subsumption under the general concept of art. The special talent is coordinated with the alleged or real irrationality of music as a kind of charisma, a latter-day copy of the priestly one, said to distinguish those admitted to the special musical domain. Favoring this faith are psychological peculiarities of music: it has been observed that people who are psychically normal, according to scientifically accepted criteria, may nonetheless be unable to make acoustic distinctions as elementary as that between high and low tones. This contrasts with our relation to the visual world, which coincides initially, after all, with the world of empirical things; even the color-blind see what is light and what is dark. Such observations are the probable bases of the conception of musicality as a particular gift of grace.

But the conception itself is fostered by archaic, irrationally psychological moments. Strikingly strong are the affects with which men cling to that charisma or privilege of musicality—or clung to it, at least, for as long as an understanding of music was expected of the educated class. Shaking the privilege of musicality was viewed as blasphemous—by the musical, who felt debased, as well as by the unmusical, who could no longer use nature's denial of something as an alibi before the cultural ideology. Yet this indicates a contradiction in the musicality concept harbored by public opinion. The right, indeed the necessity, of music is hardly ever questioned, least of all in places where the principle of the exchange society has thrived—the rationality principle from which music is removed, according to the ideology. Nowhere is musical life so fostered and music so highly praised as an integral element of culture as in America, the land of not just a positivistic mentality but of real positivism.

In Ernst Krenek's operetta *Schwergewicht oder die Ehre der Nation (Heavyweight, or The National Honor)* a prizefighter's wife and her lover persuade the fighter that their intimacies are a necessary part of training for a dance marathon record. "Yes, yes," he says, "records must be." Somewhat along the lines of this logic, music is officially approved even if one cannot quite see why it must be. What exists rates highly with the reified consciousness, simply because it exists. The contradiction to the essence of music as something not to be nailed down, something literally rising above mere existence, could hardly be carried farther. At the same time such naiveté of the otherwise so hardboiled hides a need for music as something other; it is not entirely eradicable from the activities of self-preservation. From the start, however, the general conviction of the necessity and promotability of music has an ideological effect. In its implicit affirmation of the existing culture, to which music also belongs, it thanks music for its own affirmation. Against the universal dissemination of music, which keeps reducing its distance from everyday life and thus undermines it more and more, abstinence and a closed season would be in order. Eduard Steuermann once said rightly that nothing does more harm to culture than its cultivation. Yet asceticism is not only prevented by the economic interest of music sellers but by the avidity of their customers.

The benightment of public opinion about music insulates it from such insights. Music, the art of music, strikes it as a kind of natural datum. The very man who holds on to the truth content of music will not be flatly certain of its necessity; rather, he will see what music it is, how, where and when it appears. The not so infrequent aversion to music I have mentioned in the context of conductor and orchestra is not just rebelliousness on the part of those who are *amusisch*, or the rancor of experts fed up with having to do things instead of being able to do them freely. That *taedium musicae* also keeps faith with its concept, as opposed to musical inflation. Abstinence from music may become its proper form. The Schönberg school's consistent inclination to prevent performances of its own works or to sabotage them at the last moment was not mere eccentricity.

The complex relation of rationality and irrationality in music comes together in a major social tendency. The irrational moments of the process of living are not removed without trouble by the advance of bourgeois rationality. Many are neutralized, shifted to special fields, and integrated. They are not only left undisturbed; irrational zones are often reproduced socially. The pressure of increasing rationalization—one which, lest it become unbearable to the affected, must make rational provision for heartwarming aspects—calls as much for that as does the always still blind irrationality of rational society itself. To be able to preserve its particular character, the rationality that has been realized only in the particular requires such irrational institutions as the church, the army, the family. Music, and all art, takes its place in their line and thus fits into the general context of functions. Beyond that it could scarcely keep alive.

But objectively too, in itself, it comes to be what it is—something autonomous—only in a negative relation to that from which it comes to be distinct. If it has been smoothed into the functional context, the constitutive moment of its objection to the context disappears—and yet that moment constitutes the raison d'être of music; if it has not, it deceives people about the omnipotence of the context, thereby ingratiating itself with it. This is the antinomy, not just of music, but of all art in bourgeois society. Only on rare occasions has that society come out radically against art as such, and then mostly in a spirit, not of rational, progressively bourgeois tendencies, but of feudally restorative ones like those of Plato's *Republic*. From the twentieth century I know only one emphatic attack on art, Erich Unger's book against poetry.[1] It dates back to the mythological-archaicizing exegesis of Judaism by Oscar Goldberg, whom the figure of Chaim Breisacher in Thomas Mann's *Doctor Faustus* made famous. In general, art will rather be opposed by orthodox theologies, primarily Protestant and Jewish ones, than by spokesmen of the Enlightenment.

In outlying, old-line Lutheran or Calvinist congregations it may still be deemed sinful for children to waste time on artistic things, including music. The oft-cited motive of innerworldly asceticism seems to be stronger in strict and patriarchal forms of early Protestantism than in fully developed capitalism. If for no other reason, the latter is tolerant of art because art lends itself to the process of exploitation: the fewer frontiers are left, the more alluring it is for investors. That explains the quantity of musical life in America, exceeding everything that can now be found in Europe. But precisely in America, in conservative and status-conscious milieus, I observed at times a frank hostility to music, something generally alien to the enlightened consciousness which under liberalism tends to laisser faire even toward art. The professors at a large American university—large, but locally segregated from the metropolitan center—looked upon opera-going as unserious, to say the least, so much so that European emigrés on the faculty with whom I wished to hear *Salome* preferred not to risk it.

For all its provincialism, this sort of public opinion honors music more than does tolerance without commitment. It views music as something pointing beyond solid extant orders—Ernst Bloch called it the world's blasting powder—while noncommittal tolerance is symptomatic of the contradictoriness of public opinion. It is illuminated by facts like this: logical positivism, many of whose schools will blacken any thought that cannot be redeemed by facts as "art," as "conceptual poetry," shrinks nonetheless from a critique of the concept of art, accepting it without another glance as a branch of everyday life. From the outset, art is thus deprived of all claim to truth; theoretical tolerance confirms the work of destruction which practice, swallowing art as entertainment, carries out anyway. As happens often in the life of a concept, the philosophical contradiction reflects the real contradiction of a society which insists that there shall be no Utopia,[2] although without a utopian image, however faded, the society could not endure.

Because, as we said, music must be, most people have their own views of it. Depending on the circles interested in its various types, there exist several tacit but nonetheless effective public opinions on things musical. Their stereotypicality rests on their dissemination, and vice versa. The chances are that they not only color the phrasings but serve as the predeterminants, or at least as one of the components, of seemingly primary forms of reaction; this might be a matter for testing. Countless individuals are apt to hear according to the categories made available to them by public opinion; the immediate datum itself is inherently mediated.

Such a public opinion lights up in a definite accord between those who talk about music. Presumably it is that the more articulate, the more thoroughly music, and the relation to music, blends with a consolidated cultural ideology, as in the realm of the conservative institutions of official musical life, for example. If its invariants were successfully distilled, they would probably be recognizable as special cases or ciphers of more general, socially effective ideologies. A man with musically sound views always arouses the suspicion that they may issue from sound views elsewhere, comparable to the prejudices that go with bondage to authority. Theoretically, the skeleton of their opinion might be construed and then scientifically translated into characteristic theses apt to stimulate affirmation or denial in the circle of test subjects.

Models of such statements would be, for those who consider themselves openminded about modern music, for instance: "Yes, I can still go along with Alban Berg, but Schönberg—that's too intellectual for me."

Or, from the lips of the practically inclined: "I don't think this music will ever be as popular and comprehensible as the classics."

Or, for cultural pessimists: "But where will it all end?"

Or, for a less clearly circumscribed circle of persons: "These are all transitional phenomena."

Or, "This newest music is just as cold and merciless as our world. Where is the humanity, the feeling?"

Or an especially popular phrase: "You still call that music?" with its supposition of an eternal picture of music instead of its actual, historic one. Many of these invariants of public opinion are based on an opaque but utterly intolerant conception of normalcy.

The conception becomes tangible in the dimension of musical dynamics. Extreme fortissimo is denounced as noise, as antimusical; a pianissimo inspires coughs, if not laughter. To the idea of sensual pleasurableness, acoustical extremes, and thus all extremes, are taboo. Supposed noise was not the least of the reasons which some sixty years back caused an educated philistine to rail against Liszt, Strauss, and Wagner. Sensitivity to noise in music is the musicality of the unmusical, and at the same time a way to ward off expressions of pain and to attune music to a moderation that belongs to the sphere of cheerful and refreshing subjects, to the sphere of bourgeois vulgar materialism. The public musical ideal frequently becomes entwined with that of comfort. The reception of a matter of the mind is made to suit physical ease. In the realm of musical reproduction this sort of public opinion usually rejects intentions that conflict with the habituated ideal performance; doing absolute justice to the matter will be censured as willful. At the same time one fully perceives the reproductive artist's ability to project something, also his technical quality; the experience of the matter is by no means radically cut off by the opinion. Hegel's line that public opinion merits respect and disrespect applies in music too.

Common sense will not want to dispense with the argument that the eternal recurrence of the clichés of public opinion might simply denote their truth, after all—just as in a desolate rainy season everyone complains about the weather. But the analogy does not hold water. The subject's commensurate position relative to music would be to its concretion. Where the judgment is not motivated by that but by the automatic hundredth repetition of abstract verbalizations, one must suspect that the subject did not let itself be

143

touched by the phenomenon at all. What bears this out is the fact that those stereotypes, judged by unimpeachable characteristics of what they depreciate, are false. Schönberg's music is by no means "more intellectual"—if the word does not make us flinch—than Berg's; his truly revolutionary works were outbursts of an unconscious in quest of manifestation, comparable to the automatic writings of literature, rather than anything having to do with esthetic reflections. Such reflections were far from Schönberg's mind; his whole habitus, of the person as well of an oeuvre unshaken in the premises of its own possibilities, was that of an artist naive *tant bien que mal*. What makes Berg sound less intellectual to public opinion is simply a nature that was less abrupt than Schönberg's in excreting the more familiar forms of expression; Berg himself felt most uneasy to be played off against Schönberg under that category in which he sensed the *parti pri* for moderation.

The question where all this will end is nothing but an alibi for those who avoid facing the matter here and now. One's own ignorance is rationalized as a farsighted philosophy of history; being out of touch with the object becomes an intellectual superiority over the object. The talk of inhumanity and coldness tacitly assumes the desiderate that music ought to warm—without considering that by no means all past music did, and that precisely this effect has meanwhile sunk to the lowbrow level. Besides, the new music, like the traditional one, contains both highly expressive and highly detached pieces; like all music, it is a force field of constructive and mimetic moments and no more exhausted in either kind than any other such field.

Hardly any of the stock concepts of musical public opinion will stand up. They are mere ideological stragglers of obsolete historic stages. Originally, once upon a time, many of the main categories were moments of live musical experience; many still preserve a trace of truth. They have become fixed, however, have turned into independent symbols of thinking as one is expected to think, have been insulated against deviation. Out of that which in periods of more strictly structured societies with smaller population figures used to be a circle of *connaisseurs de la cour et de la ville,* a dubious process of socialization has made an agglomerate of those who approve a system of norms extraneous to what they have heard.

What comes to matter more than expertise is familiarity with, and zealous repetition of, accepted judgments. The farther a broad public's estrangement from advanced production, the more welcome the interjection of public opinion categories.

Phenomena which as concrete music are obscure to the audience will be unresistingly subsumed under the ready-made concepts; knowing all about those will serve as a substitute for the musical experience. Even in the realm of traditional music, identification with opinion often manages to hide the lack of a relation to the thing itself. Socially this kind of listening will largely take its bearings from the group to which the individuals view themselves as belonging. They do not necessarily admit to the taste they consider the best; sometimes they profess the one they ought to have according to their self-appraisal. Particularly inclined to go by public opinion are people who are swamped with music without having been prepared for it by tradition or specific education. They get into a process of false collectivization: of a collectivization estranged from the object.

The situation of musical public opinion would probably emerge only in another context. We would have to see what has become of the concept of public opinion as such, one of the central concepts of Locke's doctrine of democracy. Jürgen Habermas has several times investigated the dynamic of that concept in social reality.[3] One of these studies was confined to a surveyable circle of intellectually emancipated bourgeois, as it echoed until far into the twentieth century in the conception of the role of so-called notables. This element, materially qualifying but at the same time restrictively elitist and thus undemocratic, has been lost by the concept of the public in modern democracies, with a balancing objective removal of the social inequalities to which that concept used *sans gêne* to confess.

The problematics of public opinion showed already in an aporia that was topical for Rousseau in particular: that the average value of individual opinions, which democracy cannot do without, frequently deviates from the truth of the thing itself. This has been exacerbated in the course of total social evolution, also in public opinion about music. Formally, the possibility of opportunity for everyone to hear music and to judge it is superior to the privilege of segregated circles. It might lead beyond the narrowness of a taste whose social narrowness was often esthetically restrictive as well. In fact, however, that broadening, that extension of freedom of opinion and its use to people who under the circumstances can scarcely have an opinion, counteracts their material commitment and ultimately undermines their chance to form an opinion at all.

What commends itself as the democratic potential of opinion degenerates into the pressure of a retarded consciousness on the advanced one, to the point of threatening artistic freedom. De Tocqueville's diagnosis of the American spirit comes to be true on all continents. Since everyone can pass judgment without being able to judge, public opinion comes to be both amorphous and rigid, and thus invalid. Today its spongy and yielding side finds crass expression in the fact that there really are no more musical partisans in public opinion, like the ones of Gluck and Piccinni or of Wagner and Brahms. They have been succeeded by schools squabbling in the cenacle, while all that has remained public is a vague aversion to everything suspected of being modern. But it is not individualism that explains this inarticulate state; it is not a condition in which groups are no longer formed because everyone makes his own judgment and there can be no common denominators. On the contrary.

As less and less specific and simultaneously encompassing views crystallize in the mass of listeners—if this should really ever have occurred in music—they put up less and less resistance to their intentional and unintentional social manipulation; in this respect musical opinion is no exception from other ideological departments. Slogans launched by opinion centers and by the mass media are taken up in a hurry. Some, like the call for the clear and distinct form called intelligibility, date back to an age in which there was still such a thing as a decisive opinion of the cultural upper stratum. Removed from live dialectics with the object, they are degraded to "manners of speaking." The opinion-making centers reinforce that, drilling it in once more in their turn. While citing the consumer, they are careful not to expose themselves for anything but the consumer consciousness that exists anyway. What is constantly presumed to be in flux, subject to so-called changing fashions, is probably approaching a stationary state. What is supposed to be as subjective as opinion would be reducible to invariants we can count.

Of course this does not settle the question of primary and derivative opinion. As has been repeated countless times, the influence mechanisms, as Mannheim called them, are far more powerful in the thoroughly administered socialized world than at the peak of liberalism. The very concept of influencing is liberalistic, however, construed after the model of subjects who are not just formally free but intrinsically independent, and who are appealed to from outside. The more doubtful the validity of that model, the more obsolete the talk of influencing; the separation of inside and outside falls where no inside is constituted any more. The distinction between imposed opinion and that of the living subjects loses its base. Their current views are probably more confirmed in their average value by the centralized organs of public opinion than directly received from those media as something alien—and indeed, in their planning the media always take the receptivity of their ideological customers into consideration.

Ideological processes tend like the economic ones to regress to simple reproduction. True, regard for customers is itself ideological insofar as it puts up rules of the free market game and presents the masters of opinion as devoted servants. But, just as Gurland has shown that the compromise structure survived in the economic policies of the totalitarian state, we see it surviving in ideological centralism. The organs of public opinion cannot limitlessly force on people what those people do not like. Until the sociology of education and the critique of ideology offer more concrete demonstrations of economic links, the question of cause and effect within the superstructure remains somewhat idle. As moments of the totality, the distinct moments of the superstructure condition each other. We can neither reduce the subjectivity of opinion-holders to the subjective processes of the formation of opinion—which are themselves still secondary processes—nor the other way round.

Official musical opinion has its institutional organ in the critics.[4] Hiding behind the ingrained tendency to knock the critics is the irrationalist bourgeois art religion; the tendency is inspired by people's fear lest critical thinking deprive them of one more uncontrollable segment of life, and finally by the aversion which all bad positivity feels to the possibility of being shaken. This prejudice itself is a piece of public opinion, and the critics deserve to be defended against it. By shielding music from consciousness and entrenching it in the half-truth of its irrationality, the hatred of critics injures music, which is as much a matter of the mind as its penetration. Yet the rancor of men who deeply feel their own exclusion from this matter finds its target in those who—wrongly, most of the time—consider themselves cognoscenti. In music as elsewhere, the intermediaries are held liable for a system they are merely symptoms of.

The universal objection that all criticism is relative, a mere special case of a mentality whose misuse of the mind depreciates any mind as worthless, does not say much. The subjective reactions of a critic—which critics, to document their sovereignty, sometimes lay to chance—are not opposed to objectivity of judgment. They are its premise; without such reactions music is not experienced at all. It is up to the critic's ethic to raise his impression to the rank of objectivity, by constant confrontation with the phenomenon. If he is really competent, his impressions will be more objective than detached evaluations by dignitaries who are strangers to music. Yet the spot of relativity that stains all judgments about art is not sufficient to obscure the difference in rank between a Beethoven movement and a medley, between a symphony by Mahler and one by Sibelius, between a virtuoso and a bungler.

The sense of such differences must be carried to the full discrimination of well-founded judgment. But something else, which in the end proves false before an emphatic idea of truth, is closer to truth than an abstention from judgment, the shrug that would dodge the intellectual motion which is the motion of the thing itself. Critics are not bad when they have subjective reactions; they are bad when they do not have any, or when they undialectically stick to them and use their office to put a stop to the critical process that is the duty of their office. This arrogant type of critic flourished in the era of impressionism and Art Nouveau; it was more at home in literature and the fine arts than in music. Today it is apt to be eclipsed by those who either do not judge at all any more or do it merely en passant, after appraising the situation. The decay of criticism as an active force in musical public opinion is not manifested by subjectivism but by the shrinkage of a subjectivity that mistakes itself for objectivity, in faithful concordance with overall anthropological trends.

There is no more emphatic argument for the rights of critics than their abolition by the Nazis, the obtuse transposition on the intellect of the difference between productive and unproductive labor. Criticism is immanent to music itself; it is the procedure which objectively brings each successful composition as a force field to its resultant. Music criticism is required by music's own formal law: the historic unfoldment of works and of their truth content occurs in the critical medium. A history of Beethoven critique might show how each new layer of the critics' consciousness of Beethoven unveiled new layers of his work, layers which in a certain sense were not even constituted prior to that process. Socially, music criticism is legitimate because nothing else enables musical phenomena to be adequately taken in by the general consciousness. Even so, it takes part in the social problematics. It is tied to such institutions of social control and economic interest as the press—a connection not infrequently extending to the critics' position, all the way to consideration shown to publishers and other notables. Within itself, moreover, criticism is subject to social conditions which clearly make its task more and more difficult.

Benjamin once defined that task in an epigram: "The public must always be wrong, and yet it must always feel represented by the critic." [5] This is to say that critics must contrast the truth, which is objective and thus intrinsically social, to the general consciousness that has been negatively predesigned by society. The social insufficiency of music criticism is drastically illustrated by its ever-increasing failure to solve that task. In the peak period of liberalism, when the critics' freedom and independence were respected—the figure of Beckmesser is the invidious retort to their prestige—some of them dared to defy public opinion. In Wagner's case it was a reactionary step, taken for the sake of the *tempus actum;* but for all the obtuseness of his anti-Wagner position the much-reviled Hanslick held on to an element of truth, to the purely musical *peinture* that was not honored again until much later.

Critics such as Paul Bekker or the dubious Julius Korngold still retained some of the liberality of their own opinion against the public one. It is on the decrease. Once the audience's public opinion about music really turns into bleating, into a reiteration of clichés to demonstrate one's own cultural loyalty, many critics feel more strongly tempted to bleat along in their fashion. It has little to do with schools. Many musical phenomena affect critics like cues, triggering lines which do have something to them but cannot be automated without deteriorating into performances of what everyone expects. They are hardly less conditioned reflexes than those of the entertainment listeners. When such a man encounters Schönberg's *Gurrelieder*, for example, he will—if only so as to prove to his readers that he is an expert—promptly start talking of the most obvious things, those that strike the deafest of ears: of post-Wagnerianism, of an alleged over-enhancement of the Wagnerian orchestra, of an end of the neoromantic style.

But the critic's task would only begin where these statements end, with a demonstration of what is specific and new in the early score, which Schönberg never disavowed; for the laggards' glee in chiding the works of his youth as lagging he had nothing but mockery. A far-reaching formation of melodies, a richly graduated harmonization, the constitution of independent dissonances by the carriage of voices, a soloist-type loosening of the sound in Part Three, far beyond the impressionistic procedure, and finally the indescribably bold emancipation of counterpoint in the last canon—all this is more significant for *Gurrelieder* than the warriors from *Götterdämmerung* in Part Three or the Tristan chord in *"Lied der Waldtaube."* Above all, however, an occurrence familiar from traditional music: that something new and original was invented, said, composed in the accustomed idiom. According to the fearless logic that takes hold of *Gurrelieder*, Mozart could be dismissed as a mere Haydn epigone.

Calling attention to this does not help. They will not be broken of the habit, not by any analytical demonstration, and they invariably call *Wozzeck* a late flowering of the *Tristan* chromatics, praise Stravinsky on account of elemental rhythmic force—as if the artificial use of shifted *ostinati* were identical with primal rhythmic phenomena—and certify Toscanini's faithfulness to a work[6] even where he neglects the metronome indications given by Beethoven. Critics are even less obliged to give up their Nibelungen hoard of minted judgments since the independence of their position, without which criticism would be senseless, frees them also of possible factual control. The less commensurable the new music remains to an audience that has lagged behind and has been fed standard merchandise, the more will that audience accept the critics' authority without question, on the one condition that even when behaving in modern fashion they will indicate by nuances that they do agree with public opinion.

This is what their elegance adjusts to. It is enough to report on events in a tone that will confirm the reader in his belief that they are events; one must respect the respectable and may brush off those who have no power behind them. Materially uncontrollable by the public, the critics' authority becomes a personal one, an additional agency for the social control of music by standards of conformity, draped with more or less good taste. The qualifications for a music critic's job remain irrational. If a man is well-versed and has kept some interest in music, his isolated journalistic writing talent will mostly suffice; the crux—a knowledge of composing, an ability to understand and judge the inner form of structures—is hardly called for, if for no other reason, because there are none who might judge that ability itself, who might criticize the critics. But incomprehension enters into the judgment: its falseness will be enhanced by the resentments of the uncomprehending.

Whether and to what extent music critics will adapt themselves, intentionally or not, to the overall policy of their papers remains to be analyzed. In so-called liberal papers this is probably rarer than in those with conservative or religious ties, for instance; in the Weimar Republic there were striking exceptions on both sides. In the totalitarian press the critic is merged *sans façon* with the apparatchik. In their culture supplements in particular, liberal papers like to grant space to more acidulous views than will be found in the main section; this possibility, the prototype of which was the old *Frankfurter Zeitung*, is itself part of liberalism. Still, it too must probably observe the limits of "going too far." If moral outrage at extreme manifestations is today no longer good form, such extremes will be treated with condescension or amusement. It reflects the depoliticization of the mind at large—itself a political act, even in culture.

The state of criticism should not be deplored, as used to be the custom; it should be deduced. If the critics themselves are musicians—in other words, if they are at home in their subject and not falsely above it—they are also all but inevitably captives of the narrow immediacy of their own intentions and interests. It took the magnanimous genius of a Schumann to formulate a critique like that of young Brahms, or the judgment about Schubert, then not yet bruited about. The reviews written by major composers are largely vicious. Hugo Wolf was as blindly biased against Brahms as the professorial Brahmsian critics were philistine failures where the Neo-Germans were concerned. Debussy suffered of the self-righteousness of the antidilettante who keeps forgetting that in musical cognition competence is not a *terminus ad quem* but has to prove itself by surpassing itself.

The expert with his *déformation professionelle* is the counterpart of the hidebound layman. Yet any man whom the subject preoccupies less than it did those composers is today, at least, eliminated on that ground. Lessing's insight that the critic does not have to do better is certainly still true. But music has become so much of a métier sui generis, one whose laws range from succinct technical experience to musical good manners, that it really takes someone seriously involved in production to make distinctions in it; immanent critique alone will bear fruit. Professional critics who are not capable of it—which means most of them—are relegated to ersatz sources, mainly academic institutions that qualify them with diplomas or titles without being of much help in their task. Yet the more dense and ramified the grid of musical life and its administrations, the more will the reviewer turn back into what a dusty nineteenth-century legal term called him: a reporter. The change does not merely mean resignation on his part; it means missing the objectivity to which he would seem to submit.

For the sole art in art is what is more than any facts that might be reported. Delicately understood, the genuine experience of music, like that of all art, is as one with criticism. To carry through its logic, to define its connections, means always also to perceive it in oneself as the antithesis of falsehood: *falsum index veri.* Now as ever, knowledge and the capacity to discriminate are directly one. Their *locum tenens* would have to be the critic, and he fills that role less and less. It is not only due to the fact that compositions keep growing more brittle for one who does not dwell in their own foxhole. Rather, considering the needs of prompt topicality and wide publicity, the prevailing forms of music criticism would hamper the critic even if he were up to the task. The best part of musical cognition slips between the institutions of musical life. Besides, even the culture industry's literature of appreciation, which rapidly expands in Germany as everywhere, gravitates toward the purely informative type.

Even the function of expertise, wherever it survives by any chance, is undergoing changes. Richard Strauss in Munich was already suffering under the mentality of "We're from the city of Wagner; we're modern anyway." And Vienna, where the new music originated, is still occupying the developmental rung of 1900: "We hold the franchise on music culture; no one can fool us." Without expertise, without a habitual knowledge of the familiar, the new that is taking shape can hardly be understood; but that knowledge by itself tends to congealment and self-seclusion. In young industrial areas one often finds a more open public opinion with less material understanding. Corresponding to this on a larger scale is a certain shift of the musical center of gravity from Europe to America; what makes John Cage so fascinating for young European musicians could probably not have evolved without the premise of an absence of tradition. Here too, the most recent music is joined by a potential of regression, of a reformation to primitive stages. Shadowlike, it accompanies social progress. Brecht's barbarian futuristic demand that the mind will have much to forget seems unwittingly and unwillingly fulfilled in public opinion about music, fruitfully and destructively at once.

10

NATIONS

At music festivals and similar events official gentlemen continue to make encomiastic speeches on the international character of music, on its bridge-building between peoples. Even in the Hitler era, when the Nazi music politicians tried to replace the International Society for Contemporary Music with a backward-directed organization, there was no shortage of such professions of faith. They have something pleasurable about them, as when countries engaged in cold warfare against one another participate in joint earthquake relief operations, or when a European doctor demonstratively cures natives on a distant continent. Such outbreaks of brotherhood testify that nothing is too bad to allow something universally human to flower, though the humane holidays do not even slightly inhibit what goes on socially and politically, day in, day out. Not in musical nationalism either; its testimonials run parallel. In great times, the chosen people of the moment customarily aver that they and they alone hold the franchise on music. The contradiction is stubborn enough to cause some sociological reflection.

For sociology the nation is a problem anyway, and in the most emphatic sense. On the one hand the concept of the nation contradicts the universal concept of the human being, from which the bourgeois principle of the equality of subjects is derived. On the other hand, nationality was the premise of realizing that principle, something without which bourgeois society at large, a society whose idea contains universality, was all but unthinkable. Bourgeoization in the broadest sense, including cultural aspects, occurred through the nationality principle or at least on its basis. Residues of this are actually or allegedly specific national moments today. In the end, social contradictions continue in national conflicts. This already happened in imperialism, but it also applies to the "nonsimultaneity" of highly industrialized states and more or less agrarian ones, and nowadays to the problems between great powers and the so-called developing countries. The ideological function of music within society is inseparable from this. Since the mid-nineteenth century a country's music has become a political ideology by stressing national characteristics, appearing as a representative of the nation, and everywhere confirming the national principle.

Yet music, more than any other artistic medium, expresses the national principle's antinomies as well. In fact, it is a universal language without being Esperanto: it does not crush the qualitative peculiarities. Its similarity to language does not depend upon nations. Even far distant cultures—if we do, for once, employ that horrible plural—are capable of mutual understanding in music; that a well-trained Japanese should be a priori unable to play Beethoven properly has proved to be pure superstition. Still, music has national elements to the same extent as bourgeois society as a whole. Its history, and that of its forms of organization, essentially occurred within national boundaries.

But this was not extraneous to music. Despite its universal character—which it owes to the absence of firm concepts, the very lack that distinguishes it from the spoken language—it did show national characteristics. Realizing those was part of its full experience, perhaps of its universality itself. It is a known fact that Weber became very popular in France—not directly on account of his humane content, however, but by virtue of a national German one whose difference from French tradition was relished there like an exotic dish. Conversely, our perception of Debussy is adequate only if we are aware of the French tinge in his musical cadence, similar to the Italian tinge we often hear in opera. The more it is an idiom that resembles a linguistic one, the closer will music come to national definitions. The Austrian touch of Schubert and Bruckner is no mere historical factor but a cipher of the esthetic phenomenon itself.

To any naive follower of a consciousness schooled by German classicism and its evolutionary tendency down to the moderns, Debussy's miniature formats would have to appear as arts-and-crafts bric-à-brac, and the suavity of his colors as sweet hedonism. This is how Pan-German schoolmasters used to react to French music. To hear Debussy correctly one must hear how those

155

miniature formats which arrogant Germans tend to confuse with genre pieces pass judgment on the metaphysical claims of German music. Part of Debussy's musical physiognomy is the suspicion that grandiose gestures usurp a spiritual rank more likely to be guaranteed by asceticism toward those gestures. The preponderance of sensual sound in the so-called impressionist music involves playfully pensive doubts of the Germans' unshaken trust in the autocracy of the spirit. But the critical and polemical features of Debussy and all Western music are thus coupled also with a shutting of eyes to essential aspects of German music. In the thirties there was a parodist who called himself Bétove. I do not know whether he was English or French; in any case the wisecracks he performed on the piano, evoking storms of applause, made it easy to imagine how not just Wagner but secretly even Beethoven sounds beyond the Rhine: like self-righteously barbarian bombast, an esthetic habitus devoid of urbane manners. Against such inanities on either side all mention of the universality of music has something threadbare about it. Music is not a simple state of affairs, is not directly to be obtained, but needs reflection on the separating national elements.

One objection raised time and again against the sociology of music is that the nature of music, its pure being-in-itself, has nothing to do with its entwinement in social states and conditions. What facilitates this *dèsinteressement* is that in music we cannot put a finger on social states of affairs as we can in a nineteenth-century novel, for instance, although the sociology of art in nonmusical realms long ago turned into an interpretation of modes of procedure instead of sticking merely to tangible contents.[1] Max Scheler, in the case of mental states of affairs, crudely separated their sociologically conceived relations to factuality—their "roots in being," as this was called in those days—from their allegedly pure intellectual content, heedless of the fact that those "real factors" merge with the content itself. And now, forty years later and bereft of philosophical claims, the comfortable noblesse of that sociology of knowledge enters into an opinion of music—an opinion whose bad conscience views purges as necessary to preserve the musical realm from extra-artistic sullying or from abasement to an ideology for political ends.

But what refutes this apologetic inclination is that the object of musical experience makes a social statement of its own; that the content, once robbed of this element, will shrink and lose that very indissoluble and inextinguishable something whereby art becomes art. It is that national element, that rejection of the German spirit, which essentially constitutes Debussy's spirit. To feel him without it would not only strip the fiber of that music of the very thing it is; it would also diminish it. Debussy would be resettled in the sphere of salons and social pleasantry, a sphere to which he has neither more nor less of an affinity than great German music has to the sphere of violence and self-aggrandizement. Where Debussy, without laying emphatic claims to the absolute, is more than a divertissement, it is the national tone that makes him more. It links him with those emphatic claims by including them as rejected.

This is no piece of information, however, no speculation about Debussy, but an aspect of the compositorial figure. The man who fails to notice it is shutting his ears, as an expert in the field, to the part of music that does more than epitomize the field. If we call this surplus the universality of music, access to it would only be granted to those who perceive the definite social nature of music, and thus its limitation. It does not become universal by abstraction from its spatial-temporal content; only through its concretion. A sociology of music would consist of cognitions that grasp its essentials without exhausting themselves in its technological facts. There is, of course, a permanent mingling with those facts. To be worthy of its object, musical cognition would have to be able to read the inflections of the musical language, the nuances of its form—in other words, to read technological facts so that they can be used to define elements such as the national one of Debussy.

It is only since the rudiments of bourgeois nations exist that national schools with full characteristics have unfolded. National or regional centers of gravity and their migrations will be discoverable in the Middle Ages too, but there the differences surely were more floating. Wherever national traits are more clearly recognizable in the Middle Ages, as in the Florentine *ars nova,* they crystallized in bourgeois centers. The late medieval Dutch schools that extend down to the Reformation would probably be difficult to conceive without the fully developed urban economy of the Low Countries; the tracing of such contexts would be among the foremost tasks of a cooperation between sociology and the history of music. Not until the Renaissance dissolved medieval universalism did national styles come to be more distinct. The nationalization of music paralleled its bourgeoisization. Italy was the font of what may—in a not quite unjustified, though strictly limited analogy—be called "Renaissance" in the history of music; Germany, about the year 1500, was lagging behind.

German music of those days sounds like one of a different national type but was, rather, a music of retarded humanism. It was the humanist movement which then delivered the national, perhaps from the womb of older popular traditions. The very traits that make the German choral composers around 1500 seem specifically German—as opposed to a certain rational transparency in the rising Italian music—are medieval traits. Even as a continuing productive force the German element in music always kept an archaic, prenational touch. This very touch would later fit it for the language of humanity; what was prenational in it kept recurring until it transcended the national. How deeply the national category is ingrown in the history of the inmost complexion of music could perhaps be fully illuminated only by reflecting on the centuries-old productive tension of Latin and German in music, and on the tension between nationalism and the traces of universalism that were kept alive amid political and economic German reaction.

The controversy whether Bach belongs to the Middle Ages or already to the Modern Age is undialectical. The revolutionary force with which his music thrust beyond the national limits of direct social perception was as one with that present medieval tradition which in the absolutist era did not unprotestingly bow to the demands of each single bourgeois state. Its urban refuge was Protestant sacred music. But it was only Bach's absorption of the bourgeois-national and urban music of past centuries—Italian and, later, French—that lent such powerful eloquence to his musical genius. What raised Bach above the consumer music of his period, above the genteel style inaugurated chiefly by his sons, was that bit of medievalism which in him grew into the thoroughly polyphonous construction of the modern homophonous language. But the heritage came to be binding only because he did not raise it retrospectively but measured it against the developed bourgeois-national musical languages of his time, the Italian and French. In Bach, the national element is truly voided into universality.

This should explain no less than the primacy which German music held until close to the mid-twentieth century. In Germany, even since Schütz envisioned the unity of monody and polyphony, a prenational stratum and a national one actually imported from the Latin countries have mutually pervaded one another. This makes out a crucial premise of that concept of musical totality which around 1800 let music converge with the speculative systems and their idea of humanity—and which in the "founder period" * of German music was of course partly responsible for its imperialistic overtones as well.

From the early days of the bourgeois era the interaction of music and nation involved not only the productive aspect of the nationality principle but its destructive one. A slogan widely circulated since Oscar A. H. Schmitz is that the British are a people without music. That in *musica composita,* at least, the Anglo-Saxon people have for centuries not matched the creativity of others is obvious and not to be undone by folkloristic rescue operations. The original genius of Purcell, often cited to the contrary, does not suffice to refute that judgment. But it was not always valid. In the Elizabethan age an early national state favored by insular location passed its national limits anticipatorily, so to speak, in products of the mind, and music too was caught up in this intellectual movement which in sixteenth-century England surely did not lag behind the one of all Europe. The idea of music echoes throughout Shakespeare's work; at the end of *The Merchant of Venice* it becomes a phantasmagoria of what music itself did not catch up with until centuries later. The blanket exclusion of Englishmen from music is a pure resentment theory of German nationalism, an attempt to deny the inner kingdom to the older, more successful empire.

There is no denying, however, that the British musical genius dried up from the early seventeenth century on. Most probably the

---

* *Gründerperiode* is the German word for the years of hectic economic as well as colonial expansionism which followed on the founding of the Second German Empire in 1871. —Transl.

fault can be attributed to the rise of Puritanism. If those are right who hold that *The Tempest*, the poet's abdication, is at the same time a protest against that religious trend, the work's musical spirit would be most closely akin to that interpretation. It sometimes seems as though the pressure of the economic frame of mind of inner-worldly asceticism had forced British musical impulses to seek refuge in a zone of safety from the anathema that hung over music as falderal, that degraded music, wherever found, to falderal: Keats and Shelley are the *locum tenentes* of nonexistent great English composers. A nation's specific political-ideological fate can suppress its musical vigor until it withers; productive musicality, as an intellectual faculty mankind was late to acquire, is evidently most sensitive to social pressure. There is no prophesying the long-range effects which the Nazi dictatorship that helped reactionary fustian to the top will have had on German musicality. In post-1945 production, at any rate, Germans no longer hold that primacy of which Schönberg, when he formulated the twelve-tone technique, thought he had assured them for a hundred years.

How deeply the humanity and universality of music entwine with the national element they are transcending is exemplified by Viennese classicism, notably by Mozart. The German-Italian synthesis in his compositions has been diagnosed without pause—mostly, of course, with reference to the fusion of mere categories such as opera seria, opera buffa, and *Singspiel,* also perhaps to the combination of southern cantability with the obligatory German way of composing, with the filigree technique of Haydn and the orchestral one of the Mannheim School. But the national moments permeate each other all the way into the smallest cells and the "tone." Some of Mozart's instrumental pieces sound Italian without any pseudomorphosis to the aria: slow movements in piano concertos, like the Andante in C Minor from the E Major Concerto (K. 482) or the one in F Sharp Minor from the A Major Concerto (K. 488). These pieces, however, are by no means detachedly classicistic according to the *convenu* of Mozart the Apollonian. Rather, they are the first to anticipate and then sustain the romantic tone, in as Venetian a manner as that city's *imago* could probably light up to a German only. The classicism in it is a *fata morgana*, not a present thing.

The national moments in Mozart relate dialectically to each

other. The sensually southern one is broken by a spirituality that removes it by taking hold of it and thus lends it a complete voice. Southern amiability, which centuries earlier had smoothed the provincial and gross side of the German form of musical reaction, is now, as the spiritualized picture of a substantial, unsplit life, recovering its own from the German or Austrian. That element of *cantabile* which we know was inspired by Italian song, and which delivers Mozart's instrumental music from the rattling mechanics of rationalism, turns itself into a carrier of humanity. Conversely, however, extending the German construction principle past the Italian melodics helps achieve that unity of diversity which is legitimized by the fact that the particular which it produces and grates on is itself no longer a concrete flourish. If the great music of Viennese classicism and its successors down to the second Vienna School can be understood as an interaction of universal and particular, then this idea was bequeathed to it by the productive interaction of the German and Italian in Mozart.

The universal is the total construct dating back to Bach, with whose "Well-tempered Clavichord" Mozart was familiar through Swieten; but the particular, in the language of classicist esthetics, is the naive element of direct song from the effective art of the Italians. In Mozart this loses its accidentality and particularity by finding the way to an encompassing whole by itself. But the whole is humanized by that element: it receives nature within it. If great music is integral in the sense of neither insisting on the particular nor subjecting it to totality but allowing the latter to arise from the impulse of particularity, then such integration originates as an echo of the German and Italian moments in the ascending musical language of Mozart. This too absorbs the national difference, but in each instance it develops one moment from the other, from the one it is not. The seraphic expression of Mozart's own humanity, manifested on the operatic stage in the Sarastro complex of *The Magic Flute* and in the last act of *The Marriage of Figaro*, took shape in that national duality. The humane is the reconcilement with nature by virtue of nonviolent spiritualization. This is precisely what happens to the Italian in Mozart, and he in turn left it historically to a national center, to Vienna.

Until Brahms and Mahler that city continued to absorb important musical forces. The central musical tradition that aims at

161

integral form and is profoundly akin to the idea of universality, the antithesis of the nineteenth century's national schools, this itself was lent a national touch by Vienna. Many of Mahler's and Berg's themes talk in Viennese; even Webern secretly—and therefore so much more emphatically—speaks the idiom. The primarily very different temperaments of West or North Germans such as Beethoven and Brahms were attracted by it as if the humane breath which their unruly or uncommunicative music longed for had been tied to the place like some local spirit. The Viennese dialect was the true world-language of music, and what it conveyed was the craftsmanlike tradition of motive-thematical work. This tradition alone seemed to assure music of something like immanent totality, something like the whole, and Vienna was the home of the tradition. It fitted the bourgeois century as perfectly as did classical economics, in which the totality of the competing interests of all individuals was presented as the interest of society as a whole.

The genius of Vienna which dominated musical history for almost 150 years was a cosmos of the higher and the lower, transfigured by a poet for music, Hofmannsthal. It was the congruence of count and coachman as the social model of artistic integration. That retrospective phantasm was socially not realized in ancient Austria either, but the conventions of life stood for it, and music fed on those. Ever since Haydn, and most strongly in Beethoven, one could feel it as a unit of spirit and nature, of the artificial and the folksy—as if Vienna, the city that had not quite kept pace with the rest, had saved an arena in which music could remain untouched by the split in bourgeois society. What that great music was anticipating, as reconcilement, it had read on the walls of that anachronistic city where feudal forms and bourgeois freedom of thought, unquestioned Catholicism and philanthropic enlightenment, got on well together for so long a time. Without the promise emanating from Vienna, deceptive as it might be, the most high-flying musical art of Europe would scarcely have been possible.

But however dubious this unity in bourgeois society was even in Vienna, that enclave which knew it was doomed, the balance of the universal and the national could not be maintained in music either. In Beethoven's, at times even in Haydn's music, we hear a rumble of the lower, the not quite domesticated: the elemental as cover for something social. Only the smile which in the masters' case befalls it from the heights of sublimation will tame and confirm it as one. Where it drops out of the framework it serves the greater glory of that unity by being comical.

In Schubert, then, where the complaisant Viennese humanism relaxes the total discipline of the classicist way to compose without abandoning it, the national moment stands on its own for the first time. Its Utopia, one of an inextinguishably concrete coloring, refuses to fit into the bourgeois universe. Beethoven's chthonic stratum, his nether world, is dug up and made accessible. Schubert's *à la hongroise* is already a stimulus, "out of the ordinary," but at the same time it bears that untouched, unintentional stamp of noncompliance with the civilizational side of integral music, with the side that is too culture-immanent and estranged from the living subject. In Schubert this element is still moving loosely on a world theater that tolerates divergence like the stage of Ferdinand Raimund, with the pretense of unbroken unity dropped from the start. This is why Schubert really knows no breaks.

After Schubert, that cachet of the particular was quickly isolated and posited in the so-called "national schools" which in the nineteenth century took up the cause of the antagonisms of the several national states and made it their own. In this process the qualitative differences between peoples, those not exhausted in the general musical concept, came to be transformed into commodity brands on the world market. The national musical components lagging behind the international rationality, notably behind that of communications, were exploited as natural monopolies by states whose rivalry was artistic too. This could not help depressing the musical level. In Schubert the national element still had the innocence of the dialect; thereafter, thrusting out an aggressive chest, it bore benighted witness to the nonreconcilement of bourgeois society.

Music has a direct share in the change of functions that turned the nation from the organon of bourgeois emancipation into a shackle of productive strength and the potential of destruction. What had sometimes been the color of unmaimed humanity in music, marred by no ceremonial and by no abstractly commanded order, is bewitched now, made a particularity that installs itself as something higher, and becomes a lie. What an Austrian, Grillpar-

163

zer, said about the road from humanity via nationality to bestiality might be transposed on the history of national music from Schubert to Pfitzner.

Even so, till far into the nineteenth century, militant nationalism kept a touch of better days when it was steeping itself in motives of the bourgeois revolution. A listener must stop up his ears not to hear Chopin's F Minor Fantasy as a kind of tragically decorative song of triumph to the effect that Poland was not lost forever, that some day—as that line probably went in the language of nationalism—she would rise again. But what triumphed over that triumph was an absolute musical quality that could be no more nailed down than confined within national frontiers. That quality cremates the national moment that kindled it, as if the march, the epode of a piece invented on a scale as large as a Delacroix canvas, were the song of liberated mankind—just as the finale of Schubert's C Major Symphony once resembled a festival decked in the bright pennons of all peoples, something less exclusive than the "Song to Joy" in which the lonely are vilified. Chopin's work, dating from his late period, may well be the last in which a nationalism attacks oppressors without celebrating an oppression of its own. All subsequent national music is poisoned, both socially and esthetically.

Everything that goes under the name of "folk music" has served the sedimentation of the most diverse historic strata. Precapitalist rudiments hibernate in it at times; in fully industrialized countries those are not so much melodies as a certain spontaneity of making music heedless of the rationalized norms. Added to this are debased cultural goods, also—since the popular *lied* of the nineteenth century—ready-made commercial ones, and finally organizations of the folk-costume-society type; thus the harmonica players were rounded up by a strong industrial interest. Where branches of musical life organize programmatically, a fusion with *Weltanschauungen* is never far away.

Today, in Europe, the vitality of unsteered folk music-making probably varies still between the several countries. Where an individual composer's great achievement came to be the musical ideal, as in Germany, there is less collective spontaneity than in Italy. In the Mezzogiorno, in spite of everything, the human language seems not wholly separated from the musical medium.

The somehow archaic musicality of the people, something substantial in the Hegelian sense, preceding reflection—down there, meanwhile, this is chiefly active in a material which once upon a time was itself part of the individualist sphere: in operas. In Italy they have remained popular to a degree inconceivable in northern countries. Also worth recalling here are the Neapolitan songs that strike so curious a balance between art *lied* and street ditty; they found their apotheosis on Caruso records and in the novels of Proust. There is something to the ancient observation that the musical culture of a single objectified work is hard to unite with the culture of a musicality distributed, as it were, throughout society. What really constitutes the difference, how far it extends, and whether it is now leveled off after all—all this would remain to be determined. Even in Austria, under the rule of a tacit ego ideal, expecting someone to be musical is more a matter of course than in Germany, let alone in England.

In countries with a living musical collective consciousness—which need not be folkloristically tinged at all—one can speak of musical life in a more literal sense than where music runs autonomously counter to the immediate life of the population. Once successfully sublimated, it is potentially removed from people by its objectification. And yet the musical collectivity is not simply noncontemporaneous, not an intact past historical stage, but an enclave within modern society, colored by that society even while contrasting with it. The primitive and infantile consolidates itself as an impotent and doubly evil protest against civilization. It was precisely in the Germany of fascism that the preindustrial moments of folk music zealously lent themselves to postindividual organization. They brag about their own naiveté, a prototype of what came to the top as "blood and soil" ideology. They know why they like to stick to instruments that do not have the chromatic scale at their disposal, one of the most crucial accomplishments of the whole modern musical rationalization process. Folk music has long ceased to be simply what it is; instead, it mirrors itself and thus negates the immediacy it is so proud of—like innumerable texts of "folksy" and in the final analysis shrewdly devised songs. It has become a false consciousness that is past rescuing.

But so has the later art music in the national style. This too sins no less against itself than against the nature it inscribes on its banner: by processing the natural, by manipulating that which claims to be spontaneous. Such extreme folkloristic tendencies of the twentieth century as were embodied in composers as important as Bartók and Janáček should not, under this aspect, be simply regarded as continued evolutions of the late romanticist national schools. This was their descent, but their resistance to manipulation resembled the protest of oppressed peoples rising against colonialism. Much as the early Bartók has in common with his compatriot, Liszt, his music is as strongly opposed to the parlor gypsydom prepared for metropolitan consumption. His own folkloristic researches were polemics aimed at the gypsy music manufactured in cities, a product of national romanticism's decay.

Once more, temporarily, the national element became a musical productive force. Having recourse to actually uncomprehended idioms not processed by the reified Western music system paralleled the revolt of the new avant-garde music against tonality and the rigid metrics coordinated with it. During World War I and in the early twenties Bartók truly had his radical period. In the same spirit, documents of Bavarian folk art showed up in the Blaue Reiter group, not to mention the crosscurrents between Picasso and the Negro sculpture as interpreted by Carl Einstein. It did not last, however. Reactionary implications of folklorism, notably its hostility to differentiation and subjective autonomy, prevailed. What was a masked ball in the nineteenth century, a kind of ideological drapery, prepares in folklorism for the bloody fascist earnest of a musical state of mind that tramples on universality and barbarically imposes its own limits, its happening to be this way and no other, as a higher law.

Yet intramusical reaction and nationalism already join hands in such typical products of national late romanticism as Tchaikovsky and Dvořák. There the national moment is represented by themes that either were or seemed to have been borrowed from folk music. That music is heavily accented, under orders of the determining ideology; whatever is not a theme in the sense of a nationally characterized single melody declines to a mere transition or, in the bad products of the species, to noisily blown-up fillers. But this upsets the idea of symphonics, of unity producing itself from diversity. In the consciousness of such symphonics mankind breaks up into a potentially hostile multiplicity of nations, and so do the symphonic movements split into single themes and the connection slapped on them. The sole remaining organizing factor is the schema, not work from within. The structures approximate the medley form. Song hits have become the heirs of nationally tinged thematics; the legitimate successor of Rachmaninoff was Gershwin. That after fascism's defeat, in countries this side of the Iron Curtain, the folkloristic currents in music subsided testifies to their untruth, to the mendacity of that spiritual exertion of "natural" associations of men in a society whose technological rationalism condemns the manifestations of such associations to fictitiousness even where they may perhaps keep vegetating.

The most important and most fatal form of musical nationalism in the nineteenth century was the German. Richard Wagner exerted a power over other countries that harmonizes exactly with the newcomer-country's success in world markets—too exactly to let us believe in mere coincidence. Wagner already was an article for export, like Hitler. Though lagging behind the West in world-economic terms until the boom of the Bismarck era, Germany had hardly any more live folk music left; it was necessary for German musical romanticism to conjure up something of the kind, perhaps as early as in *Der Freischütz*. In Brahms we find themes of unsurpassed beauty—the second from the introductory Allegro of the D Major Symphony, for example—which sound the way folk songs may be imagined by a reflected consciousness but have never existed in fact.

Altogether, up to Borchardt's translation of Dante, German romanticism inclined to an esthetic surrogation of the national because in German history the nation's birth was a miscarriage, as was bourgeois emancipation. Brahms wrote piano pieces that cite unwritten ballads from a distant past and yet are compositorially so genuine it would be hard to convict them of the anachronism. Wagner—even more in *Die Meistersinger*, his socially probably most effective work, than in the Nordic *Ring*—heats this intention into a Teutonic phantasmagoria. It was well suited to persuading all the world of the German people's supremacy, just as the Frenchman Gobineau and the Briton Houston Stewart Chamberlain proclaimed it in Wagner's name. That Germany had no longer a present living tradition of folk music, that its image could be completely remodeled in favor of agitational effectiveness, as it were—this was just what permitted the irresistible tone of *Die Meistersinger*, along with its evil.

It is a work strutting with genuineness and health, indescribably rich and articulated, an artifact par excellence, yet at the same time replete with infectiously swampy miasmas. The national sprouts airy roots; it turns into the magic garden of a man Nietzsche saw through as the "Klingsor of all Klingsors," because that whose existence is averred does not exist. The national exaggerates itself rhetorically to make us forget the falseness of its message, and that in turn redounds to its effect. The "Mastersingers" got a whole nation drunk on themselves, esthetically anticipating with their transfigured mirage, under the social conditions of liberalism, what the glorified ones would then inflict politically on mankind. The striking principle of symphonics, that power of integration which in Viennese classicism meant humanity, becomes the model of the integral state, the seductively commanded self-aggrandizement.

It was Nietzsche, of all men, who to this day has made the greatest contribution to the social cognition of music: he found the words for these implications of Wagner's. If musical sociology were to deny itself this tool as merely speculative it would remain as far beneath its object as beneath the level of the Nietzschean insight. The aspect of extroverted totality which separates symphonics from chamber music has turned in Wagner's case—except for the original chamber orchestra version of the *Siegfried Idyll* he wrote no chamber music—into political extroversion. In my own treatise *Zur gesellschaftlichen Lage der Musik* I approached the sociological interpretation of *Die Meistersinger* from the text of the work:

In *Die Meistersinger,* one of the most informative and for good reason socially most popular works, the rise of the bourgeois entrepreneur and his "national-liberal" reconcilement with feudality becomes thematical in a sort of dream transposition. In the wish-fulfillment dream of the entrepreneur who has "arrived" economically it is not he whom feudal lords receive but the rich bourgeoisie that receives a feudal lord; the dreamer is not the bourgeois but the knight, whose dream song at the same time restores the lost precapitalist immediacy as opposed to the rationalistic rules of the bourgeois "masters." The bourgeois individual's suffering under his own simultaneously alienated reality is the Tristan side of *Die Meistersinger*; in the hatred of Beckmesser, the petty bourgeois, it joins the consciousness of an entrepreneur aiming at global expansion, one who feels the existing circumstances of production as shackles on the productive forces and whose romantic picture of the feudal lord may already hide a yearning for monopoly in place of free competition. And indeed, the outcome in the festival meadow is no competition any more, only its parody in the clash between the knight and Beckmesser. In Sachs's and the knight's esthetic triumph the ideals of the exporter and the private investor are still in balance.[2]

This remains true even if the finished text of *Die Meistersinger* had in fact kept faith with the one Wagner drafted prior to his disappointment at the failure of the bourgeois revolution. The net result of the opera is indeed the exact national-liberal goal: the alliance of the feudal upper stratum with the industrial bourgeoisie, the triumphant class that proceeds to organize in monopolistic form and forgets a liberalism with which the topmost captains of industry have already broken. This, not less than the sense of national superiority over the competition in world markets, gave the work its concordance with the jackboots of the world spirit. In *Die Meistersinger*, as Nietzsche put it, the German Reich once more defeats the German mind.

To be sure, such reflections stay outside the musical framework. The approved musicology, which no sooner reaches its intramusical limits than it will use programs and texts as crutches, should of course not condemn that deficiency. Though the content—even where it is ideological, and indeed precisely there—cannot be simply deduced from the text, it is not indifferent to the text. Whatever in music cannot be fixed to a category like the nation is so channeled by Wagner that the musical gesture, one of permanently roused elation, will in its effective context be associated with the nation and with nothing else. Even today, after the catastrophe, it is hard to escape from the terrifying grandeur of *Die Meistersinger*. The music drama's unity is no mere artificial hypothesis; it has prevailed as a phantasmagorial totality. An analysis that has fully mastered the Wagnerian ideology would be able to identify it in every last scroll and ramification of the *Meistersinger* score—a paradigm of musical sociology carried to the end. The irresistible demagoguery of the Nuremberg festival drama is located more in the music than in the text. The effect of Hitler's speeches was not so much one of meaning either.

But the music—that in the second act, above all, on the basis of which one may study the bounds of the category of genius itself—the music does not simply create a national fiction. What Wagner has done with artistic rationality is to conjure up and manipulate a half-submerged and forgotten collective world of images. If there is no longer a tradition of German folk music—in *Die Meistersinger* only the cobbler's song by Hans Sachs really imitates a nonexistent folk song—something else has survived: a genuine, specifically German musical accent. It was fully discovered only in romanticism; in *Die Meistersinger* it is probably the famous bars about "the bird who sang today" that make up its essence. Nietzsche's description of Wagner as "almost genuine" alludes to that. Good luck brings back what has been forgotten; but what makes a social untruth of it is the rationalistic disposal whose own contradiction it is. There too, Wagner's music in itself anticipates something of fascism; a sociology of music that defines the ideological in music, in its immanent form, will inevitably also be critique. Wagner was both heir and assassin of romanticism. In the habitus of his music it became collective narcissism, the intoxication of endogamy, a hash of the objective spirit.

Wagner's music and that of his school—the neo-German school which also included such differently-minded composers as Bruckner, Strauss, Mahler, even the early Schönberg—literally "conquered the world," as the newspapermen's phrase goes. It thus involuntarily prepared the ground for a sort of artistic cosmopolitism. Hitlerite nationalism performed a similar somersault: not only did the reaction to it give us our first glimpse of a total conception of Europe; it also created the mass basis for that conception. From the case of a Europe ephemerally crushed under Hitler's heel one could learn that the differences between nations have become historically obsolete, that today they are no longer differences in the essence of the scrambled human beings. Wagner's worldwide expansion encouraged programmatic nationalism in other countries' music as a defense, not just in Debussy but throughout neoclassicism. Absorbing Nietzschean motives, this movement arose right after World War I as an antidote to Wagnerian self-representation and self-intoxication. In Jean Cocteau's treatise *Le coq et l'arlequin,* the manifesto of neoclassicist esthetics, *l'arlequin* is the word for the spirit of all German music. It is mocked as a clown because it lacks self-control and measure.

Like a spiral, nationalism has kept reproducing itself on all sides in widened form. While since the last third of the nineteenth century, at least, all music had a chance to become internationally known, the forms of public reaction in the several countries shrank nationally. Pfitzner, whose own music lacks all the qualities he meant to safeguard in a specific national one, never spread beyond Germany—and there, by the way, he did not get to be really at home either. But even composers of Bruckner's and Mahler's rank have remained German topics. In other countries they are laboriously cultivated by societies dedicated to them; so is Reger, upon whom renewed reflection seems overdue. The length of their works, which exceeds the sociably tolerable; the accumulation of sonic means inherited from Wagner and frowned upon, as obtrusive, in the West; the violent style of performing that music, one that is not well-bred, as it were, and was only recently censured by Pierre Boulez as the *style flamboyant* of Berg and Schönberg—all of this leads to the verdict.

Most of the newer German music was felt to be passé and backward in the disenchanted world, just as Hegelian metaphysics seemed to the Anglo-Saxon positivists. The very quality to which its universality was attached, the transcending, the refusal to be satisfied with finiteness which pervades Mahler's music all the way into its idiomatics, for instance—precisely this is resented as megalomania, as bloated self-exaltation on the subject's part. What will not renounce the infinite is said to be manifestly paranoid and domineering; in comparison, modest resignation is called a higher humanity. This is how nationally-colored ideologies affect even the sublime questions of philosophical musical esthetics.

Cognition must not simply take sides if it is not to remain in its own national bondage. It must rise above the sterile antithesis by defining its moments of truth as well as the bad dichotomy it expresses. It is true that the Western ideal of music, an ideal honed against the German tradition, threatens to withdraw from music what makes it art and more than art—to depress it to the level of an ornamental decoration amid the extant, and perhaps even to view that as heroic discipline of taste. But it is equally true that the great music of that German style which makes for unity from Beethoven down to the Schönberg exiled by Hitler—that this music, too, has its ideological side; it maintains its objective appearance as the absolute here and now and immediately, as a warrant of transcendence, and on that ground claims authority pure and simple.

It was by metaphysics that German music became great music, but as a carrier of metaphysics it is a bit of usurpation like metaphysics itself. It shares that guilt of the German spirit which confuses its particular achievements in art and philosophy with its social realization and thus serves the ends of those who obstruct real humanity. Beyond the German historic landscape, people no longer perceive the force with which the phenomenon was shaped by its metaphysical content; they only note that content's crashing pretentions. The Hegelian sensual semblance of the idea fades into its own parody, a tasteless, uncouth puffery. Critically, each of the two unreconciled conceptions is right against the other, but neither is right by itself; the German one's ailment is *hubris,* the Western one's, too realistic an adjustment. But the only way to explain the enduring gap between them is that the musical languages, as they took shape as national ones in the late nineteenth century, can hardly be well-understood in supranational terms.

This is best exemplified in the feebler composers. Edward Elgar, to whom Britons evidently really like to listen, has no resonance at all in Germany; Sibelius has but a scant one. In England and America he is accorded high honors, though the reasons why were never demonstrated in succinct musical terms; it surely was not the great demands of his symphonics that frustrated all attempts to launch him elsewhere. More than thirty years ago I once asked Ernest Newman, the initiator of Sibelius's fame, about the qualities of the Finnish composer. After all, I said, he had adopted none of the advances in compositorial technique that had been made throughout Europe; his symphonics combined meaningless and trivial elements with alogical and profoundly unintelligible ones; he mistook esthetic formlessness for the voice of nature. Newman, from whose urbane all-round skepticism someone bred in the German tradition had much to learn, replied with a smile that the qualities I had criticized—and which he was not denying—were just what appealed to the British.

Newman's humble view of music criticism, of which he was the Anglo-Saxon matador, corresponded with that attitude. To him, and to the distinctly bourgeois Western mentality for which he spoke even as the most knowledgeable Wagner scholar, music did not have the pathos it had to a Central European mind. Music too, including the music one experiences as serious, is appraised in those countries according to the consistent exchange principle which values any being as "for something else." The ultimate outcome is art as a consumer commodity. But the principle does contain something else as well: a corrective against the German art religion, the fetishism of transfiguring the work of art, a man-made social product, into an "in-itself." The Wagnerian line, "To be German means to do a thing for its own sake," becomes an ideology as soon as one proclaims it. Such differences are shared by the modes of spontaneous musical reaction; the question to ask is whether music such as Mahler's, which no one can accuse of any sort of nationalism, can be adequately interpreted by people for whom the Austrian musical idiom is not part of their substance.

And the new music which German nationalists harassed as corrosive, rootless, and intellectual, the music in which fascists and neofascists find an indestructible object of wrath, as when radio stations that promote it are denounced for wasting the taxpayer's money—even that music was entangled in national conflicts, in most curious contrast to Germany's racist and culture-conservative ideology. Roughly speaking, the parties at the music festivals of the International Society for Contemporary Music between the two World Wars coincided with national groupings. What is now regarded as specifically new music was then confined to Germany and Austria and essentially represented by the Vienna School of Schönberg, Berg, Webern, and some others, also by Krenek and vaguely by the young Hindemith until, in *Das Marienleben*, he confessed to neoclassicism. The radicalism which not only brought innovations in such single sectors as harmonics or rhythmics but revolutionized the entire compositorial material; the revolt against the accustomed language of music as a whole—this was Central European. We may include the Bartók of that period; Stravinsky's most advanced positions had already been vacated by 1920.

Internationally such totally consistent radicalism was considered a German specialty. The posture of Schönberg, who reshaped music purely out of itself, without mundane considerations, was viewed as the fruit of unleashed speculative subjectivism, and also—not without justification—as a manifestation of German thoroughness. He not only shocked audiences; he mercilessly overtaxed them at the same time. Two things were sensed in Schönberg's extremes: the end of a tradition which people wished to hold on to although they had really ceased to believe in it, and the heritage of the obligatory compositorial manner of Viennese classicism, the panthematic procedure in which the potential of the twelve-tone technique lived. In their aversion to this music pan-Germans concurred with anti-Wagnerian neoclassicists, and with the folklorists of the agrarian countries.

The Austrian avant-garde from which the impulse had come, after all, was tolerated on music festival programs, but the majority of pieces were clumsily mimed nineteenth century or primitive carryings-on with motoric stomping. The Schönberg School itself fed the German sense of tradition; while it was being defamed under the Nazi dictatorship, Alban Berg wrote a glorification of Schönberg as a German composer. Webern's stubborn naiveté never let him doubt that Austrians were musical by the grace of God. The movement which so thoroughly plowed up the material and language of music that national moments finally disappeared —this movement itself, in its origin and evolution, was nationally limited and drew its energies from national peculiarities of compositorial procedure. That's how dialectical the history of music is.

There is no question that since 1945 the modern movement has liquidated national differences. Analogous observations can be made in the fine arts, to some extent also in literature. The internationalization of music proceeded apace, synchronized with the political decline—for a time, at least—of the principle of national states. Musical and social tendencies seem to be more tightly fused than before. The world's division into a few great power blocs can, of course, be musically traced in the crudest style differences. The reasons have nothing to do with art. Faced with the suppression of modernism in the realm of Soviet power, the West officially had to discard the shackles which cultural conformism had kept on music until they were dictatorially ordered in the East. The cultural Iron Curtain is so much a requisite of our present bloc society that any relaxation of the taboos on modern music—as occurred in Poland, for example—instantly acquires a political aspect. The compulsory politicization of all things musical in either camp amounts to an administrative social integration of music that will hardly benefit the new music.

Meanwhile, an international musical language this side of the Iron Curtain rings out unmistakably at the concerts of the Kranichstein circle, and this is not explicable by political mimicry. It may well express the depth of the connection between music and society, rather, that social tendencies such as the split into large supranational systems are immanently "represented" in works, purely by their own gravity. Thus neoclassicism—in modern music the counterprinciple to the atonality culminating in twelve-tone technique and serial composing—lost its power of attraction because of productive sterility as well as by theoretical critique; it was probably also too visibly entangled in reactionary ideologies for the younger intellectuals among composers to want to be compromised by it after the fall of fascism. In the end even Stravinsky used the serial technique, whose way to prepare the material really does make it incompatible with national peculiarities and irrationalities. What postromantic currents kept trickling until the Hitler era could not stand up to technological progress. I do not mean to say that all of this was theoretically thought through by composers; involuntariness is the best proof that a tendency is socially authentic. A gifted composer in northernmost Lapland, Bo Nilson, had never heard contemporary music except for a couple of radio broadcasts; he reached extreme electronic and serial consequences all on his own.

Still, the national schools leave their traces in the compositorial International of today. Where a river flows into another, its water is thus sometimes recognizable for a long stretch, by its color. A German touch in Stockhausen's work will be as noticeable as a French one in Boulez; in the first, it is the inclination to think things through to the end, the resolute turn away from any thought of possible effect, no matter how remote and indirect, also the gesture of strict exclusiveness. Within an accomplished common consciousness, not to be revoked by anything short of political disasters, it might be possible for national differences to be further abraded on each other in a state of second innocence, no longer in competition but in productive critique. The age of ideological nationalism in music is not only socially obsolete but rendered out of date by the history of music itself.

The Vienna School, driven from its homeland by the Nazi regime, found refuge partly in America, partly in France. On its migration it came to approach Western categories, not merely due to the temperaments and esthetic intentions of the younger composers, but by virtue of its own objectivity. The serial principle terminates in a static condition, as opposed to the thorough dynamics of free atonality, and that condition was a neoclassicist ideal too, indeed already a Debussyist one. The way of composing in fields set off against each other and largely determined by color, as it followed from the latest rationalization of compositorial procedure, converges with impressionism. Boulez keeps citing Debussy, and Eimert, the German theoretician, occupied himself productively with the *Jeux*. Delight in sensually colorful sound, which in the latest music borders on sugariness now and then, is also Western in nature. Whether this is a matter of what the optimists about progress call synthesis is uncertain, of course. Tensions which in the past were manifest as national conflicts are surviving beneath the surface.

Today the radical modern production of all countries is probably more alike than the several nations' styles have ever been since 1600, down to the strikingly short-range modifications of procedure. It thus invites the derogatory term of "leveling"; militant nationalism and outrage at an allegedly threatening equalization have always been allies. We should not let ourselves be intimidated by the fear of losing individual styles. Teleologically speaking, criticism of an individual style is already implicit in the immanent commitment that is sought by every work of lasting worth, and most of all by the ones least dependent on a universally established musical language. Successful works are those in which—as Hegel already knew—the individual effort, and indeed the accidental quality of an individual's being as it is, will vanish in the necessity of the matter. Its successful particularization recoils into the universal. The stylistic unity of radically modern art does not spring from merely willing a style, not from reasoning about the philosophy of culture, but from technological desiderates we cannot reject. The origin of this style does not oppose individualization but was located in individualization itself; today's cosmopolitan musical language is clearly derived from Schönberg, who was assailed all his life as an individualistic deviate alien to the people. Unity prevailed, and most attempts to save an individual style within it, by arranging reservations, were dubious. They were marketed with less than full consistency and brought about the very thing which under their own category, that of style, is disturbing as impure.

And yet even the most recent unity has an unfortunate side. The compositions, although remaining significantly distinguishable by their success or failure, would not be so flatly alike if they did not obey an overwhelming primacy of the whole over its parts, and thus of organization over qualitative differences. They are in danger of eradicating the restiveness without which their unity could not become productive; to sacrifice this restiveness is to sacrifice the particular, and a loss of that will reduce all works to a common denominator. A retrospective light is thus cast on the very concept of style. Its unity seems blessed where it is lacking, and violent as soon as it exists. No style has ever been what its own concept postulates—the reconcilement of universal and particular —but each one has always suppressed the particular. And for all the consistency that brought it into being, the present style also shows more than a trace of that. The trace is the index of something social: that the world, while united by industrialization, transportation, and communication, is still the unreconciled world it was before. Apparent reconcilement amid all the unreconciled always benefits the unreconciled; today it bears that guilt even in esthetics.

11

AVANT-GARDE

A social analysis of the most recent music from the viewpoint of production—in other words, of the avant-garde works of our time, the time after World War II—meets with an unsuspected difficulty. The unfoldment of the social content of music is clearly a gradual process; at its first appearance that content is disguised. It does not jump right out of the phenomenon. In the beginning our attention is absorbed by technical and sonic-sensual characteristics and above all by the style or evident expressive content; this happened to Beethoven as it did to Wagner and to someone as late as Stravinsky. As the handwriting of social aspects, music will not become legible until we have ceased to be put out by those moments and they have ceased to occupy the foreground of our consciousness; until the new musical language no longer seems to be the product of an individual will but the collective energy can be felt behind the individual manifestations—the way in which the Art Nouveau pathos of loneliness has since manifested its strange universality.

The precipitation of present social conflicts in the latest music resists cognition. The socially posited dichotomy between the musical layman and the expert is no blessing for the expert either. His proximity to things threatens to be too close, at the expense of perspective. What he has missed will sometimes drop into the restive layman's lap. The anxious and disturbed expressive content of Schönberg's atonality was better perceived by its opponents than by the friends whose sheer enthusiasm for the compositorial power made them only too eager to conceive that power in relation to tradition rather than in qualitative novelty. The Hans Sachs of *Die Meistersinger*, summoning the people to revise the masters' judgment about a new music, was indeed a romantic demagogue, but he was right in seeing through the ignorance of specialized knowledge, a negative side of progress.

No prizes for the state of mind are given, then, in the critique of the prevailing musical consciousness, of its types as well as of public opinion. To favor the modern is not an a priori correct musical consciousness, nor is a critical view of it a false one. On the contrary, summary standpoints are signs of reified thinking in which the sense for specificity has withered. The opponents may rightly profess skepticism whether art is possible at all nowadays, with the obstacles even to halfway decent composing piling higher and higher. In the past, of course, as much bad music was written as today; only its shabbiness was covered up, then, by the familiarity of universal idioms and by stylistic norms which lent a semblance of context even to the stammering of clichés. What makes the most wretched of modern pieces superior to such normalcy is that its appearances are scorned, at least, that the obligation to form the piece here and now, even if the attempt fails, is accepted.

The relation to the avant-garde has a key character for musical consciousness, not because the new is *eo ipso* good and the old *eo ipso* bad, but because true musicality, the spontaneous relation to the matter, rests on the ability to have experiences. Its concretion is a readiness to deal with things that have not yet been classified, approved, subsumed under fixed categories. The dichotomy of musical consciousness that shows here is closely related to the one between a man in bondage to authority, who automatically decries modern art, and the autonomous individual who tends to be openminded even in esthetics. It is not a matter of modernistic mentality but of objective freedom: it demands that the new not be *ab ovo* dismissed. The capacities for experience and for positive reaction to something new are identical. If the concept of naiveté still had a legitimate meaning it would be this capacity. But it is critical at the same time; the very man to whom all new music is not gray like cats in the night will eventually, on grounds of identification with the matter, reject what is inadequate to its idea and therefore to his own. One is tempted to make this the definition of the expert listener.

Adequate, however, remains only what dispenses with every last remnant of harmlessness. The frightened mass reactions to the latest music are worlds away from what goes on there in purely musical terms, but they respond quite exactly to the difference between that new—now already older—music in which the subject's suffering sheds the affirmative conventions and the latest one in which that subject and its suffering hardly have room any more.[1] Fear recoils into cold horror, past the possibilities of feeling, identification, and live adoption. That horror reacts precisely to the social condition; the ablest among the young composers are aware of the sinister implication. No denying the thought of tellurian conflicts and proportional advances in the techniques of destruction. Directly, of course, what is brewing there can no more be a theme of music than can the battles which Shostakovich voluntarily or involuntarily turned into descriptive program music. But the conduct of the compositorial subject in the latest music does reflect the subject's abdication.

That is the shock it imparts, its social sting: the ineffable content hides in the formal *a priori,* in the technological way of proceeding. Without leaving a remainder, the universal of the structure produces the particular out of itself and thereby negates it. Rationality thus gains its irrational quality, its catastrophic blind spot. Under the preconceived, simultaneously opaque and resistless universality, the listening co-performance which once defined the expert and the "good" listener type becomes impossible. The dimension of time, whose formation was the traditional task of music and within which correct listening moved, is virtually eliminated from the art of our time. The universal's primacy over the particular is claimed in all artistic media and extends to their interrelation. The differences thus far respected between music, poetry, and painting are diminished as if they were merely differences in material; the precedence of the entirety, the "structure," leads to indifference to the materials. The cause of the threatening and frightening effect is that complete integration is harshly imposed on its object—as dominion, not as reconcilement.

Totality, atomization, and the opaquely subjective act of uniting antitheses—an act which rests on principles but leaves them arbitrary—these are constituents of the latest music, and it is hard to judge whether their negative side expresses and thus transcends the social one or merely imitates it, unconscious under its spell. In the final analysis there may be no instrument to probe and distinguish the two. Unquestionably, however, the latest music as a mortal foe of realistic ideology writes a seismogram of reality. The "new realism," with which Schönberg already shared many of his motives, is thought through to the end: in art, nothing shall pretend to be something other than it is. This shakes up the very concept of art as appearance. It is why the new music admits to a remnant of chance in the universal necessity, a remnant that is essentially the same as the irrationality of rationalized society. Integration comes to be directly one with disintegration.

This explains the stunning effect which John Cage's theories of chance and accidental compositions had on the serial composers. The complete accident that shows its detachment from the senses and promises something like statistical legality, and the equally unsensual integration that has ceased to be anything but its own literalness—these, as György Ligeti put it, arrive at the point of their identity. They do not, however, arrive at the reconcilement from which the "unisociety" is farther than ever, and if it were esthetically urged today it would deteriorate into a fraud. Universal and particular reappear, but they do so while coming abruptly apart at the instant of identity. The universal becomes a self-posited rule, dictated by a particular and therefore illegitimate with respect to every particular; the particular becomes a mere exemplar of its principle, an abstract accident stripped of any definition of its own, which would be thinkable only as subjectively mediated. If it were to credit itself with more than this divergence says, the new music would be a relapse into the function of ideological solace. It is true only where the antagonisms are carried out without mitigation, without tears. No artist can anticipatorily collect the antagonisms into meanings any longer, no more than the simultaneous, hardened society lets us envision the potential of the right one. The strength of protest has contracted into a speechless, imageless gesture.

The demands of this gesture are immense. Not much that is written satisfies its idea; meanwhile, the radical theoreticians of the new music admit the aging of most of the pieces produced. The abdication of the subject, the demolition of subjective meaning that shakes us in the best of the latest works, is manifested in the lesser ones as loss of tension, nugatory trifling, a parody of playful bliss—just as the leisure society, in Horkheimer's word, is a parody of realized freedom. Compositions from which the subject withdraws as though ashamed of its own survival, compositions left to the automatisms of construction or chance—these get to the borderline of an unleashed technology that is superfluous beyond the utilitarian world.

Yet tinkering is not simply the signature that distinguishes bad composers from good ones. Whatever succeeds seems to have been forced out of it by a minimum; there seems to be no disentangling the alternation of the shocked expression of emptiness and an empty, neutralized procedure. The irresistibility with which the tinkering urge seized even the most gifted of the young baffles the older generation, but that urge itself is a generally social behavior, the sensorium's attempt at a paradoxical adjustment to the wholly alienated, thinglike and congealed. The tendency is akin to the social character of children who know all about cars before learning to read and write. It is clever and regressive in one. If today's blithely advancing positivism is unself-conscious despair, a permanent state of objective despair tends to the positivistic bustle of pseudo-scientism.

The inner complexion of music has been infected by the ersatz ideal of full employment, of production for production's sake. Vanishing in it is what procedures do not exhaust, the bit of Utopia, the dissatisfaction with mere entity. Its substance, however deeply buried, was social change. The core of the sociological difference between the new music about 1960 and that of about 1920 is probably political resignation, a reflex on that concentration of .social power which either forbids the impotent to act or transforms their action into that of another power. A feeling of immutability has befallen music. It is experienced less and less as a process; it congeals more and more to the static condition longed for by neoclassicism. Total determinism, which no longer tolerates confrontation with any independent individual entity, is also a ban on becoming. Many important pieces of the latest music have ceased to sound like evolutions; they sound as if they were all cadences staying in place. One can envision a music of social entropy.

But the same applies to the social effect of the new music, compared with that of forty years ago. Although in consistency and distance from the traditional idiom it surpasses everything that came to be in those days, it does not give as much offense. That scandals have become rare, that the new music is no longer loathed as sacrilegious but rather is sidetracked to a special field for specialists has often been remarked—with too much satisfaction to render the findings credible. They lead effortlessly to the thesis of the conforming nonconformists. Chuckles register the formation of forms precisely where forms are negated, and the will to live on the part of those who find life nauseating. Philistines gloat to see that even the nonphilistines are philistines.

Replying that conformists are the ones who say that nonconformists are conformists ought to suffice for a start, although no word is safe from being swallowed by the bustle it revolts against. Another objection—that a type of music is financially supported by its antagonists, who can always hear the opposition in it very well—this too is a denunciation, not an argument. Not that the contradiction should be embellished. But it is an objective necessity, not subjective opportunism. There is no market for a music structured so as to unearth some of the essence of the social structure; public institutions which protect it have the right to negate the negation. In spite of all that, reified consciousness and avant-garde music are incompatible. Such music esthetically resembles a condition which it contradicts by that very resemblance —and that is its social truth.

And yet, something happened when the new music was received. The sneers at the apathy with which it is said to be consumed like other commodities cover resentment of the new base it is finding, a base broader than in its heroic years. The objective spirit of "gadgeteering" surely plays a part here; it is not far from the radio tinkerer to the electronics fan. Their problem is to evolve compositorial structures out of specifically electronic material. The mere charm of unaccustomed whirring sounds will be as quickly used up as any mere charm. Of all this the fans grasp little. But the delight in mechanisms creates a kind of complicity. Having taken an oath to technology, the new music will find fewer enemies among the millions of technology enthusiasts than the relatively traditionalist expressionism found among the culture bourgeois of 1910 or 1920. The resistance is not only weakened by indifference to culture— which says something about its sorry fate; it takes a generation with virtually no more substantial experience of tradition to be as openminded as the newest one is for nonestablishment art. What comes out of it—pure idiocy; reaction, once the traditional is rediscovered; or a genuine contact with what is coming to be—will probably be decided not so much esthetically as by the real course of events.

There is no biological generation gap, but there is one of collective experience. It is conceivable that all that was forgotten will make room for what has not yet been. What the new music lacks, of course, is precisely what facilitates its reception. Schönberg's, Berg's, Webern's music was made more difficult by the excessive tension in their works. They expected the same tension from an adequate listener, at a time when audiences in their own psychological situation were not up to it. This disproportion caused the laughter which in Webern's lifetime, for example, greeted his musical moments. Because the currently created music hardly knows—or at least hardly shows—that tension any longer it is less provocative, no longer something radically other than the listeners' consciousness. This becomes exceedingly plain when you attend a program which has affinity to Webern's orchestral pieces, for instance. Webern movements once rejected as sectarian follies or as "extravagant," in the bad language of the middle-of-the-road, will then have a ring of authenticity.

At the same time, reception is at least temporarily aided by organizational moments. Schönberg's Vienna School remained socially within old-fashioned liberal forms and was thus discredited as not backed by any institutional power—although this impotence may well have saved the school's immediacy and intellectual freedom. Meanwhile, however, the cultivation of new music was adapted to the social trend, with its own technological mentality assisting in the endeavor. It was one more proof that society can solve tasks with which the state of the productive forces confronts it, sometimes even when circumstances work against those forces.

The organizational talents whose time has come will also be engendered. The most extraordinary case was Wolfgang Steinecke, a recent victim of shameful recklessness, whose quiet and immense energies were dedicated to the most advanced musical production. He not only managed at the Kranichstein workshops to keep basically different and often recalcitrant individuals together for fifteen years, by no other means than the Utopia of a music that would be different in its inmost core; he also won public authority for events that sympathized with the most obstreperous. He waged no propaganda campaigns and did not have the support of an already crystallized public opinion. His was an exemplary demonstration that even in the administered world individual spontaneity can get results if it does not begin by kowtowing to the sagely rational figures in which the a priori futility of its doings is convincingly added up.

On the whole, the social situation of the latest avant-garde is paradoxical: the growth of the media of musical communication as well as the formation of relatively independent centralist authorities, which ultimately dates back to the process of economic concentration—both of these have more or less integrated the avant-garde without separating the tendencies to neutralization and those to deliverance from expert esotericism.

Socially the modern composers of today are more homogeneous than ever. Among the most sharply-defined are sons of industrialists and patricians side by side with artists born in the most straitened circumstances. The different backgrounds are not recognizable in their production and do not disturb the network of their relations; even political creeds do not separate them. Such socialization contrasts sharply with the isolation in the tightest cenacle which Schönberg's generation took for a warrant of purity. Those who believe, or who want to make others believe, that under present conditions one can still produce in individualistic seclusion have answered with accusations of cliquishness, a charge that always has a demagogic effect as long as the agitated ones know they have the more influential cliques behind them. But the socialization of unsociables serves not only their own sorely needed protection; after all, they can no more exist in dignified penury than can anyone else. Constant exchange of experiences, theories and experimental ideas, even heated battles between schools—all of this prevents congealment in whatever infallibility is proclaimed at the time.

In the serial school, productive self-criticism often compels changes of intention at the shortest intervals. The pace of its evolution speeds up as does the pace of the real one. The support of small, albeit always controversy-filled, circles is a *locum tenens* of posterity—hoped for by the new music, but no longer to be innocently trusted in by the mind. On the other hand, those who cultivate their individuality while prattling about creativeness are almost always people whose musical language feeds on the backlog of the critically obsolete, which they mistake for the voice of nature. Of all the contributions made, theirs are the least individual. But Schönberg, in his lifetime persecuted as an ultraindividualist, was absorbed in the idea of composing studios—analogous to the Bauhaus, perhaps, with which he, Kandinsky's friend, maintained cross-connections—and Stockhausen, tempted to follow through on every trend of the progressive evolution, actually produced a composition jointly with a friend. Speaking in the argot of the Federal Republic, the other's specific contribution was already conceptualized within the determination of the work. One thinks of analogies to Brecht's work in the early thirties, and to other artistic and theoretical collective productions. The social crisis of the individual has consequences reaching all the way into the genesis of works.

The collective support is modest, and a composer's social situation remains in jeopardy in spite of it. He lives almost solely on payments that are branched off from society's wealth and doled out to him, so to speak, as tips. A sense of superfluity, no matter how repressed, gnaws at every product. Now and then one compensates by forced activity. The generation of Schönberg and his disciples felt carried by a boundless need to express themselves; not unlike the Cubists before World War I, they knew that what was in them, striving to see the light of day, was one with the world spirit. This concordance with the historic trend that helped artists to bear subjective isolation, poverty, slander, and ridicule is now lacking.

In reality the individual is impotent, and nothing he accomplishes by himself and defines as his own can any longer be viewed as so substantial and important. And yet the seriousness of art requires an unquestioned conviction of its relevance. At the same time the element of subjective constraint, the expressive urge, decreases due to the constructivism in production. Both the arbitrariness of the attack and the sovereignty of planning would be incommensurable with that urge even if it were still stirring in composers. All compositions come close to composing to order; at best, the composer gets the assignment from himself. Consideration for acoustic circumstances, particular ensemble combinations, highly specialized interpreters like the amazing David Tudor—

everything tends in the same direction. Schönberg's polemically intended maxim for the neoclassicists, "The main thing is to make up one's mind," has lost its ironical character. Making up one's mind has become central.

Perhaps the automatic writings and their musical analoga were an attempt at volitional counteraction to the volitionality of art. For not even the music of the expressionist protocols was quite involuntary. Given some rationality, the amount of time required for a major composition—an amount which usually, to the composers' ire, far exceeds that needed to produce a painting, which yields greater material rewards—will always depend on purpose and planning. But the shadow of futility, of the disproportion between the decision to do the thing and its conceivable relevance, this shadow is due to the permanent state of crisis in which society finds itself.

True, the great innovations before World War I were already reflecting the decay of the social structure, but they occurred in one which outwardly was still intact. Art seemed a matter of course while the structure existed; in the blighted one it did not seem so any more. The doubts concern its possibility, no longer merely its forms. After the horrors that were perpetrated, after genocide, absurdity has come into the existence of art; not the least part of its obsession with the absurd is the attempt to cope with it. The latest music's unbridgeable distance from all empirical reality—not just of reception but of every trace of reality in expression—this distance is unwittingly posited so that music will have a place removed from its aporia. But the curse will catch up with the magnificent effort: if something segregates itself to such an extent as if it no longer had any human content, if it thus indicts the inhuman condition, it is on the point of pitilessly forgetting that condition and becoming its own fetish. That is the ideological aspect of the radically technological, anti-ideological work of art.

That composers are at their own limitless disposal, thus making production disposable, is the fact which gradually undermines it. Its fully achieved autonomy schools it for heteronomy; the procedural freedom, the knowledge of being no longer bound to anything extraneous, permits it, as a method, to adjust to extraneous ends. In other words: to sell out. The destruction of productive forces has accompanied the entire history of their emancipation.

There music is as one with the society in which it is spellbound, and whose dimmed image it is preparing. There are forces which society awakens and delivers, but it always chains them at the same time and extirpates them, if possible—and by no means only in so-called times of crisis. The emancipated bourgeois society allowed great composers from Mozart to Hugo Wolf to perish only to deify them later, as if their sacrifice had appeased the collective spirit's wrath. For a sociology of music that will not be put off with epiphenomena, the tendency to destroy the very geniuses whose concept ranks uppermost in ideology would be a worthwhile object of study.

In modern times, for all our piled-up social wealth, similar events have not been lacking. But one need not even recall the circumstances that shortened the lives of Berg and Webern, Bartók and Zenk, Hannenheim and Skalkottas. The social tendency to destroy art goes far beyond the visible catastrophe and what will then, if possible, be relished as a tragic fate by the guilty who do not want to miss the starving genius among their ideological home furnishings. The poison oozes through the thinnest capillaries of what might be better. It may be true that gifted composers are no longer really starving in the years of the affluent society—although part of the concept of the evil is that the affected ones are in the dark; if it had been known and fully grasped that Mozart was Mozart, he would not have had to live in want. Today's ways of paralyzing musical productive forces are more subtle and thus all the more irresistible.

As a rule, great compositorial talents have acquired considerable technical skills in the course of their schooling. They have learned to handle materials which are not specifically theirs, just as well-trained nonobjective painters can also draw nudes. The belief that an artist's trade includes no more than he needs for his very own is alien to art. The most productive ones are generally those with a solid traditional foundation, one that nourishes them as much as propelling themselves away from it makes them stronger. Most of them have something of the well-trained expert, including his utility. Almost without exception, what they have in mind exacts initial sacrifices, doubly painful in view of the ostentatious wealth; but at the same time this qualifies them for that social usefulness which the culture industry administers. Their technical assurance alone, the promptness and precision with which they complete assignments, suffices to recommend them; to the *routiniers* of entertainment music they are superior even in that sphere.

But talent is not, as the conventional cliché of the art religion would have it, identical with power of resistance. Sensuality, understood in the broadest sense, is a premise of any artistic talent and a force that draws an artist to a pleasurable or at least to a less straitened life. What is lacking in ascetics, even ascetics of genius, is mostly lacking in their production as well. Artists are seducible. Productivity is not pure sublimation but entwined with regressive moments, if not with infantile ones; the most responsible of psychoanalysts, like Freud and Fenichel, refused to treat the neuroses of productive artists. Their naiveté has a damaged character and yet lends them their immediacy to the material. For a long time this saved them the need to reflect on the social situation, but it often keeps them from drawing the line between levels and retaining their integrity. Their narcissism balks at admitting compromises while they have already yielded to the bustle.

The more strictly they erect the concept of autonomous art, the harder it is for the artists to grasp and hold on to. Some—and by no means only bad ones—do not even know the nature of a work of art. Elegant craftsmanship fools them about the most reprehensible; some will skid into the culture-industrial activities without quite noticing it. Under the given system they cannot be morally reproached for this, but the irreconcilable spheres of musical life cannot possibly coexist in the same individual. I do not know a single case of a composer making his living with jobs for the market and at the same time fully satisfying his own norm. The materials here and there are too contiguous; routine, the convenience of fluency, will be transferred to what demands the opposite. Spinoza could grind lenses and write his *Ethics*, but music for use and legitimate compositions will hardly work at length for the same man. The act of selling takes revenge on the unsalable—a process that should some day be analyzed in detail.

The deterioration of great composing talents under the terrorism of the East seals a trend that is already noticeable under formal freedom. Evidently, musical productivity with high pretensions is especially fragile; the social break between music for everyone and intact music is destructively repeated in the productive forces themselves. The dwindling process of musical meaning, which cannot be ignored except as an apologetic lie, undermines the subjective possibility of production. Even in the heroic period of the new music its exponents had frequently failed to keep pace with themselves; what they composed overshot their subjective spirit, so to speak, or the objective spirit of the epoch. Long before that, Wagner once wrote in very bourgeois fashion that his *Tristan* had ventured so far ahead that his task now was to fill the gap and gradually to catch up with the opera.

But connecting lines to the rear—which always run at the same time to the collectively prevailing musical consciousness—are no sooner drawn than the more advanced music will sap their strength. Composers hoping for security from such connections are the most acutely exposed to the verdict of history. But the bravest are not proof against effects of the *contrainte sociale*—rather hidden effects now and then. One might try guessing whether even in Schönberg's case the compulsion to teach for a living was not partly responsible for the didactic, paradigmatic character of some of his later works; whether it was not his inexhaustible imagination alone that preserved him from writing "how-to" music, from composing on the blackboard, as it were. But the perfect teaching aid fails as a work of art.

That pressure generates counterpressure; that social resistance will sometimes enhance a man's powers, as it did in Wagner's case; that it will not benefit an artist to be received with open arms—all this need not even be denied altogether. Being fundamentally wrong, the condition communicates its wrongness to the artist, no matter what his relation to society. An opposing one will usually be crushed; one who receives society's consent will be turned into a consenter, into his master's voice. A socially conciliatory posture is akin to mortal self-satisfaction. But not even the abstract statement that the artist is wrong whatever he does is quite true. If being an heir to millions were really detrimental to production—it hurt neither Bachofen nor Proust—today, at any rate, being a social outsider is far more terrifying. The disproportion between concentrated social power and individual strength has grown to unbearable dimensions. The schema of *per aspera ad astra*, always suitable for fraud, dissolved along with liberalism and free competition.

What remains of it is a pretext for destroying the productive forces: they just did not have what it takes.

Awaiting the gifted one who allows himself to be destroyed by surrender—"If I do commit suicide," Schönberg once said with gallows humor, "I want at least to do it for a living"—are characteristic social forms of present music. In those, "corn" has been elevated and has lost its innocence. Dauntlessly traditionalist production no longer finds much of an echo; only provincials stay loyal to it. Now as before, the circle of those interested in new music is too small to sustain it socially and economically. An intermediate zone has been set up: a production that affects a more or less modern demeanor, will even flirt with the twelve-tone technique at times, but takes good care not to offend.

There have been moderate moderns as long as there were moderns. While posturing as thoughtful and free from experimenting manias, they always had tired and feeble results, due not only to the material employed but to the more noncommittal facture. Out of this came the widespread and rather homogeneous type that fills the moat and includes some famous names. They really do not want great art any more; what is written on their products' brows as wisdom and measure, is resignation and a bad conscience. Secretly they make no claim to commitment but recompense themselves with public success—quite enduring at times—without the embarrassment of looking like backwoodsmen.

An international unistyle of such composers can be seen to emerge. Exploiting Stravinsky, they work with brief rudiments of motives that are not developed in variations but repeated with cracked wings as if the musical impulse were crushed before stirring. The model's paradoxical acuteness is replaced by an arts-and-crafts design; there is no lack of literary erudition. An affinity to ballet is no accident in these scores. They extend the line of what in the early twenties came to be called *Gebrauchsmusik*. In those days it became apparent for the first time that music does not simply divide into the two suspiciously tried and true branches of high art and entertainment. Added to them was a species derived from stage music and dramatic interludes, a kind of music that fulfills its function in contexts other than musical. The model of the old forms of stage music—even *The Threepenny Opera* was, among other things, a parodistic straggler of the farce with song and dance—continues to take effect in parasitic leanings on what has proved successful in literature, from Kafka to Shaw.

Avidly interested in dissociating themselves from the corn which in a sense they expropriate, these people show as much prudence in their choice of libretti as in compositorial bearing. Music is reduced to background music which no longer takes itself seriously, and this reduction is laid out as an esthetic platform, down to the structures in which a composition is liquidated by the simplest stomping effects—something called "rhythmics." Along with the rise of the highly concentrated and production-planning culture industry went a visible growth of the social importance of that sector. Music for use is tailor-made for the administered world; its characters triumph even where no use requires it. Great composers—as Schönberg, for one, in his musical accompaniment to a movie scene—have occasionally furnished examples of what would be possible even in this realm if it were removed from hidebound social controls.

Meanwhile, however, the new type has captured everything located between the most advanced production and the entertainment music into which the utilitarian forms—those of the movies, in particular—pass smoothly, as a matter of course. Its characteristics: dramaturgically clever entrances, easy comprehensibility, bright colors, a sense for scoring points, and the prudence not to make intellectual-musical demands—these are also the characteristics of many a work that seems to be autonomous, of operas and ballets, even of absolute music. Their utility is customer service. They administer the listener. The sphere extends upwards too: electronic procedures are sniffed at. This new type of music, a highly significant one for our time in terms of musical sociology, simultaneously brings forth a new type of composer. Planning functionally, he combines the work processes of composition, performance, and utilization. One might talk of "manager-composers."

The prototype in the late nineteen-twenties was the extremely talented Kurt Weill in the period of his collaboration with the Berlin Theater am Schiffbauerdamm. He directorially attuned composition and performance to each other, frequently arranging his production in accordance with desiderates of reproduction and consumption. Later this became the general custom in musicals;

Weill still did it under the aspect of Brecht's attempts at a montage of artistic media and at their didactic mobilization. Out of the meetings and telephone talks of the pre-1933 collective came that figure of the composer-manager who then proceeded to subordinate everything to utilization[2] even in the more pretentious realm, as was otherwise done only in the entertainment sphere. In works for the stage, this predominance of use over a thing whose meaning makes it seem to be still autonomous rests on the fact that the end product is indeed not the score but the visible performance—a relation similar to that of a screenplay to the actual film.

Showmanship, always essential in the theater, takes hold of music as well. The unquestionable necessity of testing stage works by their performance and scores by the live sound is being absolutized. In weighing the effectiveness of the media in the scenic result, the composer turns into a music director, at the expense of that ideal of "progressive composing" to which Berg's operas, for instance, are committed. The hard, brittle counterpoint of heterogeneous media according to the montage principle is "realistically tempered," as we call that nowadays. No material is wholly worked through any more; all are cut short for the sake of an assuredly effective combination. The alienating inhomogeneity turns into a calculating enhancement of each medium by the other, which in a sense assists the first from outside.

The composer conquers positions that allow him to decide and to coordinate. Richard Strauss, as a composer, along with a good many conductors came in the course of the economic concentration of artistic decision-making to hold power positions outside their own working domain; under the organizational forms of the culture industry, which extend far beyond the mass media proper, this tendency is universalized. Eccentricities of Cage's school as well as the expansion of accidental acts beyond the purely musical realm seem like polemical retorts to the expansion of administrative measures into the processes of production. If the dream of the right musical condition were the reconcilement of the separated spheres of production, performance, and reception, the managerial system of music would reflect that dream. What is apart becomes attuned to each other, but by measures that perpetuate both the arbitrary separation and the impotence of those at whom such a false rationalization aims.

12

MEDIATION

So far, what we know in musical sociology is unsatisfactory. It consists in part of largely unproductive scientific activities and in no small measure of unproven statements. Its every cognition rests upon mere analogy. A dogmatic touch remains even where motives are drawn from consistent social theory. Just to be sure of having solid ground under one's feet, theses are confined to consumer habits or permit music as a sociological topic only where it has expanded to something like a mass basis; these theses mostly yield little. More sophisticated methods of inquiry may at times be rewarded with unforeseeable results, results which do not obviate research as do such truisms as that jazz will be heard more in metropolitan centers than in rural areas, or that interest in dance music among the young will exceed that shown by their elders. But what the sociology of music promises to the unbiased, what no single inquiry fulfills and the synthesis that keeps being postponed is not likely to fulfill either—this would be the social deciphering of musical phenomena as such, an insight into their essential relation to the real society, into their inner social content and into their function.

Instead, the scientifically established sociology of music simply gathers and sorts data in what exists. Its habitus is administrative: the data it supplies about listening habits are of the type required by the offices of the mass media. Yet in restricting themselves to the role of an accepted music in an accepted society, the data collectors block the perspective of problems of social structure, of implicit ones vis-à-vis music as well as of functional ones vis-à-vis society. They know why, citing Max Weber, they boast of being value-free. An uncritical registration of what they report as facts commends them to the bustle in which they naively take their place, making a scientific virtue of their inability to recognize what is the matter with the bustle, and with the music in it.

But intentions of musical sociology which refuse to be put off, intentions which interpretively transcend mere facticity—since such intentions cannot be purely redeemed by facts they will, without much intellectual expenditure, be branded arbitrary speculations. There are social aspects of music that one would expect to be flatly plausible: the link between great music, the point of which is that it can still be experienced today, and the spirit, and thus the social structure, of historic epochs, for example; and other perspectives opened by things as far removed from any suspicion of "sociologism" as Dilthey's history of ideas. Yet even these enter a twilight zone as soon as, under empirical rules of the game, they are shown the bill and asked for incontrovertible proof that Beethoven's music really had something to do with humanity and the bourgeois emancipation movement, or Debussy's with the vital sense of impressionism and with the philosophy of Bergson.

To that hardened scientific mentality whose ethos is to blind itself to the experience of objects while studying reflexes only, the most plausible of things will be distorted into speculative dogma. As Max Weber sensed, this frame of mind rests on the loss of continuous education. Its absence poses as a criterion of truth. The question of content is cut off as idle because it escaped the uneducated establishment. The intellect, at home in the topics of the intellectual sciences, becomes a defendant in the proceedings it degenerated to, proceedings in which general demonstrability of results matters more than their use to get to the heart of the matter. Of particular disadvantage to music in this situation is its non-objectivity, which denies directly social data.

But the fault lies not only with the progressive stolidity and benightment of scientific activities. Even one who refuses to be terrorized by those will note that the sociology of music tends to atrophy one or the other of the elements that went into its name. Sociological findings about music are the more assured the farther they are from, and the more extraneous they are to, music itself. Yet as they immerse themselves more deeply in specifically musical contexts they threaten to keep growing poorer and more abstract as sociological ones. Suppose we discern a correlation between Berlioz and incipient industrial capitalism. The link—notably the kinship of the technological aspect of Berlioz's treatment of the orchestra with industrial procedures—is hard to deny. But the social moments unearthed even by extensive extrapolations are quite out of proportion to the concrete data we have on French society in those days.

Such essential features as the desultoriness and abruptness of Berlioz's idiom do indeed plainly attest changes in the form of social reaction which he underwent in musical form. But even that would still be localized on a higher level of universality than the social processes, the revolution in production methods in Berlioz's time. Conversely, one will hardly be able to deduce from our abundant knowledge of late capitalist and imperialist society the specific traits of musicians as divergent from each other as those four contemporaries: Debussy, Mahler, Strauss, and Puccini. A differential sociology of music seems only ex post facto possible, and that makes it dubious in the sense of the dictum about what wonders can be wrought by hard thinking.

Misgivings at the headlong identifications of both realms are inescapable even if one considers them necessary because the full musical content harbors socially meaningful implications; even if he is free from that reactionary cultural ideology which, as Nietzsche already chided, will not accept the fact that truth—and art is the phenomenon of truth—is something that has evolved. We need not fear that the purity of a work of art will be sullied by the traces it bears of things as they are, traces it can rise only so far above as it makes those things its measure. What must be feared is that those traces may trickle away in the thing and induce the knowing individual to get it by stealth, by construction. The index of that is the thought's resistance to the use of words like "attribution." They cover a weakness of cognition; their noncommittal character makes believe that this knowledge springs from suspension and differentiation. Such weakness of musical sociology in one or the other direction shows so regularly it can hardly be blamed on the insufficiency of individual procedure, if not indeed on the youth—aged meanwhile—of the entire discipline.

In its scientific activities sociology surmounts the difficulty as it does so many others, by classifying in agenda style. Sociology, one says, has to do with the social effects of music, not with music itself; music should be dealt with by musicology, by the history of ideas, by esthetics. Such views are a tradition in the history of sociology. To be lodged in the old universitas literarum as a new branch of learning, it was eager to delimit itself from neighboring branches—economics, psychology, history—by a so-called clean definition of its object area. Until the period of Max Weber and Durkheim, sociology kept making apologetic efforts to prove itself indigenous. In the meantime it has come to public notice where the scientific division of labor into pigeonholes leads: to reification, confusing methodical arrangements with the thing itself.

Those limiting efforts have since come down to the hyphenated sociologies—as when industrial sociology, transparently enough, is split off from the sustaining economic processes as research in alleged interpersonal relations. It is not far, then, to the postulate that musical sociology be more or less restricted to inquiries about the social consumption of music. In the realm of theory of science, it may have been due to my reflections on musical sociology that this procedure, held to be scientifically safe, misses its own object. Esthetic and sociological questions about music are indissolubly, constitutively interwoven. Not so as might fit the view of popular sociologists: that nothing but what gains broad-based social acceptance is esthetically qualified. Instead, esthetic rank and the structures' own social truth content are essentially related even though not directly identical.

No music has the slightest esthetic worth if it is not socially true, if only as a negation of untruth; no social content of music is valid without an esthetic objectification. What expresses ideology in Strauss and also in Wagner extends to such dissonances in their technique as the alogical arbitrariness of effects or the persuasive repetition—the Eastern bloc's musical kitsch is at least symptomatic of the state of socialism over there, which the composers must illustrate propagandistically. Such are the contexts that would be relevant to a sociology of music. The social distribution and reception of music is a mere epiphenomenon; the essence is the objective social constitution of music in itself. This essence is not to be put off *ad kalendas Graecas*, feigning humility until the sociology of music has all the facts which it will then interpret, and which will enable it to interpret them. For the questions it poses for the distribution and reception of music would themselves have to be determined by the ones about the social content of music and by the theoretical interpretation of its function.

The interests of any social cognition depend on whether its

points of departure are human modes of conduct and reactions in a given society or the objectified, institutional powers on which the social processes and thus the individuals depend, all the way into their supposedly irreducible psychology. Because those objectivities are not, or not adequately, given in the consciousness of individuals; because in the crucial points they are covered, rather, by the facade while their behavior can be observed, inquired about, and even measured, a science obsessed with objectivity concentrates on the subjects—even a sociology of music that has picked Max Weber or possibly even Theodor Geiger as its model.

But the objectivity of such a perspective is only apparent. For its object itself is derivative, secondary, superficial. Because today the subjects are objects of society, not its substance, their forms of reaction are not objective data either but components of the veil. In a thoroughly formed and highly rationalized commodity society the objectivity is the concentrated social power, the machinery of production, and the machinery of distribution which it controls. What should come first, according to its own concept—the living human beings—has become an appendix. A science that denies this defends the condition that caused it. This is what scientific enlightenment ought to disentangle. It is not a matter of discretion, of choosing one's standpoint or theme, whether to start with the study of the social subjects or with that of the hardened social objectivity. Procedures beginning in both places would by no means converge. Social relations are relations of social power; hence the precedence of production over other domains. Interlocking in this precedence are the crucial moments for the social dialectic as a whole: human labor, the means by which life is maintained all the way into the utmost sublimations, and the fact that some men dispose of other men's labor, as the schema of dominion.

Without social labor there is no life; enjoyment is only its product. But social disposition reduces the use of the goods produced—which popular sociology mistakes for a datum—to a means to keep the machinery of production running for profit's sake. Abstract slices which juggle this away are therefore not as neutral toward their object as their *bona fides* flatteringly tells them. What disappears for them, to begin with, is the crux: the conditions which keep people in their place and bewitch them into what they act as, and what they also become for themselves. The assured observations build up into a wall in front of the essence, which merely appears in the observations. Empiricism does not experience what it claims to want to experience.

In the spheres of distribution and consumption, of course, in which music itself becomes a social object, a commodity, the question of the mediation between music and society causes no more difficulties than it gives pleasure. It should be treated partly with the methods of a descriptive analysis of institutions and partly, in the sociology of listeners, with methods of statistical inquiry. The way to pose the problems in which the social significance of findings can be read, however, would have to be determined by the specific quality of what has been distributed and received, while administrative research likes to disregard that relation and thus forfeits the fruits of its results.

Until distribution gets to the masses, it is subject to innumerable processes of social selection and guidance by powers such as industries, concert agencies, festival managements, and various other bodies. All this enters into the listeners' preferences; their needs are merely dragged along. Ahead of everything comes the control by the giant concerns in which the electrical, recording, and broadcasting industries are overtly or covertly merged in the economically most advanced countries. As the concentration and the power of the distributive agencies increase, freedom in the choice of what to hear tends to decrease; in this respect, integrated music no longer differs from any other consumer commodities.

The guidance is accompanied by irrationality. A very small number of musicians—hardly the ones objectively most qualified—are picked for prominence. The sums invested in them in order to build them up as a brand of merchandise are so large that they themselves attain monopolistic positions which they deliberately pursue at the same time. In the machinery of musical distribution the productive forces of performing artists are transformed into means of production, after the model of movie stars. This effects a qualitative change in them. The prominent ones have a high price to pay for their monopolistic status, itself a piece of economic semblance. They are impotently harnessed to the program policy.

199

Their performing style must be polished to a high gloss if they want to maintain their position, worrying even as global celebrities about the possibility of elimination from one day to the next.

Attempts to break the monopolies by spontaneity and a refusal to make artistic concessions have never broken anyone but the performing artists. The system may make exceptions; once in a while, for a change, it may tolerate something unlike it, but not in earnest. Its power redounds as authority and prestige to the things it launches. The phonograph record in particular, the performance that is frozen like a written work, gets this authority from its pure form. It lets people be talked into buying as exemplary what is demonstrable nonsense in the reproduction of works, both contemporary and older. The results are lowered criteria of musical performance and a market flooded with embarrassing duplicates of the stars who have made the grade.

In the selection of music for distribution, and in the high-pressure advertising campaigns, customer tastes will be cited to depress the level and to eliminate what fails to conform. The decisionmakers' objective interest makes use of the listeners' will. It is what the decisionmakers go by, according to their subjective consciousness; and let no one imagine that the listeners are being raped, that on their own, as in a happy musical state of nature, they would be open to other things if the system only allowed those things to get to them. In fact, here the context of social benightment turns into a vicious circle. The imposed standards are the ones that have taken shape in the listeners' own consciousness or have at least become their second nature. Empirically there is no refuting the manipulators when their finger points at the manipulated.

The evil lies not in original gestation of a false consciousness but in its fixation. What exists anyway, including the extant consciousness, is statically reproduced; the status quo becomes a fetish. Symptoms of economic regression to the phase of simple reproduction are unmistakable even in the form of the objective spirit. Adjustment to a market that has since deteriorated to a pseudomarket has hypostatized its ideology; the listeners' false consciousness has turned into an ideology for the ideology one feeds them. The controllers need that ideology. The slightest relaxation of their control over minds has today an explosive potential, however distant—a potential that is choked off with the hue and cry of unsalability.

Trivial details illuminate the course of control through the distributing agencies. Forty years ago you could have records sent home to you on approval, in line with the customs of a liberalism which formally, at least, respected the customer's taste. Today you find the more expensive albums citing copyright laws and the like in order to keep the stores from furnishing them on approval: "Sales conditions for Germany: Rerecording our records as well as recording broadcasts of our records on tape or wire, even for private use, is forbidden. To avoid rerecordings without permission, dealers are not allowed to loan, rent, or furnish records on approval." The possibility of abuses cannot even be denied; the worst can now almost always cite irrefutable reasons—they are the medium in which evil becomes reality. In any case the pig must be bought in a poke, for listening to records in the poorly insulated cells of stores is a farce. Complementing it is the maxim that the customer is king because he can enjoy Bruckner's entire Seventh Symphony in the privacy of his home. Whether such tendencies will change with market conditions remains to be seen.

What we call production in music, or in art at large, is initially defined as the antithesis of a cultural consumer commodity—which makes it so much less possible to equate it directly with material production. The difference between that and an esthetic structure is constitutive: whatever is art in the esthetic one is not in the nature of a thing. In critical social theory, works of art are included in the superstructure and thus distinguished from material production. The antithetical, critical element alone, which is essential to the content of important works of art and opposes them to the circumstances of material production as well as to the governing practice at large—this alone forbids unthinking talk of production in either case, if confusions are to be avoided. As in most equivocations, however, the differential moments are joined by identical ones. The productive forces, in the last analysis, are human forces and as such are identical too, in all areas. The subjects on whose faculties the material form of production always depends are historically concrete, formed in their turn by the total society of their time; they are not absolutely other subjects than the makers of works of art. After all, in craftsmanlike procedures the two roles used to intermingle for long epochs.

However much the groups may be estranged by the division of labor, all individuals working in each phase are socially joined, no matter what they are working on. Their work, even the artist's most individual one in his own consciousness, is always "work in society"; the determining subject is far more of a total social subject than privileged brain workers in their individualistic delusion and arrogance would like. In spite of it all, the artistic and material state of the epoch communicate in this collective element, in the relation of procedures and materials that is objectively predesigned at each time. This is why, once the acute tensions between a society and its contemporary art are forgotten, the unity of both will so compellingly emerge; for our present experience, Berlioz has more in common with the early world fairs than with the *Weltschmerz* of Byron.

Yet as in real society the productive forces take precedence over the circumstances of production which chain as well as enhance them, so will society's musical consciousness be finally determined by the production of music, by the work congealed in compositions, although the infinity of intermediaries is not altogether transparent. In the empirical sociology of culture, which tends to start out from reactions rather than from what is reacted to, the *ordo rerum* is ideologically twisted into the *ordo idearum:* in art, being precedes consciousness insofar as the structures in which the social force has been objectified are closer to the essence than the reflexes to them, the immediate social modes of the receivers' behavior.

The largely concealed, historically delayed and interrupted primacy of production can be illustrated by remembering the case of entertainment and consumer music. That, after all, is the preeminent object offered for consideration to popular sociology. However it may try to shield itself in negative eternity from the dynamics of composing, it does remain the resultant of (a) a reified consumer consciousness, (b) the petrified invariance of tonality, and (c) elements of progress. If entertainment music were ever given the micrological attention it needs—more than autonomous art, which becomes autonomous by placing the essence in the appearance—its idiom would allow us to discover precipitations of the historic evolution of productive forces. In the so-called fads this evolution is demoted to an appearance of perpetual novelty within perpetual sameness. The paradoxical part of fashion is not abrupt change, as a prejudice makes us believe; it is the infinitesimally tempered vibration of historic unfoldment amid coagulation. Fashion is infinite slowness conceived as abrupt change.

Over long stretches of time, however, the desultory mood of disguised immutability does reveal itself as a retarded copy of dynamics. The chromatic auxiliary notes of late-nineteenth-century entertainment music, for example, tie the compositorial chromatization tendency to a lagging consciousness in that the essence literally comes to be an accident. Such depth processes are more than mere borrowings from high-level music: they are minimal victories of production over distribution and consumption. It is precisely in popular music, by the way, that the primacy of productive forces should be traceable all the way down to its material basis. Jazz, however directed, would hardly be so appealing if it did not respond to some social need; but that need in turn is created by technological progress. The compulsion to adjust to mechanized production evidently requires the conflict between that mechanization and the living body to be repeated, neutralized and imitated, in the body's leisure time. Something like a reconcilement between helpless body and machinery, human atom and collective power, is symbolically celebrated. Forms and tendencies of material production radiate far beyond production and its literal necessities. This dependence on the state of technology is of course indissoluble from the social circumstances of production. The social preponderance of material working conditions over the individuals is so great, their chance of self-preservation against it so hopeless, that they regress and in a kind of mimicry equate themselves with the inescapable. The glue of yore, the ideologies that kept the masses in tow, shrank to an imitation of what exists anyway, dispensing with its exaltation, its vindication, even with its denial. The culture industry's echo in a subjective mass culture is a kind of Monopoly game.

The very abstractness and inadequacy in the relation between sociological and musical aspects is explicable. Society is not, as a hardened dialectical-materialist doctrine pummels into its followers, directly, tangibly and, in the jargon of that doctrine, "realistically" continued in its works of art. It does not become directly visible in them; else there would be no difference between art and empirical existence, no such line as even the ideologues of dialectical materialism must eventually draw when they refer art and culture to special departments of their administration. True, even the most sublime esthetic qualities have a social positional value; their historic side is a social one at the same time. Yet society's entrance into them is not immediate; it often occurs only in rather hidden formal constituents. These have a dialectics of their own, which then, of course, reflects the real one. Conversely, however, theory too must be reminded that social reception is not one with musical content, not even with the social one for which the musical one serves as a code. Whoever ignores this remains so sober, in terms of musical sociology, that his very sobriety will lead to decretive fantasizing.

An adequate social theory of the superstructure would not be free to content itself with the *thema probandum* that the superstructure is dependent. It would have to make use of society, and eventually of the distinction between lower manual and the so-called mental labor, to grasp the complexity of the relation, indeed the hypostasis of the mind itself. While autonomous music, by virtue of that distinction, also has a place in the social totality and bears its mark of Cain, the idea of freedom lives in it at the same time. And that not as a manner of speaking but in the habitus of resistance to what has just outwardly been imposed by society. The idea of freedom, the medium of the bourgeois emancipation movement beyond which it historically points, does have its basis in the infrastructure; but the structures of its being like society and of its socially opposing society are so complex that succinct attributions inevitably yield to the arbitrariness of political slogans. The first social characteristic of autonomous music, as of all modern art, is its distance from society; our job is to recognize and, if possible, to deduce this distance, not sociologistically to feign a false proximity of what is distant, a false immediacy of what is indirect.

This is the limit which the social theory of the sociology of music prescribes regarding its proper objects, the great compositions. In fully autonomous music, society in its existing form is opposed by the turn against the imposition of dominion, an imposition disguised in circumstances of production. What society might chalk up to great music as a negative quality, its inutility, is at the same time a negation of society and as such concrete, in keeping with the state of what is negated. This is why musical sociology is forbidden to interpret music as if it were nothing but a continuation of society by other means. The best means of making the social character of that negation clear to ourselves is the fact that the totality of the socially useful and agreeable things spurned by autonomous music produces a normative canon, and thus, at each stage, something like positivity. But such norms in their supraindividual dignity are social norms, no matter how disguised.

To analyze the interlocking of superstructure and infrastructure would not only broaden our insight into the superstructure. It would touch upon the doctrine of the superstructure itself. If one managed to demonstrate a false consumption, for instance—false in the sense of conflicting intrinsically with the objective definition of that which is consumed—this would have theoretical consequences for the concept of ideology. Consumption, the use-value side of music, so to speak, could in the social totality degenerate to an ideology, and that might well extend to material consumption. The pressure to get rid of the surplus production would have turned the immeasurably increased quantity of goods into a new quality. What seemingly benefits people and in the past was only withheld from them would have become a form of fraud against them.

Ideology and superstructure would thus have to be distinguished far more vigorously than before. True, all things of the mind feed on the infrastructure; as its derivatives they are disfigured by the context of social guilt. But the mind is not exhausted in its ideological elements in the exact sense of the word; it also looms above the context of guilt. In fact, nothing but the mind will let us name that context. The social defense of an antisocial spirit is as much a task of musical sociology as its obverse, the development of criteria for ideological music instead of having labels pasted on it from outside.

Extraneously social and inward, purely compositorial trains of evolution diverge in the history of music. What happened right after Bach can be understood neither as a productive critique of his work nor as an expression of the view that Bach's impulses, scarcely even received yet by the musicians of his time, had come to an end. Rather, the turnabout was effected by the bourgeoization of music—a process heralded long before, of course, but greatly intensified about the middle of the eighteenth century, somewhat analogously to simultaneous tendencies in English literature. Nevertheless, the external and internal determinants join relatively quickly, twenty-five or thirty years after Bach's death. The dynamization of the motive-thematical labor which he had made universal and which as "labor" already exceeds the static nature of the so-called musical Baroque—this dynamization is Bach's compositorial consequence as much as that of the genteel, variety-seeking style that followed. It is as if the external determinants and perhaps an actual need of the audience had merely strengthened and accelerated whatever productive forces were ripening inside the composition. One explanation of the parallelism might be the unity of the spirit of the time. Its productive forces unfold in the same way, and as the same forces, in areas not immediately dependent upon each other. The mediation of music and society is apt to be taking place in the substructure of the labor processes underlying both realms. To follow this up would be the task of a history of music that seriously united the technological viewpoint with the sociological. What applies in terms of musical sociology is the Hegelian line that the essence must appear, in the manifest social phenomena as well as in artistic forms.

Such contrarily directed sociologists and estheticists as Karl Mannheim and Walter Benjamin have denied any autonomous, quasi-logical context of problems in the so-called history of ideas. Their critique was salutary in view of the hypostasis of the sphere "mind" that lies in the assumption of a closed history of meanings necessarily leading from one structure to the next. This amounts to asserting a special mental sphere independent of society. But legitimately as that polemic stresses the interaction of mind and society, there remains a remnant of problematic simplification. We cannot overlook the fact that art, rather like philosophy, knows a logic of progress, albeit a precarious one. Hegel absolutized it falsely; but the matter requires the existence of something like "unity of the problem." It is not unbroken and only intermittently effective; society, of which art is a part as much as the pinnacle, always keeps breaking more or less brutally into the execution of the problem context, with desiderates heterogeneous to it. At times, adjusting to its own retardation, society compels music to regress behind the state befitting the state of its problems; the reverse, the petrifaction of self-satisfied musical practices and its social correction, is well-known.

Unexplained remains the reason why from a distance, at least, there seems to be an eventual confluence of the immanent logic of the problem context and the external determinants after all. Aristotle propounded an immanent and largely stringent critique of Plato, but at the same time and in the same critique he was a philosophical exponent of the social transition from the short Athenian restoration period and the breakup of the *polis* into universal, quasi-bourgeois Hellenism. The question of the mediation of mind and society far transcends music, where it is too easily whittled down to that of the relation of production and reception. It is probably true that this mediation does not occur outwardly, in a third medium between the matter and society, but within the matter. And that on both its objective and its subjective side. The social totality, having sedimented itself in the form of the problem and of the unity of its artistic solutions, has disappeared therein. And since society is encapsulated in that form, its autonomous unfoldment also follows the social dynamics without a glance or any direct communication.

What keeps the mind moving in music, the rationality principle which Max Weber rightly recognized as central, is nothing but the unfolding extra-artistic, social rationality. This is what "appears" in music. It can, of course, be grasped only by reflection on the social totality that finds expression in the special mental fields as well as in all areas separated from each other by a division of labor. The problem's form is never unequivocal; the philosophical one according to Plato, for instance, asks for a possible rescue of ontology and, conversely, for continuance of its critique. In music one will be allowed to hear not only analogies but the same dual character: in Beethoven, for example, no less a reconstruction of a meaningful existence than the protest of a subject freed from tutelage against any heteronomously preordained meaning.

The cavities in the matter, which contain the problem's form, make it easier for society to penetrate the autonomy of procedure. Specific social needs can be transformed into ways to pose a purely musical problem. Let us go back once again to the mid-eighteenth century:

> I may point out a connection which to my knowledge has so far escaped both the historians and the sociologists of music. As frequently stressed, the turn to the genteel style was linked with the demands of a bourgeois stratum of the audience that was forming then and wanted to be entertained at the opera and at concerts. For the first time composers were confronted with the anonymous marketplace. Without the protection of a guild or of a prince's favor they had to sense a demand instead of following transparent orders. They had to turn themselves, their very core, into organs of the market; this was what placed the desiderates of the market at the heart of their production. The leveling that resulted—in comparison with Bach, for instance—is unmistakable. Not unmistakable, although just as true: that by virtue of such internalization the need for entertainment turned into one for diversity in the compositions, as distinct from the relatively unbroken unity of what is falsely called the musical Baroque. This very variety among the several movements, with the aim of divertissement, became the premise of that dynamic relation of unity and diversity which constitutes the law of Viennese classicism. It marks an immanent advance in composing, one which compensated, after two generations, for the losses caused by the initial turn in style. It was the source of a way to pose musical problems that has survived to this day. The customary invectives against commercial mischief in music are superficial. They delude regarding the extent to which phenomena that presuppose commerce, the appeal to an audience already viewed as customers, can turn into compositorial qualities unleashing and enhancing a composer's productive force. We may phrase this in the form of a more comprehensive legality: social compulsions under which music seems to be placed from without are absorbed by its autonomous logic and the need for compositorial expression, and are transformed into an artistic necessity: into steps of the right consciousness.[1]

The history of ideas, and thus the history of music, is an autarchic motivational context insofar as the social law, on the one hand, produces the formation of spheres screened off against each other, and on the other hand, as the law of totality, still comes to light in each sphere as the same law. Its concrete deciphering in music is an essential task of musical sociology. Due to such hypostasis of the musical sphere, the problems of its objective content cannot be transformed directly into problems of its social genesis, but society as a problem—as the entirety of its antagonisms—immigrates into the problems, into the logic of the mind.

Let us reflect further on Beethoven. If he is the musical prototype of the revolutionary bourgeoisie, he is at the same time the prototype of a music that has escaped from its social tutelage and is esthetically fully autonomous, a servant no longer. His work explodes the schema of a complaisant adequacy of music and society. In it, for all its idealism in tone and posture, the essence of society, for which he speaks as the vicar of the total subject, becomes the essence of music itself. Both are comprehensible in the interior of the works only, not in mere imagery. The central categories of artistic construction can be translated into social ones. The kinship with that bourgeois libertarianism which rings all through Beethoven's music is a kinship of the dynamically unfolding totality. It is in fitting together under their own law, as becoming, negating, confirming themselves and the whole without looking outward, that his movements come to resemble the world whose forces move them; they do not do it by imitating that world.

In this respect Beethoven's attitude on social objectivity is more that of philosophy—the Kantian, in some points, and the Hegelian in the decisive ones—than it is the ominous mirroring posture: in Beethoven's music society is conceptlessly known, not photographed. What he calls thematic work is the mutual abrasion of the antitheses, the individual interests. The totality that governs the chemism of his work is not a cover concept schematically subsuming the various moments; it is the epitome of both that thematic work and its result, the finished composition. The tendency there is, as far as possible, to dequalify the natural material on which the work is confirmed. The motive kernels, the particulars to which each movement is tied, are themselves identical with the universal; they are formulas of tonality, reduced to nothingness as things of their own and preshaped by the totality as much as the individual is in individualistic society. The developing variation, an image of social labor, is definite negation: from what has once been posited it ceaselessly brings forth the new and enhanced by destroying it in its immediacy, its quasi-natural form.

On the whole, however, these negations are supposed—as in liberalist theory, to which, of course, social practice never corresponded—to have affirmative effects. The cutting short and mutual wearing down of individual moments, of suffering and perdition, is equated with an integration said to make each individual meaningful through its voidance. This is why the *prima vista* most striking formalistic residue in Beethoven—the reprise, the recurrence, unshaken despite all structural dynamics, of what has been voided—is not just external and conventional. Its purpose is to confirm the process as its own result, as occurs unconsciously in social practice. Not by chance are some of Beethoven's most pregnant conceptions designed for the instant of the reprise as the recurrence of the same. They justify, as the result of a process, what has been once before. It is exceedingly illuminating that Hegelian philosophy—whose categories can be applied without violence to every detail of a music that cannot possibly have been exposed to any Hegelian "influence" in terms of the history of ideas—that this philosophy knows the reprise as does Beethoven's music: the last chapter of Hegel's *Phenomenology*, the absolute knowledge, has no other content than to summarize the total work which claims to have already gained the identity of subject and object, in religion.

But that the affirmative gestures of the reprise in some of Beethoven's greatest symphonic movements assume the force of crushing repression, of an authoritarian "That's how it is," that the decorative gestures overshoot the musical events—this is the tribute Beethoven was forced to pay to the ideological character whose spell extends even to the most sublime music ever to mean freedom by continued unfreedom. The self-exaggerating assurance that the return of the first is the meaning, the self-revelation of immanence as transcendence—this is the cryptogram for the senselessness of a merely self-reproducing reality that has been welded together into a system. Its substitute for meaning is continuous functioning.

All these implications of Beethoven result from musical analysis without any daring analogies, but to social knowledge they prove as true as the inferences about society itself. Society recurs in great music: transfigured, criticized, and reconciled, although these aspects cannot be surgically sundered; it looms as much above the activities of self-preserving rationality as it is suitable for befogging those activities. It is as a dynamic totality, not as a series of pictures, that great music comes to be an internal world theater. This indicates the direction in which we would have to look for a total theory of the relation of society and music.

The spirit of a time is social in nature, a mode of human conduct which for social reasons has parted with the social immediacy and become independent. It is by way of that spirit that the social essence prevails in esthetic production, the essence of the individuals who are producing at the time as well as that of the materials and forms which face the subject, on which it exerts itself, which it determines, and which in turn determine it. The relation of works of art to society is comparable to Leibniz's monad. Windowless—that is to say, without being conscious of society, and in any event without being constantly and necessarily accompanied by this consciousness—the works of art, and notably of music which is far removed from concepts, represent society. Music, one might think, does this the more deeply the less it blinks in the direction of society.

Subjectivity cannot be absolutized esthetically either. A composer is always a *zoon politikon* as well, the more so the more emphatic his purely musical claim. None is *tabula rasa*. In early childhood they adjusted to the goings-on around them; later they are moved by ideas expressing their own, already socialized form of reaction. Even individualistic composers from the flowering of the private sphere, men like Schumann and Chopin, are no exceptions; the din of the bourgeois revolution rumbles in Beethoven, and in Schumann's *Marseillaise* quotations it echoes, weakened, as in dreams. The subjective mediation, the social element of the composing individuals and the behavior patterns that make them work so and not otherwise, consists in the fact that the compositorial subject, however necessarily it may mistake itself for a mere being-for-itself, constitutes a moment of the social productive forces.

A sublimated art like music that has passed through the interior requires the crystallization of the subject. It needs a strong, resistant ego to objectify itself as a social slogan, to leave the accidental quality of its descent from the subject beneath. What is called soul, and what the individual defends against the pressures of bourgeois society as if he owned it, is itself the essence of social forms of reaction to those pressures; they include even the antisocial ones. Opposition to society, the individual substance which secretly begins with the fact that a work of art will free itself from the circle of social necessities, is a critique of society and thus always a voice of society too. This is why the attempts to devalue what society has not accepted are as foolish as they are ideological, whether desiring to disparage whatever music does not serve some community or merely to deny sociological consideration to any that has no mass basis.

The fact that Beethoven's music is structured like the society to which—with doubtful justification—we give the name of "rising bourgeoisie," or at least like its self-consciousness and its conflicts, is premised on another fact: that the primary-musical form of his own views was inherently mediated by the spirit of his social class in the period around 1800. He was not the spokesman or advocate of this class, although not lacking in such rhetorical features; he was its inborn son. How harmony between human productive forces and a historical trend is achieved in detail will be difficult to make out; that is the blind spot of cognition. It is always hard put to reconnect what in itself is one, what was dissected only by cognition itself, with the aid of such dubious categories as that of influence. Presumably that unity is actualized in mimetic processes, in childhood assimilations to social models—in other words, to the "objective spirit" of the time.

Aside from extremely deep-seated, unconscious identifications—the difference between Beethoven and Mozart is explained by that of their fathers—mechanisms of selection are socially relevant. Even if we were to assume a certain unhistoric constancy of human talents as opposed to social determinants—an assumption that would amount to a mere X—it is a fact that one element or another will be brought out in the subjects and rewarded by that objective spirit, depending on the state of society. In Beethoven's youth it meant something to be a genius. As fiercely as the gestures of his music rose against the social polish of the Rococo, he was backed by a good deal of social approval. In the age of the French Revolution the bourgeoisie had occupied economic and administrative key positions before seizing political power; this is what gave to the pathos of its libertarian movement[2] the costumed, fictitious character from which Beethoven, the self-appointed "brain owner" as opposed to the landowner, was not free either.

That this archbourgeois was a protégé of aristocrats fits as neatly into the social character of his oeuvre as the scene we know from Goethe's biography, when he snubbed the court. Reports on Beethoven's personality leave little doubt of his anticonventional nature, a combination of sansculottism with Fichtean braggadocio; it recurs in the plebeian habitus of his humanity. His humanity is suffering and protesting. It feels the fissure of its loneliness. Loneliness is what the emancipated individual is condemned to in a society retaining the mores of the absolutist age, and with them the style by which the self-positing subjectivity takes its own measure. Esthetically as well as socially the individual is but a partial moment, unquestionably far overrated under the spell of the personality concept of the history of ideas. Although changing the objectivities that face the artist takes a surplus of subjectivity, one not purely soluble in those objectivities, the degree to which the artist is a functionary of the tasks confronting him at each moment is incomparably larger than bourgeois superstition will admit. But in these tasks lies all of society; it is through them that society becomes the active part even in autonomous esthetic processes.

What the phrase from the history of ideas glorifies as creativity— a theological name and strictly due to no work of art at all—is concretized in artistic experience as the opposite of the freedom that attaches to the concept of the creative act. What is attempted is the solution of problems. Contradictions that appear as resistance of the material, which is historic in itself, are to be pursued to the point of reconcilement. By virtue of the objectivity of tasks, including the tasks they supposedly set themselves, the artists cease to be private individuals and become either a social subject or its vicar. Hegel already knew that their worth is proportional to their success in this self-relinquishment. What has been called the obligatory style, rudiments of which are discernible as early as the seventeenth century, contains the teleological call for a wholly, thoroughly formed composition, a call for—in analogy to philosophy—a systematic composition. Its ideal is music as a deductive unit; whatever drops out of that unit, unrelated and indifferent, defines itself as a break and a flaw to begin with. That is the esthetic aspect of the fundamental thesis of Weber's musical sociology, the thesis of progressive rationality.

Knowingly or not, Beethoven was an objective follower of this idea. He produces the total unity of the obligatory style by dynamization. The several elements no longer follow one another in a discrete sequence; they pass into rational unity through a continuous process effectuated by themselves. The conception lies all ready, so to speak, charted in the state of the problem offered to Beethoven by the sonata form of Haydn and Mozart, the form in which diversity evens out into unity but keeps diverging from it while the form remains an abstract sheath over the diversity. The irreducible genius of Beethoven's achievement may lie in his immersed vision, in an eye that in the most advanced production of his time, in the masterly pieces of the other two Viennese classicists, could read the question in which their perfection transcended itself and called for something else. This was how he dealt with the crux of the dynamic form, with the reprise, the conjuring of static sameness amid a total becoming. In conserving it, he has grasped the reprise as a problem. He seeks to rescue the objective formal canon that has been rendered impotent, as Kant rescued the categories: by once more deducing it from the liberated subjectivity. The reprise is as much brought on by the dynamic process as it ex post facto vindicates the process, so to speak, as its result. In this vindication the process has passed on what was then going to drive irresistibly beyond it.

But the deadlock between the dynamic and the static element coincides with the historic instant of a class that voids the static order and yet cannot yield, unfettered, to its own dynamics without voiding itself. The great social conceptions of Beethoven's own time, Hegel's philosophy of law and Comte's positivism, have found words for this. And that bourgeois society is exploded by its own immanent dynamics—this is imprinted in Beethoven's music, the sublime music, as a trait of esthetic untruth: by its power, his successful work of art posits the real success of what was in reality a failure, and that in turn affects the declamatory moments of the work of art. In truth content, or in its absence, esthetic and social criticism coincide. That is how little the relation of music and society can be superimposed on a vague and trivial zeitgeist in which both are thought to share. Socially, too, music will be the more true and substantial the farther it is removed from the official zeitgeist; the one of Beethoven's epoch was represented by Rossini rather than by him. The social part is the objectivity of the thing itself, not its affinity to the wishes of the established society of the moment; on that point art and cognition are agreed.

One will be free to draw some inferences on the relation of sociology and esthetics. They are not immediately one: no work of art can vault the chasm to existence—its own or society's—which defines it as a work of art. Yet no more can the two be separated by scientific lines of demarcation. What joins in the complexion of the work of art are society's *disjecta membra*, no matter how unrecognizable. Gathering in their truth content is all their power, all their contradictoriness, and all their misery. The social side of works of art, to which the cognitive effort is devoted, is not only their adjustment to extraneous desiderates of patrons or of the marketplace but precisely their autonomy and immanent logic.

It is true that the problems and solutions of works of art do not arise beyond the systems of social norms. But they do not acquire social dignity until they remove themselves from those norms; the highest productions actually negate them. The esthetic quality of works, their truth content, has little to do with any truth that can be empirically pictured, not even with the life of the soul. But it converges with social truth. It is more than the mere conceptless appearance of the social process in the works, although it is always that too. As a totality, each work takes a position on society and by its synthesis anticipates reconcilement. The organized aspect of works is borrowed from social organization; they transcend that in their protest against the principle of organization itself, against dominion over internal and external nature.

Social critique of music, also of its effects, presupposes an insight into its specific esthetic content. Otherwise it would narrowly and indiscriminately equate the structures with mere entity as social agents. If great works of art, works with an important truth content, reduce the abuse of the ideology concept to absurdity, the esthetically bad will always make up for it by sympathizing with the ideology. Immanent artistic flaws are stigmata of a socially false consciousness. But the common ether of esthetics and sociology is critique.

The interrelation of music and society becomes evident in technology. Its unfoldment is the *tertium comparationis* between superstructure and infrastructure. What it embodies in art, as something commensurable to the human subjects and at the same time independent of them, is the social state of the productive forces in an epoch, as the Greek word indicates. As long as public opinion was more or less in balance with the compositorial state, composers had to move at the advanced level of the technology of their time. It was probably in witness of the more recent break between production and reception that Sibelius was the first more pretentious composer to become world-famous far below that level. In the neo-German period one would have stood hardly a chance without mastering the novelties of the Wagnerian orchestra. The system of musical communication is too comprehensive for composers to find the technical standards easy to ignore; it is only due to violent resentment that one's embarrassment at lagging behind will recoil into its opposite. That embarrassment, of course, may dwindle as the chances of monopolistically cranking up a composer's fame increase. A striking technological retrogression occurred in France, in the post-Debussy generation; the ideal of the *métier* was not remembered again until the next, and one can scarcely help thinking of parallels with industrial developments over there.

But technology always embodies a standard of society as a whole. It socializes even the supposedly lonely composer; he must pay attention to the objective state of the productive forces. As he lifts himself up to the technological standards they merge with his own productive force; in most cases both will so pervade each other during his apprenticeship that they can no longer be disentangled. Yet these standards always confront the composer with the objective problem as well. The technology which he encounters as if it were complete is thereby always reified too, estranged from him as well as from itself. Compositorial self-criticism grates on that reified moment, eliminates it from technology again, and thus keeps the technology going. As in individual psychology, a mechanism of identification with technology as a social ego ideal evokes resistance, and resistance only will create originality. There is nothing immediate in originality. Beethoven expressed that in a truth worthy of him, in the inexhaustible sentence that much of what we attribute to a composer's original genius ought to be credited to his skilled use of a diminished 7th chord.

The adoption of established techniques by the spontaneous subject mostly brings their insufficiencies to light. If a composer tries to correct them, by posing problems in a technologically sharply defined form, the novelty and originality of his solution turns him at the same time into an executor of the social trend. The trend is waiting in those problems, waiting to shatter the shell of the extant. Individual musical productivity realizes an objective potential. August Halm—a man greatly underestimated nowadays —was almost the only one to sense that in his theory of musical forms as forms of the objective spirit, however dubious his static hypostasis of the forms of fugue and sonata may have been otherwise. The dynamic sonata form in itself evoked its subjective fulfillment even while hampering it as a tectonic schema. Beethoven's technical flair united the contradictory postulates, obeying one through the other. As the obstetrician of such formal objectivity he spoke for the social emancipation of the subject, ultimately for the idea of a united society of the autonomously active. In the esthetic picture of a league of free men he went beyond bourgeois society. As art as appearance can be given the lie by the social reality that appears in it, it is permitted, conversely, to exceed the bounds of a reality whose suffering imperfections are what conjures up art.

The relation between society and technology cannot be conceived as constant in music either. For a long time society found no technical expression other than to adapt technology to social desiderates. In principle there were hardly any independent demands and criteria of musical technology prior to Bach's thoroughly shaped compositions; how the Dutch polyphony fared in this respect remains to be explored. It was not until technology had ceased to make its social use its direct measure that it became a proper productive force: its methodical, labor-dividing separation from the total society was the premise of its social development, just as in material production. The dualism of material technology —it is something autonomous, moving in line with the canon of rational science, and it is a social force—is also the dualism of musical technology. We owe many a technical accomplishment, like the invention of the accompanied monody in the late sixteenth century, to a "new sense of life," as the amply embellishing phrase goes—namely, to direct changes in the structure of society, changes that do not date back visibly to technical problems of late medieval polyphony. Rather, it was a collective subcurrent which surfaced in the *stile rappresentativo*, having been suppressed by the polyphonous art music. Bach, on the other hand, whose technical innovations were not broadly received, were not even given all their due by Viennese classicism—Bach accomplished them purely by the ear's compulsion to process, purely and thoroughly, what the theme of a fugue on the one hand and the harmoniously meaningful conduct of thorough-bass on the other mean on their own.

The congruence of that technological development with the progressive rational socialization of society did not become visible until the end of a phase at whose onset no one dreamed of it. Technology is differentiated by two conditions: by the state of the material and by that of the modes of procedure. The first might be crudely comparable to the circumstances of production a composer is getting into; the second, to the totality of the developed productive forces against which he checks his own. Yet both obey the interaction. The material is always a product of the procedures, interlaced with subjective moments; the procedures must necessarily be in definite proportion to their material if they are to do justice to it. All these states of fact have both an intramusical and a social side and are not causally and equitably dissoluble on one side or the other. At times the genetic contexts are so complex that all attempts to disentangle them remain idle and leave room for innumerable other interpretations. More essential than what comes whence, however, is the content: how society appears in music, how it can be read in its texture.

Postscript—
Sociology of Music

A question to be raised here is what a complete sociology of music, as distinct from a mere introduction, ought to look like. Its conception would have to differ from a systematics designed to develop or present, in strict continuity, something which in itself is discontinuous and not uniform. Nor could a method bent on a dubious completeness be expected to fit the phenomena as a schema of external order. Rather, a finished musical sociology should take its bearings from the social structures that leave their imprint on music, and on what we call musical life in the most general sense.

The social question about the relation of productive forces and circumstances of production can be applied to musical sociology without doing violence to it. What we mean there by "productive forces" is not just production in the narrow musical sense, i.e., the activity of composing, but also the work of living reproductive artists and the whole unhomogeneously compounded technology: the intramusical-compositorial one, the playing capacity of the reproducers, and the modes of mechanical reproduction which are today of paramount importance. Opposed to those, as circumstances of production, are the economic and ideological conditions to which each tone, and the reaction to each tone, is tied. In this age of consciousness- and subconsciousness-industries the musical mentality and taste of audiences is also an aspect of the circumstances of production, in a measure the exploration of which would have to be a central task of musical sociology.

Musical productive forces and circumstances of production do not simply face each other as antagonists. Instead, they interact in many reciprocal ways. Even in the socially particular sphere of music, circumstances of production can be changed, to some degree even created, by productive forces. The models are the transformations of public taste by great productions—abrupt ones as wrought by Wagner, for one, and imperceptibly slow ones in the entertainment music in which compositorial innovations, though diluted and neutralized, nevertheless leave their traces. For the present it was scarcely raised as a problem whether and to what extent the changes in public taste are actually determined by those in production, or whether both are equally dependent on a third factor whose cliché is the "changing spirit of the times." It seems plausible that the full bourgeois emancipation of the period around 1800 brought forth both Beethoven's genius and an audience to which he appealed. The question probably permits no clear-cut alternative; perhaps only the most discriminating analyses of contemporary reviews might do justice to the phenomenon. . . . Sometimes musical productive forces will explode the circumstances of production that have been sedimented in taste: jazz, for instance, which swept all nonsyncopated dance music out of fashion and demoted it to the realm of nostalgia.

Conversely, circumstances of production may shackle the productive forces, and in modern times this has become the rule. The music market has turned down progressive music and thus called a halt to musical progress; unquestionably the compulsion to adjust has made many composers suppress in themselves what they really would have liked to do—and by no means only since the mid-nineteenth century. What is called the alienation—a term that is gradually becoming hard to bear—of advanced production and audience would have to be reduced to its social proportions: as an unfoldment in which the productive forces cast off the leading-strings of circumstances of production and ultimately move into blunt opposition.

Let no one deny that this in turn has consequences for the production itself, that the specialization it is driven to can diminish its autonomous substance. A musical sociology focusing on the conflict between productive forces and circumstances of production would deal not only with what comes to be and is consumed but also with what does *not* come to be and is scuttled. Social pressures did and still do, perhaps, bar the unfoldment of important talents. Even the greatest were impaired. Some of Mozart's works in almost every category are written the way he really would have wished, and for all the unity of style they differ crassly from the ones he toiled over. Not only the productive force of individual artists is fettered, but the one potentially contained in the material. Stirring from the sixteenth century on was a desire for dissonances; an expression of the suffering, simultaneously autonomous and unfree subject, it was forced back time and again, down to the days of *Salome, Elektra,* and the atonal Schönberg, and mostly, as in Mozart's so-called "Musical Joke," was permitted satisfaction only in disguise, as humorous parody.

Now and then the circumstances of production have also enhanced the productive forces. Richard Strauss would not be conceivable without the rise of the German grande bourgeoisie and its influence on taste and institutions. Antitraditionalist qualities, subjective differentiation in particular, were as much elicited by the bourgeois music market as they later were socially limited in the course of the historical dialectic to which the bourgeoisie itself was subject, and finally revoked under totalitarian regimes. Even the autonomy of great music, the means of its most emphatic opposition to the dictates of the marketplace, would hardly have evolved otherwise than via the marketplace. Musical forms, even constitutive modes of musical reaction, are internalizations of social forms. Like all art, music is as much a social fact as an inner self-shaping, a self-liberation from immediate social desiderata. Even its socially unintegrated side is social in essence, confirming that emancipation of the subject whose idea was once envisioned by the bourgeois libertarians. The freedom of art, its independence of the demands made on it, is founded on the idea of a free society and in a sense anticipates its realization.

This is why the sphere of production[1] is not simply a basis for musical sociology as the sphere of production is a basis for the process of material living. As a matter of the mind, musical production is itself socially mediated, not something immediate. Strictly speaking, the only part of it that is a productive force is the spontaneity that is inseparable from the mediations. From the social point of view it would be the force that exceeds mere repetition of the circumstances of production as represented by types and species. Such spontaneity may harmonize with the social trend, as in the young Beethoven or in Schubert's songs; or it may offer resistance, as Bach and again the new music of today do, to submission to the market. The question to be raised is this: *How is musical spontaneity socially possible at all?* For it always contains social productive forces whose real forms society has not yet absorbed. Socially, of course, the objectification that generates musical texts has been largely preceded by what we now call musical reproduction: by the playing and singing of music.

Extremely crucial for any musical sociology is a task now being undertaken in several places: the exploration and analysis of the *economic base* of music, the element in which its relation to society is actualized. This concerns primarily questions of musical life: the extent and the effects of its determination, not only by economic motives but, more deeply and importantly, by economic legalities and structural changes. Fruitful, for instance, is the question whether forms of musical organization, composing, and taste were affected by the transition to monopoly capitalism. Whatever music may be summed up under the concept "fetishism of means" is likely to go back to the function of the "technological veil" in monopolism.

Musical interpretation and reproduction brings music close to society and thus has special relevance for the sociology of music. Economic analysis will have to deal chiefly with this sphere; it is there one can probably best put a finger on the components of a market that always remains in existence, and on the components of monopolistic manipulation. Technical requirements, the demands of a reproduction adequate to the composition, clash with the public's demand for glamour, perfection, and beautiful voices. The latter are cast for affects, to a degree exceeding all expectations. If you say from the musical point of view, for example, that even in opera beautiful voices are means of presenting the composition rather than ends in themselves, you will be answered in a tone of outrage out of all proportion to the rational gist of the controversy. The study of such outbursts and of their psychogenesis promises more insights into the function of musical activities in the psychological household of society than will result from inquiries about immediate likes or dislikes.

The reproduction of works, which delivers them to the market-place, alters their function. In principle, except for the most obstreperous works of the avant-garde, the entire upper sphere of music can turn into entertainment music. The false consciousness of the reproducers, their objectively demonstrable inability to give the thing an adequate presentation—an inability shared by some very famous names—is socially wrong and simultaneously enforced by social circumstances. The right reproduction would amount to social estrangement. In principle, nothing but opposition, cancellation of its social contract, will still gain for music its content of social truth.

Something to be vigorously scrutinized is how the economic base, the social setup, and the production and reproduction of music are specifically linked. Musical sociology must not be content to state some structural congruence; it has to show how social circumstances are concretely expressed in types of music, how they determine the music. What this calls for is nothing less than a deciphering of music, that wordless and conceptless art. The realm in which the effort is most likely to succeed is technology. It is in the state of technology at a particular time that society extends into the works, and there are much closer affinities between the techniques of material and artistic production than are acknowledged by the scientific division of labor. The dissection of labor processes since the manufacturing period and the motive-thematical work since Bach, a simultaneously splitting and synthesizing procedure, are profoundly congruent; with Beethoven it is even more legitimate to talk of social labor. Society's dynamization by the bourgeois principle and the dynamization of music mean the same; yet how this unity is realized is quite obscure for the present. It may be quite correct to cite one and the same spirit as having jurisdiction in both places, but this is more a circumscription of the problem than a solution. Explanatory formulas are not infrequently mere masks to hide the thing that needs explaining.

Music is ideological where the circumstances of production in it gain primacy over the productive forces. What should be shown is what can make it ideological: engendering a false consciousness; transfiguring so as to divert from the banality of existence; duplicating and thus only reinforcing that existence; and above all, abstract affirmation. One may postulate that intramusical ideologies are recognizable by immanent discord in the works; the intention of my *Versuch über Wagner* was to combine, as far as possible, a critique of Wagnerian ideology with the intraesthetic critique. But diagnosis and analysis of ideologies do not exhaust

223

the music-sociological interest in them. The same attention should be paid to the ways in which ideologies prevail in practical musical life, i.e., to the ideologies *about* music. Today ideology is apt to be entangled with violent naiveté. Music is unthinkingly accepted as a proffered consumer commodity, like the cultural sphere as a whole; it is affirmed because it is there, without much reference to its concrete nature. Checking such theses would be up to empirical research. It would be a partial aspect of its broader task: finding out to what extent the so-called mass taste is manipulated; to what extent it is that of the masses themselves; and to what extent, where it must be ascribed to the masses, it reflects what was drilled into them for centuries—and more yet, what they are social-psychologically constrained to feel by the total situation.

As far as musical sociology concerns itself with the ideological content and the ideological effect of music it becomes part of a theoretical critique of society. This imposes an obligation on it: to pursue the truth of music. Sociologically that amounts to the question of music as a socially right or wrong consciousness. Musical sociology would have to illuminate what it means to pursue the manifestations and criteria of such consciousness in music. We do not yet have enough analyses of what is rightly called "corn," the musical equivalent of mendacity; nor do we have analyses of the truth content of authentic works. Also to be researched are the historical, social, intramusical conditions of musical consciousness. One inescapable problem is whether in music there can be a clear-cut separation of a socially correct consciousness from ideology, or whether—which seems more plausible—the two permeate each other, and if so, why. The affirmative moment of all art, and that of music in particular, is inherited from the ancient magic; the very tone with which all music begins has a touch of it. It is Utopia as well as the lie that Utopia is here now. It would take an explication of the idea of truth to lend theoretical dignity to the sociology of music.

The question of the truth and untruth of music is closely linked with that of the relationship of its two spheres, the serious one and the lower, unjustly termed the "light Muse." The division probably originated in the social division of labor and in the oldest class relations, in which refined matters were reserved for the rulers and coarse ones for the populace. Ritual differences may have entered into the esthetic one. The division gradually congealed, was reified, finally came to be administered, and finds its echo among the listeners who seem to be insisting on either one or the other. Since the last rudiments of prebourgeois musical culture have withered, the spheres no longer touch. Administration and planning of the lower is the new quality into which the overwhelming quantity of entertainment music has recoiled. The antithesis of productive forces and circumstances of production becomes flagrant in the dichotomy: the productive forces are pushed into the upper, quasi-privileged sphere, are isolated, and are thus a piece of the wrong consciousness even where they represent the right one.

The lower sphere obeys the predominant circumstances of production. A critical sociology of music will have to find out in detail why today—unlike a hundred years ago—popular music is bad, bound to be bad, without exception. To be discussed in this context is the question raised by Erwin Ratz: how music can be mean. Meanness too is a *fait social*, incompatible with the immanent claim of any musically animated sound. Entertainment music no longer does anything but confirm, repeat, and reinforce the psychological debasement ultimately wrought in people by the way society is set up. The masses are swamped with that music, and in it they unwittingly enjoy the depth of their debasement. The proximity in which popular music besets them violates human dignity along with esthetic distance. It would be up to empirical research to develop methods subtle enough to track down such enjoyments and to describe their course.

Problems of this sort belong to the reception research of musical sociology. As a whole it has to go by categories and theorems objectively oriented on the matter, so as then, on its part, to correct and broaden the theorems. First to be clarified would probably be questions such as that of the difference between reception and consumption: in other words, wherein the assimilation of hearing music to the relation to material consumer goods consists; what esthetically adequate categories fall by the wayside; what new ones—one might think of sporting types—may possibly come into being. Passing mention might be made of the difficulty of distinguishing the new qualities from older ones since binding studies about the older qualities are not available. It is not even certain whether music ever was adequately received outside the

225

fraternity of artists or whether such reception is a wishful image, conceived only as a negation of the present state of things.

Let me throw out some suggestions for a line of empirical inquiries designed on the basis of the theorems of my "Introduction" and from the outline sketched here. Historically one might compare technological changes in selected typical works with the changes in material technology, and also with those in forms of social organization. Questionable in this complex are the causal links; one would expect interdependence rather than strict dependence of one on the other.

Success with something like an analysis of musical content—in music, which has no immediately objective content, this would of course have to consist in materially deciphering facts of the "form"—could lead to efforts to determine just what parts of the resulting content are perceived, and how. Subjective research in reception would thus be meaningfully combined with object-directed analysis.

Radio Research has familiarized us with investigations concerning likes and dislikes, preferences and aversions, and these should now be related to the preferred or rejected qualities of music in itself. This might help to get an empirical grip on its ideological effects. It is hardly an accident that none of this was ever done even though the ways to pose the problems have been known for almost thirty years. Resistance comes from two facts: that the individual reactions and habitual behaviors to be researched are not conscious, and that most people—again due to cultural conditioning—are unable to put their musical experiences into appropriate words.

Added to this are idiosyncrasies on the researchers' own part. The alleged empirical inaccessibility of the dimension in question, the "deep stuff," is often merely a pretext to keep from jeopardizing the conservationist character of music and its alliance with very tangible interests. At first one will be able to approach the really meaningful questions of musical reception only indirectly, perhaps by establishing correlations between the musical likes and dislikes of the persons questioned, their extramusical ideologies, and their overall psychology.[2] A simpler way would be to have music described by test persons, to compare the description with the results of an object-directed analysis, and thus to recognize ideological elements in reception.

226

A study of the language people use in talking about music would unquestionably be worthwhile. It is a defensible hypothesis that this language consists in the main of socially prefabricated clichés that serve to screen a living relation to the matter. At the same time it is replete with ideological contents and psychological rationalizations which in their turn may affect the reception. A primitive experiment, yet instructive already, would be to take three groups —one made up of listeners to serious music, one of listeners to entertainment music, and a third of people who do not care—and to question them, not about music, but about their ideological views.

For some of these procedures there are models that would have to be repeated with representative samples and designed in line with a principle. I am thinking, for instance, of the attempts of Allport and Cantril to test immediate and manipulative-authoritarian factors in the effect of music, both serious and light. Also one should do what Malcolm McDougald did at the time, only in less personalized a manner: one should make descriptive analyses of the techniques of manufacturing hits with the aid of the mass media and locate the bounds of manipulation and the minimum requirements for its success. "Promotion research" would be especially interesting since the techniques that win prominence for a pop singer are presumably not very different from the ones that do it for a politician.

Empirical musical sociologists like Alphons Silbermann see the point of departure for all of musical sociology in the experience of music. Yet this concept must not be dogmatically accepted. It would have to be checked out on different types, most usefully, perhaps, in intensive individual case studies: in how far a musical experience actually occurs; in how far it is a ritual; by what means this supposedly first experience is socially mediated. The chances are that the primary thing will prove in fact to be a highly derivative one, and in that case the alleged musical experience should no longer be used as a basic category in a sociology of music. Instead, the guidelines are, on the one hand, presently prevailing cultural and anthropological qualities and, on the other, forms of organization and mechanisms with an effect on musical life, in which generally social mechanisms are disguised.

Suitable rudiments from the viewpoint of social psychology

could probably be found in the theorems developed by this writer in a series of writings on jazz. Empirically one would have to trace the extent to which jazz, in the household of the masses, actually plays the role implied by its own structure—an adequacy which is no more a matter of course than the general one between a work and its reception. The exegeses of that music would have to be verified or falsified much further than was possible in their exposition. It could be done by including other branches of the culture industry, perhaps, branches independent of jazz but displaying analogous structures—as indicated, for example, in Herta Herzog's formula for the so-called soap operas: "Getting into trouble and back out again." Other ways would be comparison with Hollywood comedies or reference to the encompassing total schema of the "dirigist" mass culture.

Finally, the very widespread resistance to serious music and the social-psychological importance of hostility to music as a whole should probably, by means of clinical studies, be combined with characterological problematics and the general critique of ideologies. Just as diseases were able to tell us many things we did not know about the healthy organism, the social phenomena of hostility to music and estrangement from music would probably cast light upon the social function of music today, and also on its "dysfunction."

Suggestions of this sort sketch out a preliminary concept of the interrelation of the realms of musical sociology as well as that of the possibilities of dealing scientifically with much that has been developed here from thought and experience. It can, of course, not always be expressed according to the approved scientific rules of the game, no more than a critical theory of society can be couched in categories of the traditional one.

Frankfurt, October 1967

NOTES

1. TYPES OF MUSICAL CONDUCT

1. The concept has been specified and unfolded in *Der getreue Korrepetitor*, Frankfurt, 1963, pp. 39 ff.
2. Cf. Theodor W. Adorno, *Dissonanzen*, Göttingen, 1963, pp. 9 ff.
3. Cf. Theodor W. Adorno, *Philosophie der neuen Musik*, Frankfurt, 1964, pp. 182 ff. [*Philosophy of Modern Music*, New York, 1973.]
4. Cf. Max Horkheimer and Theodor W. Adorno, *Dialektik der Aufklärung*, Amsterdam, 1947, pp. 212 ff. [*The Dialectic of Enlightenment*, New York, 1972.]
5. Jürgen Habermas et al., *Student und Politik*, Neuwied, 1961, pp. 171 ff.

2. POPULAR MUSIC

1. As noted in the Preface, many ideas expressed in the following chapter were previously laid down in an English essay ("On Popular Music," *Studies in Philosophy and Social Science*, Vol. IX, No. 1, p. 17 ff., written, "with the assistance of George Simpson," while Adorno headed the music division of the Princeton Radio Research Project). The terms of that essay are used in this translation. The German chapter title is *Leichte Musik* (light music). —Trans.
2. The German word here is *U-Musik*, Adorno's own disparaging abbreviation of *Unterhaltungsmusik* (entertainment music). To appreciate the derogatoriness, one must consider the differing etymologies of the English and German words. The "enter-" in "entertainment" comes from the Latin *inter* and denotes a relation, while the German prefix *unter-* means "under" and implies inferiority. To stress the point, the other sphere, mostly termed "serious music" in the English essay and therefore in this translation, is generally called "the higher" in the German text. —Trans.
3. Abner Silver and Robert Bruce, *How to Write and Sell a Song Hit*, New York, 1939.

3. FUNCTION

1. Cf. Theodor W. Adorno, *Moments musicaux,* Frankfurt, 1964, pp. 167 ff.

4. CLASSES AND STRATA

1. Heinrich Regius [pseudonym of Max Horkheimer], *Dämmerung; Notizen in Deutschland,* Zürich, 1934, p. 11.
2. Theodor W. Adorno, *"Zur gesellschaftlichen Lage der Musik,"* Zeitschrift für Sozialforschung, I (1932), p. 105.

5. OPERA

1. Cf. Theodor W. Adorno, *Klangfiguren,* Berlin and Frankfurt, 1959, pp. 32 ff.
2. Cf. Walter Benjamin, *Schriften I,* Frankfurt, 1955, p. 336 f.
3. The radius of opera, like that of theater as a whole, must of course be seen in the right proportion, i.e., relative to the mass media. "Compared with other cultural institutions such as radio and motion pictures, the theater, especially in a metropolis, has a very small effective range. The broadcasts of the Hessian Radio, for example, can reach almost every inhabitant of Frankfurt. Families without a radio set are a rarity, and movie houses are so numerous in Frankfurt and offer so many performances that every Frankfurt resident over 18 would be able to go to the movies about 22 times a year. The municipal theaters, on the other hand, do not have enough seats to sell annually for each adult resident to go to the theater even twice a year. Indeed, Frankfurt residents who are not in a theater club or some similar organization would have to wait about a year and a half for a chance to get into one of the two municipal theaters." (Manuscript in the statistical department of the Institut für Sozialforschung, Frankfurt, p. 46.)
4. Cf. Max Horkheimer and Theodor W. Adorno, *Sociologica II,* Frankfurt, 1967, pp. 168 ff.
5. According to an inquiry published in 1949 in the Quarterly Statistical Report of the State Capital of Hannover, "the so-called 'intellectual strata' including . . . professionals, higher civil servants, and executive employees" among subscribers prefer "unequivocally the drama. Independent businessmen, other civil servants, workers, and service employ-

ees, on the other hand, are more interested in opera subscriptions" (manuscript in the statistical department of the Institut für Sozialforschung, Frankfurt, p. 20). Without doing violence to this dichotomy, one may be permitted to interpret it as that between upper bourgeoisie and lower middle class. According to the customary criteria, the well-to-do included in the second group are not considered part of the educated stratum.

6. CHAMBER MUSIC

1. Social psychologists have observed a tendency on the part of countless, sometimes organized, individuals to attach affective values to these gadgets, turning the play with the tools into an irrational end in itself.

7. CONDUCTOR AND ORCHESTRA

1. This text was long formulated and had repeatedly been read in public before June, 1962, when the British weekly *Observer* carried Robert Craft's interview with Igor Stravinsky on the same subject. The concurrence of the critical conclusions reached by men of such different ways of thinking speaks for itself.
2. Cf. Elias Canetti, *Masse und Macht,* Hamburg, 1960, pp. 453 ff. [*Crowds and Power,* New York, 1963.]
3. Cf. Theodor W. Adorno, *Quasi una Fantasia,* Frankfurt, 1963, p. 60.
4. Cf. Theodor W. Adorno et al., *The Authoritarian Personality,* New York, 1965, pp. 664 ff. and 669 ff.
5. Cf. Theodor W. Adorno, *Versuch über Wagner,* Munich and Zürich, 1964, p. 26.
6. I would not wish to withhold my recent observations of a type of younger orchestral musician differing notably from the one described here.

8. MUSICAL LIFE

1. It is different in America, where one meets scientists who must strain even to imagine experiencing music otherwise than by radio. The culture industry has become much more of a second nature than thus far on the old continent. The substantial consequences for the sociology of music have yet to be uncovered.

2. Cf. Theodor W. Adorno, "The Radio Symphony," *Radio Research,* 1941, New York, pp. 110 ff.

9. PUBLIC OPINION AND CRITICS

1. Erich Unger, *Gegen die Dichtung; Eine Begründung des Konstruktionsprinzips in der Erkenntnis,* Leipzig, 1925.
2. Cf. Adorno et al., *The Authoritarian Personality,* pp. 695 ff.
3. Cf. Habermas et al., *Student und Politik,* pp. 11 ff.; Jürgen Habermas, *Strukturwandel der Öffentlichkeit; Untersuchungen zu einer Kategorie des bürgerlichen Gesellschaft,* Neuwied, 1962.
4. Cf. Adorno, *Klangfiguren,* pp. 248 ff.
5. Walter Benjamin, *Schriften I,* p. 341.
6. Cf. Adorno, *Klangfiguren,* pp. 72 ff.

10. NATIONS

1. Cf. Arnold Hauser, *Philosophie der Kunstgeschichte,* Munich, 1958, pp. 1 ff.
2. Adorno, *"Zur gesellschaftlichen Lage der Musik,"* p. 368.

11. AVANT-GARDE

1. Cf. Adorno, *Quasi una Fantasia,* pp. 339 ff. and 365 ff.
2. Cf. Bertolt Brecht and Peter Suhrkamp, *"Anmerkungen zur Oper 'Aufstieg und Fall der Stadt Mahagonny,"* in Bertolt Brecht, *Stücke,* Vol. III, p. 261. Cited in Hans Magnus Enzensberger, *Einzelheiten,* Frankfurt, 1962, p. 118.

12. MEDIATION

1. Theodor W. Adorno, *"Soziologische Anmerkungen zum deutschen Musikleben,"* Deutscher Musikrat, Referate Informationen 5, February, 1967, pp. 2 ff.
2. Cf. Max Horkheimer, *"Egoismus und Freiheitsbewegung,"* Zeitschrift für Sozialforschung, V (1936), pp. 161 ff.

Postscript

1. The writer's error in his essay *"Zur gesellschaftlichen Lage der Musik,"* published in 1932 in *Zeitschrift für Sozialforschung,* was his flat identification of the concept of musical production with the precedence of the economic sphere of production, without considering how far that which we call production already presupposes social production and depends on it as much as it is sundered from it. This alone has kept the writer from reissuing that essay, the draft of a finished musical sociology.

2. Rudiments of such research now exist. At the University of Marburg, Christian Rittelmeyer of the Department of Psychology has shown empirically that the brusque rejection of progressive art, notably of music, accompanies complexes of a character structure tied to authority, such as rigid dogmatism and "intolerance for ambiguities"—which is to say that thinking in black-and-white stereotypes prevails among the sworn enemies of all things modern. Rittelmeyer went on to "investigate the effects regarding intolerance and an aversion to modern art which curricula in *'musische Bildung'* (works of art and the like) and in specific cultural education (specific visual aids) had on comparable groups," and he "came to the preliminary conclusion that the former method" (i.e., *musische Bildung*) "will either raise these values or leave them unchanged, while the latter will lower them." In the meantime we have received more concrete analyses of hit songs and the mechanisms of identification from Gunnar Sønstevold and Kurt Blaukopf (*"Musik der 'einsamen Masse'; Ein Beitrag zur Analyse von Schlagerschallplatten,"* in *Musik und Gesellschaft,* ed. Kurt Blaukopf, Karlsruhe, 1968, No. 4).